PARENTS OF INVENTION

PARENTS OF INVENTION

The Development of Library Automation Systems in the Late 20th Century

Christopher Brown-Syed

Foreword by W. David Penniman

LIBRARIES UNLIMITED

AN IMPRINT OF ABC-CLIO, LLC
Santa Barbara, California • Denver, Colorado • Oxford, England

Library of Congress Cataloging-in-Publication Data

Syed, Christopher.
    Parents of invention : the development of library automation systems in the late 20th century / Christopher Brown-Syed ; foreword by W. David Penniman.
        p. cm.
    Includes bibliographical references and index.
    ISBN 978–1–59158–792–7 (pbk. : acid-free paper) — ISBN 978–1–59158–791–0 (ebook)
    1. Integrated library systems (Computer systems)—History. I. Title.
Z678.93.I57S94   2011
025.04′—dc22   2011011067

ISBN: 978–1–59158–792–7
EISBN: 978–1–59158–791–0

15 14 13 12 11   1 2 3 4 5

This book is also available on the World Wide Web as an eBook.
Visit www.abc-clio.com for details.

Libraries Unlimited
An Imprint of ABC-CLIO, LLC

ABC-CLIO, LLC
130 Cremona Drive, P.O. Box 1911
Santa Barbara, California 93116-1911

This book is printed on acid-free paper ∞

Manufactured in the United States of America

Contents

Foreword

When Tracy Kidder wrote his book *The Soul of a New Machine*, he focused on the people who were, in fact, the soul of the machines being developed. Mr. Kidder lived with the family of one of the players, Tom West, and left a lasting influence just as any participant observer might do. Tom West's daughter, Jessamyn, went on to become an automation consultant in the library field.

When Chris Brown-Syed "lived with" Geac as one of its early employees, he both contributed to and was influenced by the innovative company, just like any other participant-observer. He now puts his magnifying glass to the development of the Geac enterprise and the environment in which it evolved. With his intimate involvement in this endeavor, it is not surprising that he, too, is drawn to a primary focus for the story. In his own words, "This story is mainly about those people and the technical challenges they faced and overcame."

Dr. Brown-Syed knows full well the complexities of the intersection of people, information, and technology (now accepted as the domain of "informatics") and how the "people" component can determine the success (or failure) of an innovation. He was one of the faculty members in a pioneering school of informatics and taught the first cadre of students in that program. He knows something about the risks (and rewards) of being a pioneer.

In the book you now hold, Dr. Brown-Syed brings both a scholarly and a dramatic detail to the people and chain of events around the development, marketing, and application of local library systems at a time when automation was beginning to find its own within the library community. As with his subsequent labors in the area of informatics, he was also a "pioneer" in library local system development. This book, then, is as much his story as it is the story of others in "the game." Again, in his own words,

This story is about a systems development facility haunted by a ghost and frequented by insomniac programmers in pajamas with burning desires to solve problems and how such solutions were achieved. It is also about the sometimes fierce competition among ILS vendors.

In telling this story, it is not surprising that Dr. Brown-Syed mentions the Online Computerized Library Center (OCLC) early on. The founder of this goliath, Fred Kilgour, was a student of innovation. He often spoke of the complexities surrounding bringing new ideas or inventions to the stage of "innovation" where their application could become useful. It is ironic that this giant of a bibliographic utility did not play a larger role in the library local system arena during the period covered in Dr. Brown-Syed's book. While the existence of the centralized collections of bibliographic records facilitated local systems endeavors, the systems themselves sprang from other sources. Mr. Kilgour always dreamed of a "local system" that was not local at all, but resided centrally for all to draw from. He was thinking "in the clouds" and, as usual, was ahead of his time. I think he would be an avid reader of this book and its study of the people behind an innovation that was right for its time.

As for the concept of innovation (as opposed to invention), it should be clear upon reading this book that, while invention may spring like a burst of insight from an inventor's head (or like Athena, the goddess of invention, springing fully formed from the head of Zeus), innovation takes longer and is messier. Innovation involves trial and error and the balancing of many players' interests and egos. It is about adding value. It is about marketing as well as technology. And, it is always about people and their concern with changing others or being changed themselves—and change is never easy. In the realm of library automation, many innovations have been "done to," not "done for," libraries, librarians, and library users. Consider the disruptive technology of Google™ as well as the World Wide Web itself. These innovations have dramatically influenced how people acquire and accept information of all forms. Before these innovations evolved, other innovations on a less dramatic scale were being pursued, such as the one described in this book. While the scale may not have been nearly as dramatic as that of the Web, there was drama nonetheless. Dr. Brown-Syed captures this drama in his highly readable story with many characters and many subplots. The chapters of this book unfold the tale in a mix of technical detail and personal recollection.

As described in *The Innovator's Dilemma* by Clayton Christensen, disruptive innovations play havoc with the status quo. They touch a nerve of unmet need for customers and displace what had comfortably occupied a niche (large or small) in the marketplace. These innovations start slowly and often build from the bottom up. Over time, these innovations displace the current providers in the marketplace, providers who ignored the disruptive changes underway until it was too late. Following the evolution of such changes from birth through adolescence to maturity—and death—is a significant undertaking. It is also one worthy of capture and study. Dr. Brown-Syed provides just such a study. There is much to be learned here about information, technology, and people, and about libraries.

Studying the human aspect of innovation (and it is mostly a human story) not only is a good read, but also is informative in a way that carries a message for all who are concerned with the future of libraries. That message is perhaps best summarized in Louise O'Neill's concluding remarks to this book, where she says,

Not only must librarians influence human software vendors and developers, but also they must now prepare themselves to shape and even lead the development of technology that replicates and automates librarians' expertise in bringing people and information together. (Chapter 8)

By quoting one of the concluding statements of this book, I have given away neither the plot nor the ending. I have, I hope, merely piqued the reader's interest in the story that follows.

W. David Penniman, PhD

Commonly Used Terms and Abbreviations

ABLE	Application Building Language and Environment; Geac's main banking platform
BCU	Branch Control Unit, a multiplexer used by Plessey to connect multiple terminals over one telephone line
BPS	The Geac Bibliographic Processing System, written for the Series 9000 computer
C	A computing language used extensively in the UNIX environment
CLANN	College Libraries Activities Network of New South Wales
CLSI	A major Boston-based vendor of Integrated Library Systems, acquired by Geac in 1993
CPU (1)	Central processing unit; the part of a computer that performs the work
CPU (2)	Computer Professionals Unlimited, a Detroit-based engineering service
DEC	Digital Equipment Corporation
DOBIS	Dortmunder Bibliotheksysteme, a vendor of Integrated Library Systems
DRA	Data Research Associates
Geac	A Markham, Ontario–based vendor of Integrated Library Systems (not an acronym)
GLIS	Geac Library Information System
GLUG	Geac's report generation language, considered "safe" for use by customers
HUGO	Language in which the Geac Library Information System was written
IBM	International Business Machines
III	Innovative Interfaces Incorporated

ILS	Integrated Library System
NOTIS	Northwestern Online Totally Integrated System
OCLC	Online Computerized Library Center, a worldwide bibliographic consortium based in Columbus, Ohio
OLTP	online transaction processing
OS	Operating system; computer programs that allow a computer to perform basic functions
OSI	International Standards Organization's reference model for Open Systems Integration
PDA	Personal digital assistant; any of several handheld computers designed to assist with personal schedules, directories, and other office functions.
PDCU	Portable Data Capture Unit, a handheld backup and inventory device used by Plessey, Geac, Follett, and many other vendors.
PDP	A series of mini-computers manufactured by Digital Equipment Corporation
Psion	A British manufacturer of handheld computing devices
UGLI	A language superseded by HUGO
UNILINC	A multi-type library consortium based in Sydney, New South Wales, Australia
UNIX	The computer operating system developed at AT&T Bell Labs
UTLAS	University of Toronto Library Automation Systems
VAX	A series of computers manufactured by Digital Equipment Corporation
VUBIS	Library automation system manufactured by Infor/Extensity, successors to Geac
ZOPL	Geac's primary proprietary computer language

Acknowledgments

The story of library automation would fill many volumes. This tale reflects only one aspect of it, the flurry of creativity during the 1980s, the heyday of mini-computers, which saw technical challenges surmounted and standards and practices established that are still relevant three decades later. Many people assisted with this book by graciously consenting to be interviewed in person or online, or by contributing material over the Internet. They include Keith Thomas, Wendy Schick, Michel Vulpe, Don Bagshaw, Marlene Harris, Gene Damon, Jean Dickson, Michael Monahan, Paul Nixon, Bill Manson, Keith Pybus, Liz Fenwick, Diane Koen, Rona Wade, W. Christopher Martin, Linda Scott Zaleski, Tom Preble, Martyn Clay, Ian Williamson, Maria Loranger, W. Christopher Martin, Mike Himelfarb, Carol Hogarth, George Kelbley, Don Kaiser, Rob McGee, Peter and Susan Wesoly, and Peter van den Boschm. Several friends, including NNF, DCA, MET, JK, LP, JWE, SJ and TLL, read parts of the manuscript, lent their encouragement, or supported the project in other ways. John Boich and Lionel Gregory provided a good word now and then. Many family members, including Colin, Kiera, and Betty, deserve thanks for their patience and understanding. Anyone who has been omitted inadvertently is asked to please accept my thanks and apologies. My heartfelt thanks are due to Blanche Woolls, without whose faith, encouragement and editorial skills, this project would never have got off the ground. Special thanks to Louise O'Neill of McGill University for contributing Chapter 8 of this work. If despite the best efforts of all contributors and well-wishers, errors of fact or interpretation remain, they are mine alone.

Interviews

Many people contributed to this book by electronic means. In-person interviews were conducted with the following individuals.

Harrison Cheung	July 2008
Jean Dickson	May 2008
Elizabeth Fenwick	October 2008
Linda Farmer	February 2009
Marlene Harris	May 2007
Diane Koen	June 2008
Bill Manson	October 2008
Rob McGee	September 2009
Michael Monahan	July 2008
Keith Pybus	February 2009
Wendy Schick	August 2008
Keith Thomas	December 2008
Michel Vulpe	January 2009
Rona Wade	June 2008
Linda Scott Zaleski	August 2008

Introduction

This book was begun with two purposes in mind. The first was to fill a gap in the literature of librarianship, which for the most part neglects or glosses over the automation of those day-to-day processes that are viewed as being of no particular scholarly concern, and are taken as givens. Today, they are known as Integrated Library Systems, or ILS. That they can be taken for granted is evidence that they work, for the most part. Getting them to work, however, involved a considerable amount of logic and programming, and tailoring them to individual library systems still takes management and policy decisions that every administrator will have to face.

The second aim was to describe a particular phase in their development, one that coincides roughly with the dominance of mini-computers. Smaller than mainframes but still costly, mini-computers fell within the financial reaches of large libraries or local consortia of smaller ones. However, libraries posed data representation, processing, and communications challenges. Libraries, banks, and other agencies performing online transaction processing required specialized software that had to be built from scratch. I find this era of great interest, because it saw unparalleled cooperation among programmers, librarians, archivists, and ILS user groups. This book is, therefore, both a history and a reference for modern library students and managers. It seeks to explain the workings of systems that they still require to run their enterprises, and to cast light upon a particular period in computing history.

The historian's task is not merely to chronicle past events, but also to offer plausible explanations of them: historical theses. The thesis advanced in this book can be summarized succinctly. Beginning in the early to mid-1970s, and continuing through the early 1990s, advances in computing technology made conditions ripe for an extraordinary period in software development, during which a market segment—libraries and archives—actually drove the agendas of ILS vendors. With the demise of mini-computers and the rise of microcomputers, the economic and technological factors that coincided with this period of innovation ceased to apply. Drastic reductions in the cost of computing, and dramatic increases in technical capacities, forced vendors to adopt new business models in order to survive. Systems that had been priced in the hundreds of thousands—or, in some cases, the millions—were becoming available for tens of thousands of dollars.

Consequently, an era of ad hoc innovation and cooperation gave way to one of off-the-shelf solutions, and corporate mergers and acquisitions largely supplanted research and development in the ILS marketplace. However, the standards, automated procedures, and best practices that were developed, and the customer expectations and the ethical concerns that were raised during the period, still apply, and modern managers need to understand them if they are to make informed ILS purchasing and ongoing systems administrative decisions.

This book is based on documentary evidence and on a series of interviews with former employees of companies like Dynix, Endeavor, Geac, and NOTIS, and CEOs of libraries who bought and often helped develop their products. It also draws upon the author's personal experiences as an employee of the companies Plessey and Geac. It is an account of a period in the history of science and technology, but also a human story. During the heyday of the mini-computer, the 1980s, maverick start-up companies like Geac, for which several of my sources worked, soared to the ranks of the Fortune 1000 by selling hardware and software to an unlikely group of customers—a largely nonprofit and, arguably, professionally isolated cadre of librarians and archivists.

The concept of an ILS was developed at least a decade before this period begins, by people working in major research libraries, connected with universities. That work is documented thoroughly in publications such as the *Journal of Library Automation* and the ongoing series of proceedings of the *Illinois Clinic on Library Applications of Data Processing*. Mini-computers had been employed in library applications since the early 1970s, but it was not until the end of that decade that companies like Plessey, CLIS, and Geac were able to commercialize or "productize" them successfully. That involved making them scalable and tailorable to a wide variety of customers, with the same basic needs but many local requirements. As mini-computers achieved prominence, and commercial vendors came on the scene, a generation of highly creative young programmers, guided by managers who had the conceptual background, and working closely with client sites themselves, brought their formidable skills to bear upon this special set of problems, In many instances, they worked directly with customers, often for months at a time, and in a few instances sketching out software solutions on proverbial dinner napkins. Thus, the account presented herein may sometimes appear to be at odds with the prevailing literature. Some technical aspects of the systems discussed may appear in different guises, depending upon the perspectives from which they are being examined.

The overall plan of this book was influenced by the Soft Systems Methodology (SSM) of Peter Checkland, first defined in his 1981 work, *Systems Thinking, Systems Practice*,[1] which seeks to explain human activity systems, and the engineering systems embedded in them, from the points of view of various categories of stakeholders. They include the "customers," defined as those who potentially benefit from or suffer from some activity; the actors who perform it; the "transformation," or actual work being done; the belief set or Weltanschauung that underlies the activity; the "owners," defined as those who could halt the process; and the environment in which the activity takes place.

However, this is not strictly an SSM treatment of the period—it is a historical examination. As such, it advances a historical thesis: that the period of the ascendency of mini-computers, which stretched roughly from the early 1970s through the mid-1990s, was the occasion of a remarkable creative collaboration among librarians and computer engineers. Furthermore, it suggests that during the period, library automation was breaking new ground, stretching the limits of existing technologies, and setting standards that remain vital today and that created a significant niche within the computing industry.

Chapter 1 discusses the earliest phase of this quiet revolution, characterized by theoretical work, in which practical systems implementations took place. Standards for bibliographic records, and the rise of bibliographic utilities, are among the achievements of this first phase.

Chapter 2 explores the integrated library systems of the 1970s and 1980s from the perspectives of customers, and relies heavily upon the accounts of chief librarians and others who were directly involved in implementing ILS in their institutions. Chapter 3 explores the transition from librarian-customer to employee of a computing vendor, from the points of view of customer support and project management staff. Chapter 4 describes the vendor workplace with the aid of a small survey of former employees, and, again, with recourse to interviews. The social environment of the computing companies of the day, and their systems of rewards, are explored and discussed. A more prosaic look at the realities of working for a vendor during an explosive period of growth is presented in Chapter 5. Chapter 6 examines the ILS systems of the day from a more technical, or designers', perspective, seeking to explain the complexity of the engineering challenges that were prescribed by librarians, and met by engineers and librarians working in concert. Chapter 7 examines the era from a more business perspective, again relying heavily upon the narratives of a few of the many key players in the industry. What is perhaps remarkable is that many of the people who contributed to this book played so many different roles, as customers, support staff, software engineers, and company executives, and often performed several roles without any formal acknowledgments. A remarkable burst of creativity characterized the period. In her afterword, Chapter 8, Louise O'Neill explains some of the legacy left by the era, discusses the work being done in library automation today, and provides insights into the future of library automation.

Given the fluidity of the day, those customers took on design roles, formally or informally, guiding the process as much as reaping its rewards, and forcing vendors to adhere to their standards and to incorporate into systems functionalities useful only within librarianship. This demanded radically new programming approaches. For a brief time, librarians and archivists stood at the forefront of computing, actually setting the development agendas of vendors. The constantly shifting groups of programmers, salespeople, engineers, customers, and user groups who put this small revolution together were the parents of invention.

NOTE

1. Checkland, Peter. *Systems Thinking, Systems Practice*. Chichester, UK: Wiley, 1981.

1

Origins of Magic

Civilization advances by extending the number of important operations which we can do without thinking about them.

—Alfred North Whitehead[1]

Any sufficiently advanced technology is indistinguishable from magic.

—Arthur C. Clarke[2]

The origins of one sort of "magic," the history of integrated library system (ILS) automation that could mechanize every aspect of running a library, began when mainframe computers were the only computers available. For convenience, it can be thought of as having evolved through three eras.

An era of conceptualization, characterized by pioneering design work, and carried out in an environment of mainframe computers, printed output, and purpose-designed computer terminals for circulation

An era of commercialization, characterized by mini-computers, magnetic tape transfers of data, and "dumb" video display terminals that did not contain microprocessors, typically linked via dedicated telephone lines

An era of consolidation, characterized by microcomputer workstations, relational databases, client-server architecture, and Internet communications

ERA OF CONCEPTUALIZATION

The 1960s and 1970s with their mainframe computing environment can be associated with ILS development in college and university libraries, and the largest public libraries, and it often involved participation in automation consortia. These consortia shared the costs of mainframes, and later mini-computers, and sought to optimize their members' computing knowledge. During this period, the literature of librarianship demonstrates how bibliographic data representation became standardized and the specifications for bibliographic data representation and for what would become ILS were worked out. The main means of exchanging bibliographic data, or even records of circulation transactions, was reel-to-reel magnetic tape. Transaction records were captured by scanning punched cards and processed on mainframe computers overnight while the library was closed. Those mainframes, which cost millions of dollars, were typically run by a campus or municipal computing center, and the processing was largely beyond the control of the libraries themselves. The mainframes of that time, along with their peripheral devices like card readers, tape machines, printers, and disk drives, typically filled large rooms, access to which was tightly controlled. Much of the development work done during this period was done by the institutions themselves, not by commercial library automation vendors.

Beginning in the late 1970s and early to mid-1980s, "turnkey" systems based on mini-computers were beginning to enter the commercial market. Using smaller machines, which still needed rooms controlled for temperature and humidity, librarians began to offload the work of processing from campus and municipal computing centers and to build increased functionality into their systems. Mini-computers required staffs of operators to initiate and monitor the processes they carried out, and while it had been introduced to a very few computing centers, the Internet was not widely accessible. Communication was still conducted using magnetic tape and dedicated data lines. Writing in 1978, Hiltz and Turoff described a "Network Nation," but it was made up of many disparate networks that required "gateways" to communicate with each other.[3]

Regional consortia continued to provide economies of scale. Commercial library systems, first for circulation, then eventually for cataloguing and public access, allowed librarians more latitude in defining specifications for system performance and functionalities. As well, librarians could do the bulk of the processing in their own facilities. User groups, made up of customers of particular vendors, exercised considerable say over system functionality. This was important, because the main focus of the computer industry at the time was upon scientific, military, and business applications and not on the sorts of information found in libraries or on transaction processing.

While many programmers, software companies, and library practitioners involved in ILS development were aware of the body of theoretical literature that had been emerging, some of these new mini-computer-based systems evolved with little reference to the theories developed in the earlier phase. Library consultant Rob McGee, who was himself associated with the pioneering work behind done in Chicago, quite rightly traces the origins of the integrated library system concept to the early issues of the *Journal of Library Automation*. McGee says, "Charles Payne defined the original concept at Univ of Chicago, in a proposal that received national R&D funding in 1965–66.[4] The first 'proof of concept' systems were implemented at the University of Chicago, and the University of Toronto."[5]

Frederick Kilgour founded the OCLC Online Computer Library Center and developed the World Cat database in the early 1970s. By 2006, the database contained over 70 million entries for books and other library materials, and a billion listings for them at libraries around the world. In 1967, he established the first computerized library system at Ohio State University in Columbus. He was the founding editor of the journal, *Information Technology and Libraries*.[6] The history of integrated systems is well described in a wide range of articles, which have appeared in the *Journal of Library of Automation* over the years, under the editorship of Fred Kilgour. Kilgour provides a synopsis in a 1970 article, "History of Library Computerization."[7] Another important source of "shapshot" descriptions of experiences, conjectures, and projections may be found in the proceedings of the Clinic on Library Applications of Data Processing, held annually at the University of Illinois at Urbana-Champaign.

By the time Geac and the other earlier companies got into the business, during the first major period of commercialization, ILS vendors were re-inventing existing systems, or at least, implementing existing concepts, using different, newly available and largely proprietary technology. McGee remembers predicting that it would just be a matter of time before the rapidly advancing computing industry provided better solutions.

The cost of a mini-computer system could range from a few tens of thousands to millions of dollars, so large libraries and consortia continued to be the major ILS customers. Until the next decade, Internet communications protocols were not widely adopted, and the main way of reaching a remote computer was over dial-up modems and telephone lines. Higher speed, dedicated lines and better communications protocols were being introduced, but widespread connectivity was still in the future.

The late 1980s and 1990s can be thought of as an era of consolidation. These decades saw the widespread adoption of microcomputers and client-server environments, end-user computing, graphical user interfaces, faster machines with vastly more memory, and the Internet's communications protocols. Since individuals could now perform online searches and compose research papers on their desktops, the era saw the development of personal bibliographic software to keep track of citations. The mini-computer-based systems became massively integrated, incorporating almost all of the major functions required by libraries, new micro-based systems, and "distributed" automation solutions. While librarians were certainly aware of the theoretical work being done, commercial vendors often developed their systems without much recourse to the published record. Again, customer input was both essential and influential. Design problems were gradually resolved, cost issues were ameliorated significantly due to wider market conditions, and the various start-up companies that had ventured into the library market achieved maturity. There was a gradual consolidation of companies characterized by a flurry of buyouts and mergers. Products matured and became similar in their functionalities.

Systems that could deliver information over the Web instead of using purpose-built terminals and catalogue software became an expectation. By the turn of the millennium, the open-source software movement, social networking, and the interactive Web 2.0 all contributed to an era of end-user involvement, and ushered libraries into the current environment. As the Australian librarian Tony Barry had confidently predicted in 1992, the information environment of the future would look like the network that was then best accessed using a menu-driven and text-based search tool called Gopher.[8]

Library automation had begun piecemeal with separate systems for cataloguing, for database searching, for acquiring materials, for discovering the things that libraries owned, and for lending their resources to patrons and having those resources returned. Due to the enormous cost of mainframe computers, and the necessity of keeping them locked away in air-conditioned, dust-proof rooms tended by people in white lab coats, few libraries could afford their own. During the 1960s and 1970s, "computing" was synonymous with mainframes and with companies that built them, like IBM and UNIVAC.

In 1967, Nigel Cox and his colleagues, a group of librarians, had written,

Man has . . . advantages [over the computer] . . . which he may well retain even into the far-distant future . . . [G]iven his abilities, he weighs less than any computer yet designed or even envisaged:

there seems no likelihood that an electronic computer capable of so great a variety of computational facilities can be encompassed within 150 lb. [M]an needs far less energy. [M]an is the only computer yet designed which can be produced entirely by unskilled labour . . . The push-button library is still well in the future. The librarian who visualizes himself or his readers sitting at a console and conducting a dialogue with a computer by means of a typewriter keyboard and a television screen . . . should set these dreams aside for a while . . . On-line interrogation of large stores (to use the standard computer jargon for such a situation) exists in some applications now, and its use will increase, but such installations are costly and their utility must be proven beyond doubt . . . before this cost can be justified even for a large library.[9]

When Cox and his colleagues were writing this, printouts and punch-cards were still the dominant computer communications devices. During the 1970s and 1980s, local library automation systems, and the vendor companies that packaged them, became commercially viable, and newer terminals became available, ones with television screens. The dreams that Cox alluded to were fast becoming a waking reality. During the time between the late 1970s and the early 1990s, most of the technical problems associated with library automation were solved, and the solutions still underpin the systems in use during the early 21st century. It has been an interesting path but not necessarily one to which librarians today give much thought.

The steps along the way to the automation of everyday library processes are of no more current interest than Edison's thinking as he went about inventing light bulbs, Marconi's preparations for sending transoceanic radio signals, or Bell's experiments with early telephones. Perhaps this is because library automation works well enough that we no longer think about what life was like without it or about the people who designed, used, and perfected the hardware and software. However, historians delight in such things, arguably because of the "legacies" they left behind, like standards and expectations of system behavior.

ERA OF COMMERCIALIZATION

The cost of computing had dropped drastically in the 1980s, while the power of computers increased dramatically. Librarians began to purchase or lease, singly and in groups, their own mini-computers. Most of these newer, smaller computers still required air conditioning and stable supplies of electrical power, and they were still costly. Only the largest university and public libraries could afford their own mini-computers, and the software programs required were still being invented. By today's standards, the capacity of those machines was still miniscule, their internal memory and their peripheral disk drives still being measured in kilobytes, thousands of letters or numbers, whereas scarcely two decades later, millions or billions of bytes would be the norm.

To a large extent, the programming concepts, the data storage and communication standards, and the overall functionality of integrated library systems were defined during this mini-computer era. The information contained in libraries and the transactions performed in them were of different natures than those found in other enterprises, so much of the software had to be developed from scratch. Because the computers of the day were designed for general business or scientific functions, some vendors developed special hardware for use in libraries and similar organizations. Librarians and programmers together invented ILS and brought them to market. Because of the costs and size constraints, much ingenuity and economy of expression were required of programmers. Until midway through the 1980s, for instance, Geac's programs were restricted to 64 kilobyte partitions of memory. To put that in more concrete terms, the entire body of instructions required to drive a library circulation, acquisitions, or cataloguing operation could take up no more space in memory than the letters that make up a typical book chapter or graduate term paper.

Arguably, the motives that prompted programmers and clients alike to devote long hours of unpaid overtime to solving library automation problems are at least as interesting as the systems they developed. Much of this book is about their lived experience, which at times contrasts with the official record.

This story is about a systems development facility haunted by a ghost and frequented by insomniac programmers in pajamas with burning desires to solve problems and how such solutions were achieved. It is also about the sometimes fierce competition among ILS vendors and how they obtained a court injunction to prevent a competitor's sale in Florida. It covers how the bidding process worked when ILS systems cost millions of dollars; how library user groups lobbied vendors and created their own user cultures, badges, and newsletters; and how they stimulated the adoption of standards and functionalities. It also includes the narratives of some of the librarians who played major roles in the design and implementation of large database products, such as Ovid and Thomson, which are still in high demand.

This story is mainly about those people and the technical challenges they faced and overcame. It is also about start-up companies and what happens to them during periods of phenomenal growth. Many of the people interviewed for this book worked for, or were customers and sometimes competitors of, a company called Geac. Typical of high-technology companies of the day, Geac began as the project of three engineers, and within two decades had burgeoned into a Fortune 1000 company with a worldwide workforce. Its focus was upon two "vertical" markets that had been overlooked by larger companies: libraries and banks. However, given that staff frequently migrated from one vendor to another and that vendors and clients tended to hire staff away from each other, the tale touches upon many other organizations of the period.

Geac—whose name, by agreement with General Electric in the UK, was never to be spelled in uppercase—was chosen for several reasons. First, the author had access to a wealth of published information about the company, as well as direct experience from having been an employee himself. The Web site "Ex-Employees of Geac" by William Christopher Martin and the annual reunions he sponsored for many years helped keep the group together. A Wiki or online shared database was set up to collect input from Geac's customers and employees. Although it was conceived and headquartered in Canada, it operated in several countries. Amazingly, customers in those places regarded Geac as homegrown. However, past employees and customers of other library automation vendors have also contributed their stories.

The typical high-technology firm of the day was not housed in an impressive high-rise building. Many were based in inconspicuous red-brick low-rises, along the twisty streets of suburban industrial estates. One of Geac's facilities was a small, single-story, unmarked office, largely devoid of superfluous furniture. It was messy. The front door was kept permanently locked. If you knew of the building's existence, you drove around to the loading dock and entered by the service door. The building, on the incongruously named "Riviera Drive" in Markham, Ontario, Canada, was part of a high-technology enclave the media sometimes called "silicone hill."[10] The programmers called it "The Riv."

A dozen programmers worked inside. They were male and female, mostly in their twenties and thirties. One was a former marine biologist. Another was a sports enthusiast. Another drove fast sports cars, and at least one practiced skydiving. Several were engineers; all wore blue jeans to work during the day, and, if struck by a sudden inspiration or if a crisis arose, they worked all night. Their more publicly accessible coworkers, the development and customer support programmers (who also worked overnight when a crisis arose), were housed about a mile away in a larger single-story red-brick building, tucked away in an industrial strip mall on Markham's Steelcase Road.

Holly House stood across the sea in Bristol, England. Its proud history dated back at least to AD 865, when the land may have been granted to Oftfor, bishop of Worcester, by Aethelred, king of Mercia. Passing imposing gate posts with brass plaques, visitors drove along a winding lane past carefully planted plane trees. A Victorian observatory tower stood in an adjacent field. Hollywood Tower's clock was made by Dent, the designers of Big Ben. From behind the house, past a row of greenhouses, came the occasional roaring of large cats, tigers and lions kept in a quarantine facility by the owners of the property, Bristol and Clifton Zoological Gardens. Behind tall ground-floor windows, the black screens of computer terminals glowed with green and amber writing. A hodgepodge of a dozen vehicles from a Lotus to a Volkswagen van stood along the wall. In such a setting, one might expect some sort of government intrigue. Indeed, during World War II, when the estate belonged to the White family, owners of the world's largest aircraft company, Bristol Aviation, Sir Winston Churchill had been known to relax here at weekends.

During the mid-1980s, the building was full of mini-computers. Smaller than mainframes, mini-computers were about the size of refrigerators, and they were flanked by rows of disk drives the size of dishwashers. Each disk drive typically held 675 megabytes of data, so there were quite a few of them. In the high-technology tradition that had made Hollywood Tower central to the war effort, it and its red-brick North American equivalents now housed a small and somewhat secretive group of programmers, executives, salespeople, and office staff grappling with an array of intriguing technical challenges. Their specialty was online transaction processing (OLTP), and they were using the mini-computers to automate libraries and banks.

To a great extent, it was the customers who energized and shaped the development of integrated library systems. Working with programmers, they outlined the specifications. Individually, and working through "user groups," they demanded that vendors conform to a series of increasingly demanding and complicated standards. Librarians wanted rapid, reliable transaction processing, and high standards of data integrity and security in their library systems.

Today, the information professions are sufficiently advanced that the underlying technologies that support them are seldom considered. We take it for granted that it is possible to snap a digital photograph, scan a sheet of text, retrieve a document over the Internet, or talk to one another using instant text or online video. Those assumptions underlie the service models of professional librarianship in the early 21st century, but these need tweaking, as their predecessors often did.

Librarians today take it for granted that users will be able to search library catalogues, find the proper call numbers for the items they would like, and retrieve them, either from physical shelves or from local or remote databases. Most libraries of any size and complexity have online public access catalogues (OPACs) and online circulation systems to keep track of their materials. Their staffs order materials using automated acquisitions systems, and exchange materials with other libraries using automated interlibrary loan systems. These systems are so universal that the underlying infrastructures, standards, and thought processes that went into their development are seldom even considered.

MAKING SYSTEMS AS ERROR FREE AS POSSIBLE

Even the best designed systems don't always work, especially in the beginning. As MIT's Marvin Minsky put it, "It's mainly when our systems fail that consciousness becomes engaged. For example, we walk and talk without much sense of how we actually do those things. But a person with an injured leg may, for the first time, begin to formulate theories about how walking works."[11] It is a fundamental principle of cybernetic theory that most learning opportunities come from our mistakes, from negative feedback. To know that you are on course, you must know what it means to drift off course.

While they seem to work seamlessly, the early library automation systems were, as the early releases of many types of systems, full of bugs. They were politely called "undocumented features." This is not to say that software vendors did not test their products before releasing them. Design features that seemed adequate in the lab or under testing proved inadequate in the field. For instance, one circulation system failed the first time a patron attempted to take out 256 books at the same time. The system designers had assumed that 255 books would be a reasonable maximum number for any person to check out at one time. Designers used to simpler applications found the strange world of library data a bigger challenge than they had ever anticipated. The automation of library processes, and the communication of bibliographic data, presented a range of technical, logical, and human complications that are detailed in this book.

ADVENT OF BIBLIOGRAPHIC UTILITIES

At the beginning of the 1980s, many routine library processes had been automated for some time: cataloguing, bibliographic databases, and management processes for consortia to share computing resources. These were shared with membership in a consortium that allowed many libraries to share file space on a large mainframe computer, to exchange bibliographic records, and to print catalogue cards. These groups were sometimes called a "bibliographic utility" or "automated library consortia" among vendors and librarians. One of the objectives of a consortium was often to create a catalogue containing the records of many different libraries. They combined records into what was usually called a "union" catalogue, and the new bibliographic utilities became union catalogues on a vast scale.

The most celebrated of these bibliographic utilities was OCLC, based in Dublin, Ohio. The acronym originally stood for the Ohio College Library Center. OCLC soon gained subscribers in other jurisdictions, and eventually became a worldwide entity. In 1981, OCLC celebrated its tenth anniversary. A new facility was built in Dublin, and the acronym was retained but changed to mean Online Computer Library Center. According to the 1982 *American Library Association Yearbook*, over 4,200 terminals were connected to OCLC, allowing 2,800 libraries to access about 8 million bibliographic records.[12]

Where had these records come from? Many were contributed by member libraries, and cost-sharing formulas were devised by OCLC and its rival networks, including the Western Library Network (WLN) and the Research Libraries Information Network (RLIN). Members were allowed to copy or "derive" records from one another in exchange for small fees. Similar to OCLC, WLN, which had begun in the state of Washington as the Washington Library Network, had also changed its name, as the consortium's services had extended beyond its original geographic bounds. The RLIN consortium was meant to serve a group of major research libraries, which included Harvard, Yale, Columbia, and the New York Public Library. By the early 21st century, both had merged with OCLC.

We can gain some idea of the overall progress of library automation from RLIN's example. RLIN's original concept had been based, in turn, on the BALLOTS system developed at Stanford University. The acronym stood for "Bibliographic Automation of Large Library Operations using a Time-Sharing System," a name which almost never appears fully spelled out.

According to a report issued in 1978, the BALLOTS system already supported searching, acquisitions, and cataloguing and was planning a new Network File System, an Authority Control System, a Synchronous Communications System, a Library Management Information Program, and a Book and Microform Catalog Interface.

Bibliographic utilities required a consistency in transferring their printed catalogue card records into their electronic databases. This meant that librarians had to alter their records to make them fit the database, a process called "retrospective conversion" and sometimes called RECON for short. RLIN was also considering ways to implement RECON. Decades later, this dream is more easily achieved since scanners and scanning software can complete the task in seconds. In those early days, RECON might mean a great deal of new keyboarding. A whole service industry grew up providing RECON. Libraries outsourced this mammoth task by sending their records to private companies like ReMARC.

In the mid-1970s, alternatives to printed cards were in use, but the technology for viewing them online was either prohibitively expensive or simply not technically feasible. Alternate solutions such as Computer Output Microform (COM) allowed libraries to transfer copies of their computerized bibliographic records to microfilm or microfiche. These COMs were available by the middle of the 1970s.

Reel-to-reel microfilm is not suited to random access or finding the precise thing you want quickly. The industry's answer was microfiche, a rectangular piece of transparent plastic a bit larger than a catalogue card containing tens or hundreds of pages of computer printout reduced to microscopic size. A special reader consisting of a powerful lens, a light source, and a small projection screen was needed to enlarge the fiche for it to be read by librarians. Where today one would find computer workstations, large libraries had rows of fiche readers allowing users to browse the catalogue, search for materials in other libraries, and possibly read telephone directories if they were available in this form. Some companies were even capable of creating COM fiche sets overnight from automated circulation systems, so that library circulation lists could be reasonably up to date. A visitor to the library would know what books had been borrowed before midnight the previous day and when they should be returned.

However, some staff and patrons disliked COM fiche. Eye strain and the necessity of constantly keeping the fiche in order were two problems. "The letters are small, and they jump all over the screen," lamented a user in 1981. Circulation and reference staff were kept busy reordering the sets of fiche left scattered on tables by the readers.

Membership in a consortium had another benefit: the development of "copy cataloguing." If a work had been catalogued by any member of the consortium, other members would be able to download the record into their own databases, instead of cataloguing it "from the work in hand." This would substantially change work flow in libraries, and eventually make it possible for small institutions with shortages of professionally trained staff to employ lower paid workers to catalogue their new acquisitions.

By 1983, microcomputers, or "desktops" like the IBM PC and the "transportable" Osborne (a computer housed in a box that looked like a sewing machine), were drawing library attention. However, they were being used to generate reports and perform office work, not to run the circulation, acquisitions, or cataloguing systems, because they lacked the capacity to do so.[13]

DEVELOPING NATIONAL BIBLIOGRAPHIES

During this time, the U.S. Library of Congress and the national libraries of other countries began an enormous task. They wished to create national bibliographies that would represent the intellectual outputs of entire countries. Because of legal deposit legislation, most countries had begun requiring publishers to submit at least two copies of every new book, issue of a journal, and, in some cases, material published in other media to the national library

Publishers benefit from legal deposit legislation in several ways. One of these is through Cataloguing in Publication (CIP). Even today, the legal deposit process helps ensure that works are cited properly and bolsters copyright claims. When a new book or other media production is planned, publishers can send its description to the national library on forms; and professional cataloguers in Washington, Canberra, Ottawa, London, and elsewhere can send back standardized descriptions complete with assigned Dewey or Library of Congress call numbers, authoritative subject headings, and so forth. This information can then be printed right in the book, by convention, on the verso of the title page. When a book vendor or a library purchases a new title, its high-quality description can be copied into the vendor's or library's own catalogue.

As well, national bibliographies were thought of as contributing to the record of a country's achievements. The dream, advanced by the International Federation of Library Associations and Institutions (IFLA), was of Universal Bibliographic Control (UBC). The world's librarians dreamed of recording, and making widely available, the intellectual output of the entire planet.

This was by no means a new dream. The Library of Congress' National Union Catalog (NUC), Canadiana, the British National Bibliography, and other international union catalogues had been around for decades in print form. What were new were the dreams of making them widely available by means of reel-to-reel computer tape and of making them easier to update and use. All of this paved the way for online public access catalogues. To ensure consistency in the ways in which authors' names, geographic locations, and subjects were entered into its catalogue, the Library of Congress also began to create and share "authority" files. Computer software would later make use of the Subject and Name Authorities to check new entries in a catalogue, and to revise existing ones as terminology changed.

Along with these bibliographic utilities, a few university-based and commercial library automation vendors appeared, and with them circulation systems appeared. These were applications of transaction processing that stretched the limits of computing as it was then practiced. Only two library organizations could be considered library circulation system vendors: the Dortmunder Biblioteksysteme (DOBIS) and the University of Toronto Library Automation System (UTLAS). DOBIS provided a product called DOBIS/LIBIS, while UTLAS was primarily a bibliographic utility like OCLC. It offered subscribers a shared or union catalogue, giving access to the titles held by all. But it had been creating a circulation system as well.

PROGRAMMING LANGUAGES AND ILS

During the 1970s, the University of Waterloo, located in southern Ontario, Canada, was almost as synonymous with computing as MIT or Berkeley. It had developed extensions to the popular general-purpose FORTRAN programming language called WATFOR and WATFIV and its own version of the equally popular business computing language COBOL, called WATBOL.[14] Not surprisingly, some of the early development of the ILS began at Waterloo. Much pioneering work was also done at Northwestern University and the University of Chicago. Gene Damon, a veteran executive of many computing institutions, recalls,

Looking back at my copy of the 1976 Waterloo "Circulation System Report," there is a brief bibliography at the back. It has three articles by Rob McGee on circulation system design, all I think, based on work he was doing at Chicago. It also has an article by James Aagard, another name, [who] along with Velma Veneziano, were true pioneers of library automation with their work at Northwestern.[15]

McGee himself points out that one can read about the decades of work by librarians and computer scientists documented in the *Journal of Library Automation*.[16] This journal's issues from the 1970s are particularly illustrative of developments like BALLOTS and a newfangled idea for circulation control, the use of bar-coded labels instead of punched IBM or "Hollerith" computer cards, or handwritten book cards. By the mid-1970s, commercial circulation systems that used barcodes were coming onto the market. Plessey, a long-established British general-computing firm, and the U.S.-based library vendor CLSI, would make such systems the standards of the library world, as we shall see.

The programs that computer users need are called "applications programs"; those needed to keep computers themselves running are called "systems programs." Systems programs can be written in "low-level" computing languages like IBM Assembler Language that are hard for people to understand but which run faster because they are closer to the very simple instruction sets that the machines use to operate.[17] However, while relational databases such as Microsoft Access or the various varieties of Structured Query Language (SQL) were not yet deployed, there were "file management systems" such as Mark IV. Libraries with large numbers of staff could afford programming employees and could use these systems to manage much of their routine work.[18] However, Cox's prediction that an online catalogue would be far in the future would still have seemed valid to the staff who handled reams of perforated continuous-form printouts, generated by programs written in COBOL or FORTRAN, on a daily basis.

BIBLIOGRAPHIC DATABASES, BIBLIOGRAPHIC UTILITIES, AND REGIONAL LIBRARY CONSORTIA

The decade of the 1970s saw the rise of bibliographic databases such as those marketed by Dialog and projects like Stanford BALLOTS, the introduction of stand-alone circulation systems (by companies like Plessey, and ones developed by universities, such as NOTIS), and the rise of bibliographic utilities such as OCLC. Building upon these developments but faced with the enormous costs associated with computing, regional automated library consortia began to proliferate during the next decade. They included organizations in the United States and Canada such as CRLC, FVRL, Sno-Isle, Circcess, Amigos, Bibliomation, NELINET, INCOLSA, and WOLF, to name but a few. Their role was to help member libraries implement library automation in all its forms by training staff and helping purchase hardware and software at a lesser price.

Library automation has always been a niche market within computing and consists of smaller niche markets. School libraries and smaller, often rural public libraries had different needs from larger public libraries, academic libraries, and special libraries, more or less demanding in their requirements for system functions and features. A consortium serving all of these types of libraries needed software to handle the most demanding institution in the system. The magic of the microcomputer helped this materialize.

By the mid-1980s, the microcomputer was coming onto the market. By the time the vendors had perfected systems that ran on mini-computers, the death knell of the era had been sounded. The cost of computing hardware had dropped to mere thousands of dollars, and the business models behind library automation vendors that had led the field during the past decades were no longer viable. Those that could adapt survived, and the systems they sold became more standardized in look and feel and greatly improved in capacity. The era of invention, and of close collaboration among vendors and clients, was drawing to a close. Integrated library system automation had matured.

The mainframe era had been dominated by companies like IBM, Burrows, and UNIVAC, and though they would remain dominant in the higher end of the market, smaller companies made great inroads with smaller machines. With the commercial availability of mini-computers, made by companies such as Digital Equipment Corporation (DEC), Hewlett-Packard, or Perkin-Elmer (Interdata), firms that developed and packaged that software came into being. The cost of computing hardware dropped from millions of dollars to hundreds of thousands of dollars per central processing unit (CPU), and, for the first time, cathode-ray tube (CRT) monitors were becoming relatively affordable for use in computer terminals. During the early 1970s, however, operators of some of the first mini-computers used by Plessey, a library automation pioneer, still communicated with the machine via teletypewriters, keyboards attached to printers and connected by wire to the computer.

With computing and communication technology so ubiquitous today, this should probably not be surprising. When we buy a pound of butter from the supermarket, we seldom stop to think of the process of churning butter, which once occupied hours of women's days. When we draw a pint of beer, we seldom think about the skill of the brewmaster or the control of fermentation. When we make a telephone call, we seldom pause to think about Bell, Marconi, or the other inventors whose pioneering work made our everyday acts possible. Since information and communication technologies underlie so much of our daily work and play, reflecting constantly upon their underpinnings would be counterproductive unless one were engaged in designing improved systems or specifications, or needed to know why existing ones behaved the way they did. Since much of that legacy stems from the 1980s and 1990s, from the era of commercialized mini-computer-based systems, that period will be the focus of this book. While much of the tale is told by people who were associated with Geac Computers International, and a few other companies like Dynix and CLSI, their narratives are intended to be representative. The challenges they dealt with were common among the dozen or so leading vendors that vied for the library market during those early days.

NOTES

1. Whitehead, Alfred North. *An Introduction to Mathematics.* Home University Library of Modern Knowledge. London: Butterworth, 1928. p. 61.

2. Clarke, Arthur C. *Profiles of the Future.* 2nd rev. ed. New York: Harper and Row, 1973. This statement is known as "Clarke's Third Law."

3. Hiltz, Starr Roxanne, and Murray Turoff. *The Network Nation: Human Communication via Computer.* Reading, Mass.: Addison-Wesley, 1978. passim.

4. See Payne, Charles, Rob McGee, Helen F. Schmierer, and Howard S. Harris. "The University of Chicago Library Data Management System." *The Library Quarterly* 47, no. 1 (January 1977): 1–22. Stable URL: http://www.jstor.org/stable/4306754.

5. McGee, Rob, interviewed September 2009.

6. Frederick G. Kilgour, Founder of OCLC, Dies at 92. OCLC Online Computer Library Centre. News release. August 1, 2006. Available at: http://www.oclc.org/news/releases/200631.htm.

7. Kilgour, Fred. "History of Library Computerization." *Journal of Library Automation* 3, no. 3 (September 1970): 218–29.

8. "Increasingly, we will be looking at the Net globally, which increasingly is looking like gopherspace with a few odd library things hanging off it. [I]ndividuals are increasingly publishing direct to the net, and tools to control this in an automated fashion are developing rapidly"; quote from Tony Barry, Australian librarian, 1992, quoted in Brown-Syed, *From CLANN to Unilinc*, 1996. Gopher was a text-based menu-driven search and retrieval tool that was popular before the World Wide Web. It could point to graphics, but not display them. Brown-Syed, Christopher. *From Clann to Unilinc an Automated Library Consortium from a Soft Systems Perspective.* [Thesis: PhD], University of Toronto. [microform]. National Library of Canada = Bibliothèque nationale du Canada, Ottawa, 1996.

9. Cox, Nigel S. M., J. David Dews, and J. L. Dolby. *The Computer and the Library: The Role of the Computer in the Organization and Handling of Information in Libraries.* Hamden, Conn.: Archon Books, 1967. Introduction.

10. Thomas, David. *Knights of the New Technology: The Inside Story of Canada's Computer Elite.* Toronto: Key Porter Books, 1983. p. 169.

11. Minsky, Marvin Lee, *The Society of Mind.* New York: Simon and Schuster, 1986. p. 69.

12. American Library Association. *The ALA Yearbook; A Reflow of Library Events 1981.* Volume 7 (1982). Chicago: American Library Association, 1982. pp. 53–55.

13. Walton, Robert A. *Microcomputers: A Planning and Implementation Guide for Librarians and Information Professionals.* Phoenix, Ariz.: Oryx Press, 1983.

14. McCracken, Daniel D. *A Simplified Guide to Structured Cobol Programming.* New York: Wiley, 1976.

15. Damon, Gene. Personal communication, 2009.

16. McGee, Robert. Personal communication, 2009.

17. Struble, George. *Assembler Language Programming: The IBM System/360 and 370.* 2nd ed. Reading, Mass.: Addison-Wesley, 1975.

18. Informatics, Inc. *The Mark IV File Management System Reference Manual.* 2nd ed. Canoga Park, CA: Informatics Inc. Product Development and Marketing Division, 1970.

2

Customers' Perspectives

From the accounts in this book, it will become obvious that the developers of library systems worked closely with their customers, the librarians and institutions involved. The collaboration was so close that the two groups were often interchangeable. Customers joined the staffs of vendors and vice versa. Companies began as "technology incubators" within universities, developing systems that were first for institutional use but that had later commercial applications. In the 1970s, library automation and online transaction processing (OLTP) in general did not have much currency in computing schools, arguably because machines designed to do scientific or business work were not designed to do automation and online transactions especially well. Library schools, however, were doing interesting work along these lines. The customers highlighted in this and subsequent chapters include librarians who were then employed at the Regina Public Library and the Burlington Public Library in Canada and the College Libraries Activity Network of New South Wales, Australia. In the later chapters, librarians who made the transition back and forth between vendors and customers, some based in the United States and Britain, will also present their observations. Not all of the vendors mentioned were in the business of creating automation systems to handle circulation, acquisitions, or online catalogues. Some were in the business of transferring cataloguing records from paper to digital form, and others with providing access to large research databases. This chapter provides a customer's perspective on various vendors and services, mainly as related by Rona Wade, CEO of the multitype Australian library consortium, UNILINC. First, however, let us examine the impact of an integrated library system (ILS) on a large urban municipal library in the Canadian province of Saskatchewan, as presented over local broadcast media. That the story of a new library computer rated the evening news is perhaps itself revealing of the novelty of the enterprise.

Portions of this chapter appeared in a modified form in Brown-Syed, C. "From CLANN to Unilinc: An Automated Library Consortium from a Soft Systems Perspective." [Thesis, PhD] University of Toronto, 1996.

A FIRST EXPERIENCE OF COMPUTING

"The Regina Public Library is joining the high-tech revolution," begins a segment from a Canadian television program, *This Week*, that aired early in 1985. Presenter Gordon Vizzutti continues, "From now on, a computer will not only help you find the books you want, it will automatically sign them out and of course, remind you when they're due back." Reporter Wayne Mantyka opens with the lines, "If you can't find a book at your library, you check with the card catalogue. Right? Not anymore! The card catalogue is gone. So is the newer microfiche system. It's all been replaced by the computer terminal, and the use of the computer will soon expand to other library services."[1]

Five years before, the story continues, the Regina Public Library Public Library had undertaken an automation study. "The answer was this $600,000 computer," says Mantyka, as the scene shifts to the computer room and close-ups of a Geac 8000 mini-computer housed in a pair of shoulder-high black and gray cabinets. The program's editor chooses shots of the blinking red lights on the 8000's control panel and the reel-to reel tape drives that are the most visually interesting parts of the machine. The news segment goes on to explain how barcodes on library cards and books can be used for circulation and how the system allows placing holds and blocking patrons with unpaid overdue fines. "It will allow users to find materials at any branch in the system and to know whether or not they are currently on the shelf."[2] At the time, for this library, such a feature would have been truly innovative because even if the library had been automated previously, as was the case at many universities, the systems in use would have been "batch" rather than "online." Before OLTP, patrons could not determine the status of an item without asking staff to search the day's charge-out slips, or in batch-automated libraries, without searching lengthy computer print-outs. Where libraries were automated, an item's circulation status would not be obtainable until the next day, when overnight processing had created a printout or microfiche reflecting the previous day's status changes. Knowing the status of an item in another branch would not have been possible in "real time" without telephone exchanges and the same sorts of manual searching at the remote branch.

As the segment continues, Regina librarian Janet Fielden wands patron and book barcodes; her terminal, with its black screen and amber writing, goes "beep." A message pops up saying that the book is on hold for a particular patron. The writing is in something like the Courier font, with each letter taking up the same width on the screen. Better yet, Fielden explains, keyword searching would allow you to find a book with the word "eagle" in the title, even if you had forgotten the detailed information about it. The screen display looks like this:

```
PATRON COLLECTING HOLD: JENSEN, KEN
INFORM MESSAGE ACK _a
BOOK: 3905 003263957
DUE: 85-02-19
```

After librarians Jensen and Fielden discuss some of the features of their new interactive library system, the TV crew interviews patrons and librarians on the front lines. "For many Reginans," says Mantyka, "this is their first experience of computing." Did it take long to figure out? "Oh, about 2 minutes," says one man in his twenties. "Many seniors are excited about the new system," says librarian Rosemary Obbie. And a young boy of about eight or ten, who has a home computer, says the new system is more fun. "Children attack the terminals with great glee," Obbie observes, "and people well into their 80s do too. The instructions appear on the screen."

However, the system promised even greater functionality. The new equipment would also allow patrons to access circulation records from their homes or offices. "The next step would be to allow patrons to dial-in from home," says Mantyka. Ken Jensen, then the library's assistant CEO, said. The library would have to see whether the additional load compromised ongoing operations, he said, but the new system was fully capable of allowing dial-up access.

Other high-tech innovations are mentioned. Jensen speculates that the library's collection of 33.3 rpm long-play records might be replaced by "laser disks," and Mantyka flourishes a VHS cassette. "Librarians can see the popularity of the book diminishing," he says, since people now watch more television. Mantyka addresses the camera, as the segment nears its end, "Librarians say no amount of automation will ever replace the book completely." Ken Jensen provides a concluding homage to the book: "It's such a marvelous medium. It's random-access, it's non-volatile, it's everything we want our information systems to be. We shouldn't condemn it just because it's a 500-year-old technology."[3]

After viewing the television segment in 2009, Diane Koen, associate director of planning and resources at Montreal's McGill University Libraries, observed, "What is remarkable is how little things have changed. The comments from the librarians could be written today."[4] The ILS of the new century must still perform those tasks, and the social impact is still the same, though we might take those systems for granted; that we are able to do so means that the systems now work without too many interruptions. The logic behind these systems, and their functional requirements and capabilities, have been standardized and perfected during the intervening years.

The Regina Public Library was certainly not the first of its kind to make the leap to automation. In the mid-1980s, the wall of the Education Services office at Geac's Markham headquarters was festooned with university pennants and the municipal flags of various cities, representing their customers. It read like a page from a directory of higher education: U.S. Naval Academy, MIT, St. Joseph's University, Georgetown, and York University, among others. A row of city flags represented their public library customers. At all of those sites, the company made sure one person had been designated as a project manager or systems administrator to facilitate communication and problem escalation. Interactions between customer sites and the Library Assistance Desk (LAD) involved a great deal of jargon.

While patrons at libraries like Regina might have found the system much easier to use than a traditional card catalogue, a considerable amount of learning was required of the systems librarians and computer operators who were responsible for its setup and maintenance. If a patron's search yielded no results, there were "help" screens available; but because the system's internals were so complex, those running it often had recourse to the vendor's help desk. The language that typified a help-desk interaction between customer and vendor would have been replete with jargon, and customers soon learned that a good grasp of esoteric terms meant easier communication and, consequently, less downtime.

To the untrained ear, typical instructions from the LAD could have sounded like "Sue Dyna and are you bang user eye," or "You large bang," or "You zero star star temp zero."

They would have meant that the operator should type things like "RU,!USERI" "ULARG!" and "UZERO,**TEMP,0". The system messages were often esoteric too. "Signed down to Dyna only, and God bless all who sail in her!" An operator who attempted something unusual might encounter the message "You are underprivaluged" [*sic*].

Though it was not the universal practice among vendors, Geac gave its customers complete access to all documents, scripts, and program source code much like the modern "open source" systems such as Koha, OpenBiblio, or Evergreen. Customers were free to write, in consultation with the company, their own enhancements, but they were held contractually responsible for any damage they caused. When customers' "site-specific modifications" went beyond the software's current capabilities, companies might purchase and incorporate it into later releases. The arrangement not infrequently proved mutually beneficial.

Customers often wrote manuals for the system and its components. This was the case with the GLUG report-writing software. Customers were free to use GLUG to design their own management information reports, but few had the knowledge until GLUG was explored and described in a manual. Tom Owens wrote such a manual while working in the library systems department in the University of Arizona in Tucson, and it remained the only official GLUG manual over the life of the product. Interviewed in 2009, Keith Thomas, former director of development for the company, speculates that the early successful cooperative ventures with libraries and credit unions that had shaped the company contributed to this atmosphere. He emphasizes that the benefits went both ways: "I think it would be fair to say that the provision of this information to customers was both a sign of respect for their ability and a tactical move to make them more self-sufficient, i.e. to reduce support calls."[5] In fact, as we shall see, many customers went far beyond ordinary support, using imaginative methods to actually enhance the system and to share that knowledge with the company and with other sites. Sometimes, with Geac and with other vendors like NOTIS, the distinctions between "our people" and "their people" became blurred.

Speaking at a 1985 conference, NOTIS' Jane Burke had to remind the audience that while both sides shared enthusiasm for the project, vendors were, generally speaking, "for-profit" companies, and contractual agreements should be negotiated carefully. It would be fair to say that both customers and vendors, especially the librarians working for both, were certain that something special was being created.[6]

USER MANUALS

In 1988, two programmers associated with the Geac Bibliographic Processing System (BPS), the cataloguing module written for the 9000 as a replacement for the earlier MARC Record Management System (MRMS), attempted to describe the tools and utility programs installers might need to run reports. The document was labeled "For internal use only" because anything sent to the customers would be tidied up by the technical writing team. However, any documents, programs, or scripts that were shipped with a system would be visible to anyone who knew how to find and display them, and the document "FDTOOL" was one.[7]

All Geac programs, documents, and batches (scripts) were prefixed with standard headers, which explained what they did, contained version control information, and tracked changes and updates. All lines in a header began with an asterisk, *, which computer programmers often pronounced "star." The stars indicated that the following text was a comment, not a piece of program code, and signaled the machine to ignore it. All headers included the file's name and purpose, the author's name, notes on where to find documentation, associated files, known bugs and planned enhancements, and a revision history with the dates of changes and the initials of the person making them. The document in question was called FDTOOL, and its header reads, in part, "Purpose: to assist operations / installations personnel in defining various utility programs available to the BPS system. Also useful for remembering what utilities are around to do things." The FDTOOL revision history looked like this:

```
* Revision History
* When          Who      Why
* 88 Jan 01     RS/PT    Creation date
* 88.FEB.05     PT       created uget, uset, ufind prgms
* 88-Mar 11     PT       Added major warning and
                         submitted this copy.
```

The initials were those of the programmers who had made the changes, and their "major warning" followed in a box made of asterisks:

```
Some of the programs in this document can cause loss of
data or corruption of data and should not be run by
inexperienced users.
```

There followed an explanation of the types of programs listed including statistical utilities that library customers could run for information gathering "with little or no modification," utilities for the installation and support of the system, and "general purpose programs that make life easier."

The tools document consisted of 33 pages of succinct descriptions of programs, some with cryptic names like NU, a program to convert number formats, or BPTCPD, described as "a program to display Hugo's keystroke log." To those versed in Geac's file-naming conventions, and that would have included the systems librarians and operators at customer sites, the purpose of BPTCPD would have been fairly obvious. Terminal activities were recorded in large files with names like **TCP1 and **TCP2, the prefix "BP" indicated "Bibliographic Processing System Program," and the trailing "D" suggests something to do with displaying things.

It seems obvious, in hindsight, that the company and its customers shared a common vocabulary, and worked in an atmosphere of mutual trust. Giving out the source code was really not much of an intellectual property issue since programs written in the company's proprietary languages like ZOPL or HUGO would only run on Geac hardware. To be sure, the programming language C was widely used at the time. There was eventually a ZOPL-to-C cross-compiler, and someone with programming knowledge who was bent on reverse-engineering Geac's library system could have probably done so. However, the hardware and firmware, especially those of the Geac 9000 computer, and the proprietary software were optimized for one another. Replicating the system's performance would still have been a challenge because much of the software would need to be rewritten before it ran efficiently on some other computer platform. By the end of the decade, Geac had experimentally "ported" the system to the UNIX environment by cross-compiling the ZOPL code to the C language. But history had caught up with Geac. The company switched to UNIX, but stopped manufacturing the 9000 and purchased the Advance library system, which was already running in Hawaii, and which used the PICK database engine and the UNIX operating system.

CONSORTIA CUSTOMERS AND VENDORS

Technical interactions were only one aspect of the broader collaboration among customers and vendors. The idea for an ILS had originated within the confines of universities and research libraries, but by the mid-1980s, for-profit companies had made ILS a global reality, at least for those libraries that could afford such systems. Those that could not do so as a single library might possibly rely upon a local consortium organized at the county level or even at state or provincial levels. Such consortia had existed before local automation systems, but their enhanced spending power made the acquisition of ILS for their members an attractive and viable option.

Rona Wade, who has headed Australia's UNILINC consortium for many years, recalls a series of systems installations, upgrades, and migrations from one vendor to another. She says, simply, "Cooperation made that possible."[8] Wade credits the purchasing power of consortia, as well as their being suitable test-beds for new larger-scale projects, along with the shared "spirit" of innovation.

BURLINGTON PUBLIC LIBRARY

Wendy Schick, long-time CEO of the Burlington Public Library in southern Ontario, recalls early implementations of CLSI, DOBIS, and Geac systems in her own library and those of nearby towns. The process of acquiring them and the eventual shape of those systems are probably typical of similar installations around the world. She points out that librarians at Burlington had been participating in shared cataloguing ventures before they made the move to online circulation, acquisitions, and online public access catalogues (OPACs). Nearby Hamilton, Ontario, was already a subscriber to the University of Toronto's UTLAS bibliographic database, as was the city's McMaster University. Schick described the process in a 2008 interview:

We did know of a few other libraries, like Halinet, (Oakville, Milton, Halton Hills), which was with CLSI. They invited us to join. We had our own MARC database. Our first exposure to automation was through the Hamilton Public Library, a UNICAT/TELECAT site, through a partnership with McMaster University from about 1975. We used to go in and look at their new book display.[9]

The move began for Burlington when its new CEO, Lucille Galloway, moved there from nearby Hamilton, where Charles Brisbane was the head. "Thus," says Schick,

began a story of regional cooperation. When Lucille came in 1968 from Hamilton, she had an arrangement with Hamilton that librarians from Burlington could go to Hamilton and look at their catalogue, and if they liked a book, they could order cards. Every week, we got a new set of catalogue cards.[10]

To facilitate the process, Hamilton's McMaster University entered Burlington Public as a "branch" in its UTLAS system, and Schick recalls that the arrangement lasted for about two years. "In the long run, we needed to be independent, and became in 1977, an independent public library member of UTLAS."[11]

Librarians have always been enthusiastic about new technologies. Schick recalls the birth of the Halinet consortium, which linked various libraries in what was then Halton County.

Oakville got their CLSI system when Richard Moses put a computer in the basement, and had to figure out how to pay for it. Milton and HH joined their network, but we already had a MARC database, and going with CLSI would mean losing that. CLSI didn't have a MARC database. In the end, neither did Geac . . . for a while.[12]

For Burlington, the process of implementing a local ILS began around Christmas 1979, when it was decided to issue a request for proposals (RFP). UTLAS (which had developed its own ILS) responded, as did CLSI, DataPhase, and Geac.

We selected UTLAS, but though the board approved it, they [UTLAS] had to take it to their board of governors. It would have been the first system installed outside of U of T. The board evidently said no. We were notified on Christmas Eve, 1979. They had posted a bond, to show they meant business and would carry forward.[13]

Burlington kept the money. Disappointed to say the least, Burlington's selection committee then chose DataPhase, which also figured largely in Rona Wade's UNILINC history, across the Pacific in Australia. Both DataPhase and Geac offered MARC record management systems, and Geac's was called MRMS.

We weren't thrilled with MRMS. UTLAS pulled out, we reissued or reanalyzed and chose DataPhase because it worked with the UTLAS database and preserved the MARC record, but the Burlington board refused it, and directed us to purchase the Geac system.[14]

The four-digit "agency number" for Burlington, appearing on its barcodes, is 9072. University at Buffalo's is 9071. Since vendors assigned them sequentially as contracts were signed, we can tell that Burlington immediately followed Buffalo as a Geac customer, making them both early adopters.

Like CLSI, and Plessey before them, Geac's original circulation module did not contain full MARC records. The company had purchased the rights to MRMS from the University of Guelph, with which it had a history of cooperative development work. Guelph's librarian, Margaret Beckman, had been instrumental in Geac's entry into the library marketplace. In the event, the company went on to develop MRMS as another module of its integrated system, and eventually to replace it with the BPS, and still later with entirely new systems like Advance and Vubis.

A VIEW FROM AUSTRALIA

Early in the spring of 1975, April to be precise, Australian librarian Dorothy Peake set off upon a mission to North America. She was acting on behalf of the New South Wales Board of Technical and Further Education, which administered the state's

Colleges of Technical and Further Education (TAFEs) and various Colleges of Advanced Education (CAEs). They had asked Peake to join a working party to investigate cataloguing issues. Between the months of April and June 1975, Peake made a study of online library systems in the United States, Canada, and Britain, with a view to assessing the applicability of innovations in librarianship. In a report published the following year, she observed,

The most astonishing development in North America is the growth of library networks. These are a recent phenomenon, their growth is rapid, and their implications for libraries everywhere far-reaching. It was clear to me that a quiet revolution in the formal relationships between libraries has come about through the impact of technology on libraries.[15]

After investigating the Ohio College Library Center (OCLC), IBM's DOBIS system, Stanford University's BALLOTS, the Boston-based BIBNET, the Ontario Universities Library Cooperative System (OULCS), and other networking initiatives and bibliographic management systems, Peake sought to explain "the extent to which: 1. common computer facilities can benefit library systems and improve the transfer of information within society, and 2. the impact of commercial developments in the area of information handling on libraries and library development."[16]

"Already," said Peake's report, "many hundreds of libraries throughout the world are using computers." However, in 1976, the costs of automating a library were considerable. An OCLC M-100 cataloguing input terminal cost US$4,514, and a BALLOTS terminal about US$7,000. The IBM terminals used in the Library of Congress sold for US$16,000.[17] Peake suggested adopting the OCLC Library Model 100 terminal as the Australian standard. It must be remembered that a "terminal" was simply a keyboard and a monitor hard-wired to a mainframe computer or connected to a remote computer by means of a dial-up modem over telephone lines. These so-called dumb terminals had no processors in them, and only served as a means of exchanging data with the mainframe.

Her report emphasized that bibliographic databases were merely one species of information provision service, and confidently forecast the spread and development of the network concept. While much of the report dealt with shared cataloguing, this wider vision was reflected in Peake's mention of systems to provide online ordering of materials and full-text document retrieval. These included online services provided by the U.S. National Library of Medicine (NLM), and Blackwell's book-ordering system in England. CLSI's pioneering "LIBS series" PDP-11 minicomputer-based circulation system was also described, briefly, as an example of a system to automate local operations.[18] Peake concluded on a broader, more philosophical note, citing Australia's Prime Minister Gough Whitlam's desire to promote "open government," or "free information." "The desire of workers and community groups to participate in decision making highlights the urgent need for a well-informed public ... therefore libraries are of growing importance to society particularly now that technology is available to extend their services."[19]

Peake foresaw librarians playing a major role in the process of spreading knowledge and, more particularly, in developing systems to enhance that process. "As we move toward the end of the century, the quality of life for members of society will depend on a free flow of information. Librarians and other information personnel have a responsibility and a role to play in designing systems through which this can be achieved."[20]

Within two years of Peake's investigative tour, the College Libraries Activities Network of New South Wales (CLANN) had become a reality. CLANN Limited was formed in 1978, with a AU$500,000 operating grant and a mandate to provide central technical services for tertiary education institutions in the state of New South Wales. Peake was soon appointed its executive director, a position she was to hold until 1981.

In a dedication address, the NSW minister for higher education remarked, "The beauty of the system is that the librarians will not be the only people to benefit," User access would be the "the system's greatest benefit." Peake's opening remarks stressed the importance of both people and machines. "There are two elements in a library network," she asserted. "One is an organizational structure, the other suitable hardware and software."[21]

In her address to the 1986 annual general meeting, Dorothy Peake lauded the consortium's reciprocal borrowing agreement, and pointed to CLANN's contribution of 79,694 current records to the national union catalogue (ABN) during the past year for a total of 300,000 to that point. These achievements were cast in an ethical light: "CLANN is at the forefront of developments in the provision of equality of access to users of libraries across New South Wales."[22] Thus, the end user of information was again seen as the ultimate beneficiary.

Rona Wade had taken over as executive director of CLANN in 1981. By 1985, when she described the selection process and implementation of the CLANN circulation and OPAC system, the network had over 400,000 catalogue records in MARC format in its database, linked to over 1,000,000 holdings or item (piece-level) records.[23]

CLANN GOES ONLINE

CLANN went to tender for its in-house integrated system in March 1984, and a Geac Library Information System (GLIS) was delivered the following April. Already high on Wade's agenda was the company's commitment to the emerging Open Systems Interconnection (OSI) reference model, a development that held hopes of supplementing the already developed Transport Control Protocol/Internet Protocol (TCP/IP) that would later become the underlying communications protocol of the Internet. Working with librarians in New York and other locations, Geac was testing a linked system project, which used the bottom three levels of the OSI protocol and partially compliant upper layers.

By the next year, the concepts of OSI and of local area networking were gaining in popularity in Australia, as elsewhere. In 1986, as its Mitchell CAE site made plans to distribute CLANN services over a local area network, Geac's Michael Monahan, writing in the Australian library journal *LASIE*, described how a full implementation of OSI might work in the library setting, and remarked optimistically, "The ability to achieve true international consensus on practical library networking appears within our grasp."[24] While the adoption of the seven-level OSI communications protocol has yet to become universal, another of Monahan's predictions seems apropos: "There will be a subtle shift in the function of the library as more and more systems adopt the ISO/OSI model. The library will become an intermediary in the computer information networks that many users access . . . a single access node for the local users."[25]

This confidence was shared by CLANN's Robin O'Mara and Dorothy Peake, who confidently described OSI as "the building block of the '80s," in a related *LASIE* report

(O'Mara & Peake, 1986).[26] They predicted that the new era of computer communications would enhance shared MARC catalogue systems, and would mean better interloan services and more effective interfaces with book vendors. The authors warned that OSI principles should become part of any national library infrastructure plan, and envisaged a new era of distributed processing nodes linked by the shared protocol.

It should be noted that the full seven-level OSI protocol was never actually achieved by Geac during this time frame. However, the company's Series 9000 software successfully implemented the first three layers of the OSI reference model, and presented upper layers that were compliant with but not identical to those of the model (Geac, 1986, 1987).[27]

Interviewed in 2009 during a visit to Canada, Rona Wade relates a similar tale to that of Burlington's Wendy Schick. The UNILINC consortium that she has headed for decades was formed by the College Libraries Activity Network of New South Wales (CLASS) and eventually grew to serve subscribers in neighboring states. As in southern Ontario, the CLANN/UNILINC story begins with a shared bibliographic database.

The origins of library automation in Australia rest very much with people like Jan Gettenby and Kim Juelbarck and a company called Libramatic. Jan worked for Kim. She got involved with the development of AUSMARC, which actually predates OCLC. In terms of the bigger picture, it goes back to them in Australia. CLANN had its own shared cataloguing operation, which involved coding up bibliographic records using sheets of paper. Theirs was a microfiche-based cooperative cataloguing operation, which had been working since about 1977. The system had been developed by a company called Libramatic. From a work-flow point of view, it consisted of data sheets for record inserts, copy inserts, multicopy inserts, and copy and record updating and replacement. The consortium's cataloguers filled in the sheets, conforming to AUSMARC specifications, and sent them to CLANN, where a team of keypunchers set to work. Wade explains, "It went onto disks, about 7-inches square, and the biggest challenge was to get them to North Sydney by 4 o'clock, to catch the flight down to Melbourne, so they could be added to the mainframe."[28]

From the database on the mainframe computer, they produced a monthly microfiche of the shared catalogue. By scanning the microfiche, cataloguers decided what to do with newly purchased material. Wade explains, "If your record was there already, you would do a copy insert. if not, you would do a record insert."[29]

The decision to purchase an ILS came about for CLANN in the early 1980s, after Dorothy Peake had visited OCLC in the United States and various sites in Canada. Wade joined CLANN in 1981, and by 1983 several of its members were expressing the desire for OPACs and circulation systems. Wade recalls that was "basically all you had": "There were vendors like CLSI, which was the main one we knew about. It was marketed in OZ by Libramatic, but it was really just a circ system. Some of us were thinking we ought to replace the microfiche with an OPAC."[30]

Four vendors responded to CLANN's RFP, among them Geac and Dataphase. One circulation system featured a yellow square that would appear and blink, telling staff how long it would take to process a transaction. CLANN staff called it the "yellow steam train."

"There was only one we believed would allow each library to have its own OPAC . . . as opposed to a union catalogue, with an easy click-through to the shared union catalogue. None of the vendors could do that, but Geac said they would try," she recalls. Geac's library division head gave Wade his assurances. "Hans Kleinheinz said, 'Rona, we can do it.' "[31]

Hans and sales chief Robert Desmarais traveled to Australia and came home with a contract. When that was followed by one with the Commonwealth Scientific and Industrial Research Organization (CSIRO), headquartered in Melbourne, and a third with the Royal Melbourne Institute of Technology (RMIT), Geac established permanently staffed offices in Australia. Though Geac had an OPAC and a catalogue module called the MARC Record Management System (MRMS), CLANN was not ready to make the switch from its time-tested subscription service.

We started with circulation and kept the cataloguing running on what was by now an online system called LION, with a MARC record service called LYNX, provided by a company called IDAPS. It was the best cataloguing system I've ever seen. It was fabulous. LION focused on the easiest way to get your records in, it could handle music cataloguing. With just a keystroke, you could repeat the search on LYNX.[32]

Shortly thereafter, IDAPS was taken over by a larger company that was not entirely focused on libraries, and began altering its pricing structure. Because of this, CLANN moved to an in-house cataloguing system. Once the decision was made, it all happened within a few weeks. Over lunch at a Sydney eatery called The Movable Feast, Wade asked Geac's project manager, Diane Koen, how quickly a switch to MRMS could be engineered. "We did up a plan on a serviette [a paper napkin]," she recalls.[33]

The Geac system "went live" in 1986. All 37 CLANN sites became operational within a two-month period. The following year, the network's Five Year Business Plan was approved, and cataloguing was moved from the service bureau to the in-house GLIS system. During 1987, approximately 250,000 cataloguing records were input, and 80 cataloguing terminals were in use. Also during that year, 17 new sites were added to the shared system. While reciprocal borrowing activities and contributions to the Australian Bibliographic Network were not always given in annual reports, over 100,000 reciprocal loans were recorded during the 1987 fiscal year, and the consortium's 1986 ABN contribution stood at 400,000 records, as revealed in the networks newsletters and reports.

At this point, CLANN was operating a Dual 8000 to run its circulation module; and the MRMS system and its OPAC meant they would need a third 8000. The board accepted the plan, and CLANN withdrew from IDAPS within two weeks. A mere two or three weeks after that, MRMS was up and running. "We were aware of the limitations, but it did the job," Wade says. It was not until CLANN purchased a Series 9000 computer that all of its modules, circulation, acquisitions, and the catalogue could be put onto a single machine. "It was the first time we had a true ILS," says Wade. By the early 1990s, CLANN, which had changed its name to UNILINC, had one of the largest and fastest collections of hardware in the library world, a seven-processor Series 9000, the three 8000s, a smaller borrowed 6000, and assorted other servers.

Asked to identify the most significant contribution to library automation during those years, Wade gives what may seem a surprisingly humble reply. The greatest contribution, in her estimation, was not the computer technology itself, but the data-encoding standard that allowed libraries to share bibliographic information, the MARC standard.

I think the real innovation was the MARC record and the ability to share data; that was the librarians' contribution. There's no similar record for payroll, for accounts . . . that's the library profession's true innovation, and the building block of everything that's happened since.[34]

AUSMARC

AUSMARC was the National Library of Australia's implementation of the internationally used MAchine Readable Cataloguing scheme for encoding cataloguing information, developed by the U.S. Library of Congress. Originally conceived as a format for the interchange of data on magnetic tape for the production of printed catalogue cards, MARC records became the basis for online ILS during the 1980s. MARC facilitated the implementation of OPACs. The AUSMARC specification was first issued in 1973. Subsequently additional specifications were published for books (1979 and 1981), projected media (1980), sound recordings and music scores (1982), cartographic materials (1983), and authorities files (1988).

AUTHORITY FILES

Authority files constitute a thesaurus or controlled vocabulary for recording place and personal names and standardized subject headings so that materials can be described in a consistent fashion in libraries around the world. National variations of the specification including AUSMARC, CANMARC, UKMARC, UNIMARC, and INTERMARC have gradually fallen out of use; and the LCMARC specification has increasingly been adopted worldwide. The specification corresponds to ISO standard 2709:2008, which was first issued as ANSI standard Z39.2.

However, in the 1980s, with all those national variants, anyone hoping to mount an OPAC had to invent software that would reconcile incoming formats from all those sources, and merge them together. To complicate matters, the bibliographic utilities like UTLAS, OCLC, RLIN, and WLN had already superimposed their own rationalizations upon the incoming records, and worked out slightly different solutions. Local automation systems vendors were faced with modifying a smaller handful of "site specific" modifications into a bigger handful of national formats and then merging them all into a catalogue that functioned properly.

MARC RECORDS

While all the MARCs were structurally similar, they differed significantly in usage. Every record began with a leader, a set of fixed-length fields for dates, country codes, and so forth, and then the main body of the record, which consisted of variable-length fields identified by numeric "tags" and was preceded by two "indicator" bytes. These could assist typesetting and cataloguing software in determining how to treat the field (e.g., the 245 tag, which held the work's title). The title might be preceded by the indicators "0 4." That would tell the system that the first four letters of the title, for instance, "The" and a "space," should be ignored when creating a title index. To complicate things further, INTERMARC, which was popular in France, used four indicator bytes instead of two.

Though there were 999 possible tags, only a few were in common use. Other commonly used tags were 100, personal author; 260, place of publication, including place, publisher, and date; 300, the extent of the work in pages, running times for films, or the like; and 650, topical subject heading. Some fields could be repeated. For instance, any record could have a number of subject headings, while some could only occur once in a record.

The fields were further divided into subfields, prefixed by field-separator codes and letters. For instance, a place of publication might look like this:

00 260$aLondon$bTaylor and Francis$c2009.

If the work had been published simultaneously in New York, the cataloguer would add another 260 tag.

The subfields caused the real disharmonies. $h might be used for one type of information in the United States, while the Australians might use $x. The local system software had to merge incoming records without destroying information. That might mean "mapping" the $x subfields into $h ones without clobbering anything already in the $h. The vendor also ran the risk of accidentally missing some field identified by an unusual tag number somewhere else in the record. Eventually, in Geac's case, the problem was solved with the introduction of a data specification and substitution table called BTPROD, but that would not be perfected until the early 1980s.

The average size of a MARC record had been calculated at 768 bytes, and it probably took about 128 bytes at most to describe any particular circulation transaction, so even with millions of records passing through a network hourly, today's telecommunications systems would hardly be burdened by a library system. The case was quite different during the early 1980s.

COMMUNICATION LINES

Telecommunications and computer networking presented challenges throughout the world, but especially in large countries like Australia, which were physically isolated from large computing centers or database providers in the United States or Europe. As well, high-speed, "dedicated" data lines were not yet universally available. According to Wade, setting up the integrated library system itself was only part of the challenge. Communication among automated libraries, some situated up to 800 miles from the computing center, presented an even bigger hurdle.

The communications side was even more interesting than the ILS side. When we brought LION in, we went from asynchronous to bi-synchronous lines, and we pushed the envelope in telephone exchanges, within NSW and interstate. CLANN was the reason why a number of telephone exchanges had to upgrade from old fashioned manned ones, to the digital age. That happened in about five different locations. The main one was Penrose, now part of Sydney, which was upgraded as a result of LYNX. The bisynchronous communications lines were phased out by Telstra[35] (then called Telcom).[36]

The bisynchronous data lines were expensive to maintain because engineers had to turn up onsite to service them. They were replaced by Integrated Services Digital Network (ISDN) lines, which could be maintained remotely. Many of the 150 colleges of Technical and Further Education (TAFE) were located in small towns all over New South Wales (NSW), and some consortium members were in other states. Wade observes with a degree of pride, "Our network was the reason much of the telcom system in NSW had to upgrade as early as it did."

"I'm sure that OCLC must have pushed the communications envelope in the same way in the United States," Wade says. CLANN always had the head of OTC, the overseas arm of Telstra, on its board, and through the vice chancellors of member institutions, they were able to present their case for improved communications to the telecom companies. "We were the reason that they had to communicate with the outside world, digitally."

Before the Web, before the Internet, there was no link between Australia and the outside world. AARNet certainly existed,[37] and its members, like those of the UK-based JANET, and the U.S. and Canadian BITNET and Usenet users, were mainly academics and employees of high-technology companies who could exchange mail and join interest groups, or subscribe to Listserv™ mailing lists, which were first implemented in 1986.

During the early to mid-1980s, major communications links to Australia were provided through a gateway machine in the University of Melbourne, called "munari," and others at universities like Monash. At the time, banks communicated among their head offices and maintained their own private networks, but CLANN was using the public network.[38]

INCORPORATING RESEARCH DATABASES

Another way in which librarians "pushed the envelope" was their adoption of Dialog, the online research database. Developed in 1966 by Roger Summit of Lockheed Missiles and Space for the NASA space program, the system allowed for the online retrieval of research articles from an ever-growing collection of engineering, medical, and social scientific databases.[39] The ERIC index of educational journal articles and the engineering index INSPEC were two of its important components. As services like these contained abstracts or brief summaries of articles, they would have contributed substantially to the bandwidth usage or amount of digital traffic being passed over the networks of the day. Wade credits the use of Dialog, in part, for the improvement of telecommunications cables to North America. Dialog was launched as a commercial product in 1968. It was subsequently acquired by Knight-Ridder, and in 2000 it became part of the Thompson Group of companies, which also acquired the Detroit-based Gale Research.

AARNET AND JANET

The Australian Academic Research Network (AARNet) is operated for the Australian Vice Chancellors' Committee (AVCC) under contract by an Australian PNO, Optus. In Britain, the Joint Academic Network (JANET) is funded by the government's Higher and Further Education departments, as well as the Research Council, and had about 750 primary sites in 2009.

When AARNet started in Australia, CLANN was one of the first members. Along with the CSIRO, it was one of a very few nonuniversity participants in the network. Its presence pointed out the fact that libraries were important and high-volume users of networks. As well as providing access to library catalogues, most institutions wished to provide their users with online indexes to articles appearing in journals. Online database services, such as Dialog, provided lists of journal articles and often, short abstracts or summaries of articles' contents. Today, such services often include the full texts of articles. Libraries usually pay subscription fees for database services, and fees for downloading the complete texts of articles "on demand."

According to Wade, Dialog had been adopted in Australia in the mid-1970s; but, due in part to telephone connection chargers, it had been very expensive. Nevertheless, the increasing use of research databases supported OTC's business case for improving the overseas cables.

SAGE was one of the foundation stones of AARNet. ASCnet, run by the Australian Computer Society, was the precursor to AARNet, and CSIRO had been a member. AARNNET made networking more affordable and provided increased capacity.

CD-ROM

The other innovation was the CD-ROM. In the late 1980s, it was difficult to get live communications going with the hundreds of small sites at the TAFE colleges. They would have had to use dial-up telephone connections to talk to the library network. Wade reported,

I'd heard about CD-ROM, in about 1987, and there was a Sydney company which had just started producing a CD-ROM for car-parts, as I recall. I asked if they could put a bibliographic database on CD-ROM, and they agreed to try. CLANN's CDCAT, launched in 1988, was one of the first library catalogues to move from microfiche to CD-ROM.

This meant that manual searching of a number of microfiche could be replaced by look-ups from a personal computer workstation. "We had need driving us," says Wade, "And need is a great source of innovation."

Among the most remote were ten agricultural research stations run by the NSW Agriculture Department some with populations of about 500. Before there was any other type of automation in libraries, CLANN shipped them CD-ROMs.

We had also pushed the boundaries on barcodes. We needed a lot of them. Because of that, at least 2 million items to barcode, and because we had to do a retrospective conversion, Geac invented the "smart" barcode, which printed up with the call number and the first few letters of the author's name.

THE CUSTOMER AND THE ILS VENDOR

Wade made several personal visits to the selected vendor's Canadian headquarters in Markham, north of Toronto, Ontario. She found it "not as humble as ours. . . . I wasn't coming from anything swish. But all [information technology] places look like that. OVID looked that way in the 1990s, cables strung everywhere." Wade soon discovered how important Hans Kleinheinz, vice president in charge of the Library Systems Division, was to the whole operation.

Nothing moved without Hans. He'd say, "Rona, we can do that". Could they? Did CLANN know they couldn't? Absolutely, we knew they couldn't but that they would. We got the idea that his brain was ticking over, and working out how to do what we wanted. You knew there was a brain working on your behalf. I think he drove most of the innovation.[40]

Wade also praises the technical staff upon whom Kleinheinz relied to deliver on the company's promises. Two in particular, Lambert de Visser, and Mike Himelfarb, who were eventually seconded to CLANN's Sydney headquarters for lengthy periods, draw her special praise. There were other technical "heavy hitters" in Markham or Bristol of whom the customers were aware. Michael Clark and Eric Willis are names Wade remembers well. Overall, she credits the presence of a forceful senior manager, who understood and sympathized with the issues facing libraries, with the system's success. "I knew there were heavy hitters behind the scenes who would make it happen, if Hans said so."[41]

By about 1986, CLANN knew it needed something better than MRMS. Geac's solution was GLIS 9000, which ran on the new multiprocessor, scalable Concept 9000 computer. Gone were the old restrictions on memory and disk space, and like the HAL 9000 in the movie *2001: A Space Odyssey*, it even had speech synthesis. The new software developed in-house at Markham and at Bristol, UK, was called the Bibliographic Processing System (BPS). Wade accepted the company's sales pitch with a keen ear.

BPS had holes all through it, but we had no choice. We wanted an integrated system, we didn't want all those nightly batches; it meant the item status-line was out of date, and if the [nightly] transfers didn't happen, it was noticed. There were other systems that pretended to be fully integrated. Of course they weren't. They were all cataloguing on an outside agency.[42]

Among the problems yet to be resolved was the ability to talk simultaneously to more than 512 library terminals, a feature absolutely necessary for CLANN. CLANN had upward of 700 terminals in its network scattered across the state of New South Wales and now reaching south to the national capital region of Canberra and the state of Victoria and up into Queensland. A network so diverse posed other challenges designers could never have imagined. For instance, the Australian National Gallery lent out paintings. Most libraries loan items for weeks, or possibly for academic semesters or years. The National Gallery wanted the system to allow loan periods of 20 years.

By the middle of the 1990s, people were becoming worried about the date problems caused by the approaching millennium. Programmers writing in older languages like COBOL had been encouraged to save storage space by using two-digit year numbers in dates. However, when the year 2000 came about, two-digit year fields would roll round to "00," presenting libraries with a conundrum. A book taken out in "99" and brought back in "00," would appear to have been returned before it was borrowed. Thus, no overdue notices would be generated and any fines or fees associated with the transaction would be miscalculated. Depending on the situation, the item might appear to have never left the building at all. If that loan transaction had represented a costly National Gallery painting, the results could have been disastrous.

Another solution was to use "Julian dates," which are simply the number of days past some arbitrary starting point. For instance, January 1, 4713 BCE, as measured at the Royal Greenwich Observatory, or the date January 1, 1970, which was used by the designers of the UNIX computer operating system. Using Julian dates instead of the more common Gregorian ones means not having to worry about two- or four-digit years, and what to do when a century occurs.

Wade again credits the customers of online library systems with forcing vendors to act on the Year 2000 problem After many years as a Geac customer, CLANN, now called UNILINC, went over to an ILS supplied by Data Research Associates (DRA).

We had to deal with the year 2000 problem in 1995. That forced DRA to deal with the millennium. That's what happens when a group of libraries works together. On its own DRA fixed the problem for the whole world. DRA had to confirm their ability to deal with the problem before UNILINC would sign.[43]

Lockheed Missiles and Space had led the world with its Dialog research databases. Ovid was another research service; it was UNIX based and to some degree in competition with Dialog. "Dialog could offer services to the world, why couldn't we?" says Wade. "So we did. We had OVID offering online services from a server at CLANN many years before OVID itself did. The In-country server model worked so well in Oz, all the unis, health libraries in NSW." [44]

Ovid today is a leading supplier of bibliographic data on a wide range of topics, but its first major product was a user-friendly version of the Medline database compiled by the National Library of Medicine in the United States. Medline was also one of the major offerings of Dialog. Speaking as a customer, Wade credits Ovid's successful installation at half a dozen locations in Australia with its successes in other parts of the world.

Ovid and UNILINC demonstrated what we believe was the first Z39.50 handshake in the world, at a 1995 conference in Australia—Showing UNILINC holdings in an Ovid search result. The minute we did that, the shortcomings became apparent, but it worked. We did it. We showed it was possible.[45]

"Ovid copied the Australian model in Hong Kong and the Netherlands, and UNILINC suddenly had national online services delivered to all the libraries in Australia," she asserts. "That achievement was made possible because they [Ovid] had first demonstrated that it worked at 6 libraries. You get that going, and people trust you to develop a product further."[46]

Since telecommunications presented problems for libraries not just in Australia but also around the world, many relied upon bibliographic databases, indexes, and abstracting services supplied on CD-ROMs or other removable disk media. Typically, special software had to be installed on each microcomputer workstation that would be used by the public. Companies with names like Silver Platter and ProQuest are examples of vendors that provided this innovative sort of solution. However, only a few library users could take advantage of "stand-alone" CD-ROM stations at a time. It was, of course, possible to connect via telephone lines to a computer that either held the data on large hard disks, or had a bank of CD-ROM drives called a CD tower attached to it. Disks containing the different databases had to be loaded manually onto the drives when patrons requested them. The problem with serving users in different branches or different institutions within a consortium from a central computer with a CD tower would be compounded further by the slow and costly communications lines of the day, which often had to be accessed using dial-up modems. Consortia like CLANN, whose members were already paying for telecommunications, could make the switch to online research databases with comparative ease.

We got a bigger box and ran the service for all the Ovid customers. We provided it first to CLANN for about 6 months, and they loved it . . . better than getting these CD-ROMs with 30-40 databases, and putting them into their towers or jukeboxes every month. Cooperation made that possible. All the vendors, EBSCO, ProQuest, Ovid, with their servers, ProQuest delivered disks. It would be 3 to 5 years before the vendors began running their own servers.[47]

The impetus behind CLANN, dating back to its formation under Dorothy Peake, had always been cooperation among libraries. In Wade's words, "Formal structure and cooperation over a long period of time lead to trust." In this case, cooperation came in the form of $100,000 from the consortium's board and individual member institutions, and price concessions from the hardware vendor, IBM. The cooperation sold the story to IBM. The results were impressive. Six institutions were up and running with Ovid within two weeks of the project's start, and the implementation served as a "proof of concept."

Another benefit of centralizing CD services was the physical protection of the media. As anyone who has dropped or scratched a CD knows, physical damage is a very real threat to the music or data it contains. Ovid still delivered one set of CDs to CLANN, and once loaded, they were loaded for everyone. Yet another advantage was financial. Stand-alone CD-ROM databases were sold on a site license basis, and that could mean multiplying the price many-fold if one wished to outfit a group of institutions. As well, there were labor costs associated with stand-alone CD-ROM databases and even with towers located at different branches or institutions. "Libraries had staff whose sole jobs were to load CDs into towers, constantly. Things were always going wrong with those CD-ROM drives," Wade observes.

The Australian continent is vast, and consortia like CLANN served clients in three states and the national capital region of Canberra. A multitype consortium, its members included smaller libraries like that of the Australia Council of the Arts or medium-sized but distant ones like the Orange Agricultural College. Not all of them needed online access to a central library catalogue. In 1989, to obviate the cost of dedicated telephone lines at such sites, CLANN introduced a CD-ROM version of its catalogue, called CLANN CD-Cat. The CD-Cat disks were shipped to the consortium's smaller sites on a monthly basis. If an item's status needed to be verified for intraconsortium loan, for example, it would be relatively inexpensive for the smaller sites to dial-in via modem to the central computer. CLANN CD-Cat was a "made in Australia" solution to a cost-benefit problem, and though the online database solution of a central server, as typified by the Ovid installation, gained wide acceptance, the CD-Cat remained popular. Managing one new disk a month was far less troublesome than looking after tens or hundreds of CD changes a day.

The development of networking and the development of portable media like CD-ROM were complementary processes. In 1989, the year the CD catalogue was introduced, CLANN was also granted membership in the Australian Academic Research Network (AARNet) and began to make its OPAC available to the national research community.

As the mini-computer era drew to a close and the age of distributed client-server computing dawned, new services based on the Internet were becoming attractive. It was time for UNILINC to upgrade its systems and to reexamine the underlying service concepts. While text-based Internet services had been in existence for a decade, the graphically oriented World Wide Web had been altering customer expectations since the early 1990s. Sir Timothy Berners-Lee, the Web's inventor, has described that revolution in *Weaving the Web*.[48]

While much of the innovation at UNILINC had been done in partnership with companies like Geac and Ovid, the network, under Wade's leadership, was seeking new capabilities, and the time to upgrade its ILS was at hand. Data Research Associates and Innovative Interfaces, both from the United States, and the new system from Geac called Advance, were considered. One critical goal for the network was to provide a "Union Catalogue" of the holding of all sites, while allowing the member institutions local autonomy over the records it would contain. All of the major contenders ran under the UNIX operating system. Like much of the computing world, Geac was no longer developing its proprietary OS.

When Geac tendered Advance there was no evidence that they could do both a local OPAC and a union catalogue—to limit subject headings that pertained just to a local library, including authorities. DRA was the only system at the time that we believed could do that. Innovative couldn't do it. The only major Australian library to go with Advance was Griffith University.[49]

Around the world, the 1990s saw a shift to what might be called "end-user" computing. Vastly faster more powerful microprocessors, the Internet, standardized communications protocols, and the universality of client-server architecture now allow users with laptop computers unparalleled access to information. As well, many libraries now use "patron self-checkout" terminals. These allow users to scan their own library cards and book barcodes or to scan the newer radiofrequency identification (RFID) chips embedded in books and borrower cards. Wade points out that one of the most popular self-checkout systems was "beta tested" in live operation at UNILINC.

The system in question was created by one of the current industry leaders, the American company 3M. It was deployed at 15 UNILINC locations, with the cooperation of the network, the developer, and the barcode supplier, Davis and Henderson.

Davis & Henderson developed innovative technology to print the barcodes onto 40,000 ID cards—and they did this for us. This had not been done before for a library client and hence it featured at their stand at ALA. It was costly to have the ID cards work done off shore and at our urging the Australian company who produced our normal barcodes, Leigh Mardon, also developed the ability to print barcodes onto ID cards. This was innovative in the Australian context and lead to many more applications and contributed to Leigh Mardon's success.[50]

Another capability, "smart" barcoding, again implemented with Leigh Mardon, allowed over 1 million items to be barcoded for 57 UNILINC sites. Smart barcoding meant that the barcodes did not have to be linked one by one to the bibliographic records. Instead, the barcodes could be generated from the records and affixed to the proper items.

By the beginning of the 1990s, the CLANN consortium's mandate had changed considerably. Several universities, along with special libraries, such as those of the Australia Council, the Australian National Gallery in Canberra, and the Conservatorium of Music in Sydney, had joined the network. As the mini-computer era drew to a close, a change in mandate was taking shape, and the network was renamed UNILINC.

UNILINC's mission is to enhance the provision of library and information services through cooperative action by providing cost-effective systems and services and a mechanism for using outside systems and services that enable individual member institutions to meet their objectives in this area. Their mission also includes services for approved nonmember institutions and individuals where such services promote the common interest of member institutions.[51]

By October 1991, UNILINC was no longer envisaged by its policy makers principally as a cooperative bibliographic utility with attendant activities and services. In fact, the words "bibliographic" and "library" do not appear in the mission statement. They are replaced by the terms "systems and services" and "institutions."

What was happening to UNILINC was happening in other libraries and consortia across the globe. The switch in focus, from local automation systems that were now mature to Internet-based distributed information systems, is described in the concluding chapter of this book, contributed by McGill University's Louise O'Neill.

As an interesting historical footnote, it is worth mentioning that Charles Sturt University, one of UNILINC's major members, operates a branch campus in Burlington, Ontario, a few kilometers from Wendy Schick's library. The library automation system that supports CSU's Canadian presence is provided by UNILINC in Sydney, Australia, bringing the local automation story full-circle.

Despite her ongoing optimism for innovations in computing, Wade sounds a note of caution when it comes to social media and Internet search engines because existing ones do not distinguish between high-quality research literature and other materials.

"If we're not careful, scholarly knowledge will be lost, or will become something that only high level researchers know about, which is what it was like 100 years ago, when only 'invisible colleges' knew the value of this information." However, Wade is acutely conscious of the contributions of the frenetic days of ILS development. "When I look at Google," she remarks, "it looks much like an OPAC."[52]

NOTES

1. Mantyka, Wayne (reporter), Gordon Vizzutti (presenter), *This Week* Regina, Canada: CTV Television Network, aired February 5, 1985.

2. Mantyka, *This Week*.

3. Mantyka, *This Week*.

4. Koen, Diane. Interviewed June 2009.

5. Thomas, Keith. Interviewed 2009.

6. Burke, Jane. "Automation Planning and Implementation: Library and Vendor Responsibilities." In Shaw, Deborah. "Human Aspects of Library Automation: Helping Staff and Patrons Cope." *Clinic on Library Applications of Data Processing*. Champaign-Urbana: University of Illinois at Urbana-Champaign, 1985.

7. Story, Rob, and Peter Tyson. *FDTOOL*. Markham, Canada: Geac Computers International, 1988.

8. Wade, Rona. Interviewed July 2009.

9. Schick, Wendy. Interviewed April 2007.

10. Schick, Wendy. Interviewed April 2007.

11. Schick, Wendy. Interviewed April 2007.

12. Schick, Wendy. Interviewed April 2007.

13. Schick, Wendy. Interviewed April 2007.

14. Schick, Wendy. Interviewed April 2007.

15. Peake, Dorothy G. *Library Networks and Changing Library Services a Quiet Revolution*. Sydney: New South Wales Institute of Technology, 1976. p. 1.

16. Peake, *Library Networks*. p. 3.

17. Peake, *Library Networks*. p. 91.

18. Peake, *Library Networks*. passim.

19. Peake, *Library Networks*. p. 107.

20. Peake, *Library Networks*. p. 110.

21. Peake, Dorothy. "CLANN Comes of Online Age." *LASIE* 16, no. 5 (March/April 1986): 6–11. p. 7.

22. Peake, "CLANN." p. 6.

23. Wade, Rona. "The Selection of the CLANN Circulation/OPAC System." *LASIE* 16, no. 2 (September/October 1985): 2–7.

24. Monahan, Michael. "ISO/OSI Networking in the Library Environment." *LASIE* 16, no. 6 (May/June 1986): 12–21.

25. Monahan, "ISO/OSI." p. 16.

26. O'Mara, Robin and Dorothy G. Peake. "OSI—The Open System Interface or 'The Building Block of the 80's'." *LASIE* 16, no. 3 (November/December 1985): 2–5.

27. "Geac Implements LSP Protocol." *Geac Library Newsletter* 6, no. 2 (Spring 1986). p. 1. "Geac Passes Library of Congress LSP Tests." *Geac Library Newsletter* 7, no. 1 (Winter 1987). p. 1.

28. Wade, Rona. Interviewed July 2009.

29. Wade, Rona. Interviewed July 2009.

30. Wade, Rona. Interviewed July 2009.

31. Wade, Rona. Interviewed July 2009.

32. Wade, Rona. Interviewed July 2009.

33. Koen, Diane. Interviewed July 2009.

34. Wade, Rona. Interviewed July 2009.

35. Telstra is the major telecom provider in Australia, created by the merger of the nation's domestic and overseas telecommunications entities (Telcom and OTC), in 1983. It offers a full range of land lines, mobile phones, international data communications, and television, with some services operating under the name of Big Pond.

36. Wade, Rona. Interviewed July 2009.

37. The Australian Academic and Research Network (AARNet) was launched in 1989 by the Australian Universities and the Commonwealth Scientific and Industrial Research Organization (CSIRO), under the umbrella of the Australian Vice Chancellors' Committee (AVCC). Currently in its third reiteration, AARNet Pty. Ltd. (APL) is a not-for-profit company whose shareholders are 38 Australian universities and the CSIRO.

38. This description of the role of Monash University and the University of Melbourne is based on e-mail communications with various members in the Australian academic computing community, exchanged in 2009, and on the author's personal experiences with Usenet during the period. For a history of the introduction of the Internet in Australia, see Goggin, Gerard. *Virtual Nation: The Internet in Australia.* Sydney: UNSW Press, 2005.

39. Dialog LLC. "Dialog and the Invention of Online Information Services." http://www.dialog.com/about.

40. Wade, Rona. Interviewed 2009.

41. Wade, Rona. Interviewed 2009.

42. Wade, Rona. Interviewed 2009.

43. Wade, Rona. Interviewed 2009.

44. Wade, Rona. Interviewed 2009.

45. Wade, Rona. Interviewed 2009.

46. Wade, Rona. Interviewed 2009.

47. Wade, Rona. Interviewed 2009.

48. Berners-Lee, Tim, and Mark Fischetti. *Weaving the Web: The Original Design and Ultimate Destiny of the World Wide Web by Its Inventor.* New York: HarperCollins Publishers, 2000.

49. Wade, Rona. Interviewed July 2009.

50. Wade, Rona. Interviewed July 2009.

51. UNILINC Ltd. (1991). What Is UNILINC. UNILINC Limited. [Unpublished manuscript]

52. Wade, Rona. Interviewed July 2009.

3

At the Interface: Librarians
and the Vendor Environment

The preceding chapter presented the story of ILS development from the perspective of librarians who worked primarily at customer sites. In this chapter, librarians who at various points in their careers have worked in libraries but who worked primarily for ILS vendors during the book's time frame provide their perspectives. This chapter is based on interviews with librarians who worked as trainers and project managers, and upon the author's recorded personal observations of the period.

Roles undertaken by librarians or other trained information professionals ranged from "help desk" and similar customer support duties, to preparing responses to requests for proposals (RFPs), to sales and marketing. Many occupied senior management positions at the division head or vice- presidential levels or above. However, the organizational hierarchies of many ILS vendors, like much of the computer industry of the day, were relatively "flat." Librarians, working as project managers and trainers, were often the principal contacts between customer and vendor, and relatively junior employees in all departments were given considerable latitude when representing the company. Both at headquarters and onsite, the work was frequently performed in a casual, even playful atmosphere, characterized by shared enthusiasm for what were then "cutting-edge" projects.

Today, software packages that are in widespread use, even complete ILS systems, can be installed on computers in a matter of hours or even seconds. Configuring them may take days. During the mini-computer era, physically installing software could take days, weeks, or even months. Setting up the configuration specifications often required many meetings, both internally within a library and between the library and the vendor's representative. Those representatives, either salespeople or "project managers" and "trainers," were often selected for their library knowledge because MARC records, circulation practices, and library policies needed translated into the system specifications. Then, library staff would need considerable training, usually done in modules that ran for a few days to a week, for circulation, acquisitions, serials control, cataloguing, computer operations, and other system functions. Training and project management could be done at the vendor's location or onsite. While Endeavor, founded in 1994, chose to centralize its training and its project managers rarely traveled, Geac, founded a decade and a half earlier, chose the other option. Trainers, installers, and project managers traveled frequently throughout North America, the United Kingdom, Australia, Singapore, continental Europe, and, in one instance, the former Soviet Union. The hardware maintenance staff called field engineers, or simply "Fes," were often based locally, but they too might be called upon to travel widely if their specialized knowledge was required at a remote site.

The year was 1986, and the season's blockbuster was the film *Top Gun* starring Tom Cruise. Leather aviator jackets were the fashion item of choice, and radios around the Western world resounded to the picture's groundbreaking sound track. So it was probably no surprise that planes were on everyone's minds, especially those staffers who practically lived on them as passengers during the explosive growth period of the mid-1980s. The company's new installations are chronicled in the pages of its internal newsletter, *Geaction,*[1] and its customer-oriented publications and annual reports as well as a considerable body of literature created by customers or their user groups. A notable example of a monograph written by a library customer is Westlake's 1987 guidebook for librarians installing a Geac system.[2] Examples of research articles, case studies, and brief notes written by ILS customers are too numerous to mention individually, but work by two customer-authors may be illustrative. While working at Thunder Bay Public Library, librarian Bill Hudgins penned a report on a successful circulation system implementation.[3] He went on to work for the vendor. While Michael Schuyler, a prolific librarian-author, never worked for Geac, his contributions to the literature, notably in the journal *Computers in Libraries*, began as an unfolding case study of his work at the Kitsap Regional Library during its implementation of a circulation system in the early 1980s.[4]

If any young programmers, salespeople, or support staff around Geac had caught the military fervor after watching *Top Gun*, there were several choice destinations to volunteer. The U.S. Military Academy (USMA) at West Point had been an early Geac customer, followed shortly by the U.S. Air Force Academy (USAFA) at Colorado Springs and the U.S. Naval Academy at Annapolis, Maryland. Overseas, there was the U.S. Seventh Army supported out of Heidelberg. Other interesting posts included the University of Houston, close enough to NASA's Mission Control to afford a day trip, and MIT, where Project Athena was busy laying the foundations for the wired campus and where Reagan's Strategic Defense Initiative, commonly known as "Star Wars," was the topic of considerable campus chatter. The Smithsonian Institution on the Washington, DC, mall was another.

Geac had inherited the USMA and USAFA from Plessey along with a handful of other sites. One reason was Geac's ability to read Plessey barcodes, the ones Tim Berners-Lee had been working on getting computers to read. "We never actually used them," recalls Burlington Public's CEO, Wendy Schick. "But Geac was the only company that said they could read them."[5] Since every piece of software had to have a designated wartime use, at the U.S. Army site in Heidelberg the library patron records were earmarked for potential civilian evacuations. As with Endeavor, a few years later, much of Geac's success during the period can be attributed to customer "migrations" from previous automated systems to a newer ILS.

WORKING CONDITIONS

For librarians who joined ILS vendors, the atmosphere would have been at once familiar and different. The language of conversation would have become increasingly esoteric and technical, but the customers were librarians, with similar workplace expectations. Even so, high-technology companies enjoyed reputations for eccentricity and madcap antics, reputations that they still enjoy today.

While the practice varied among departments, dress at headquarters and onsite was often casual. Not everyone wore leather jackets or "business dress" every day. The common wisdom held that librarians and their staffs felt uncomfortable around high-pressure salespeople and liked to be sold systems and trained on them by other librarians. In all, by the late 1980s, Geac alone had about 90 certified librarians in its Library Systems Division (LSD) to conduct the training. While these librarians dressed to teach support staff, others were given different directions.

Among software and sales support staff, the rule was "Wear a suit on the first day, so they know you own one. After that, dress like they do." This casual way of life did not always extend to the customer service engineers or FEs. At Tucson, where daytime temperatures routinely climb into the triple digits Fahrenheit during the summer, most people came to work in shorts and open-collared shirts. In the bowels of the library, T-shirts were quite acceptable. A decree had gone out from headquarters that all FEs had to wear ties. Tom Preble, who was the FE in charge of the University of Arizona, recalls how an executive phoned Tom Owens, then the systems chief, to remind him of the necessity to wear ties.

When it was time to add staff, librarians, software and sales support staff, and FEs, applicants were available in the mid-1980s. Many MLS graduates were on the job market, all with excellent qualifications. The same held true for programmers, FEs, and the other technical specialists a big hardware and software vendor needs on staff. With so many excellent applicants for jobs, hiring became a challenge. Some departments only advertised over electronic bulletin boards or the highly organized Usenet newsgroups. The logic was that only people who really knew something about computers would be able to reply. Word of mouth was an important source, too, as were library and trade conferences and old school ties.

In the Geac Library Systems Division (LSD) training department, those invited for interviews were also subjected to a more academic-style vetting process. Applicants would be shown some new gadget, perhaps a new software release. If they reacted with enthusiasm and asked to try out the system, they scored points immediately. If they mentioned having written an essay about automation but seemed uneager to try it, they lost.

Prospective employees would then be paraded from cubicle to cubicle and office to office so group leaders and managers from other support or development sections would be able to question them. Often, the trainers who happened to be at Markham headquarters would then take the candidate out to an expense-paid lunch. Straight talk was the order of the day at these sessions. The trainers would explain the realities of the job.

BEING ON THE ROAD

These included being "on the road" up to eight weeks out of ten, almost always in new territory and far from field engineering or software support. Trainers carried copies of the applications software and, occasionally, of the operating system. This software was on eight-inch reels of half-inch reel-to-reel computer tape, and the salesperson had to install and run the software with little or no help, especially when their assignments were in different time zones or even on different continents.

Getting computer tapes across international borders involved considerable paperwork. One customs agent unfamiliar with computing mused that, despite official stamps on their labels, someone could have unwound the tape and put a different one on the reel. The fact that the data could simply have been overwritten escaped him.

As long as the appropriate four-part forms had been completed, however, such problems were minimized.

Being on the road might mean weeks on end in hotel rooms, far from family and friends, a possible victim of boredom and social isolation. Sales staff, installers, and trainers might be expected to travel from Alaska to Massachusetts and right on to California with no stop at home. Trying to pack clothes for such diverse climates, especially in winter, could be a problem. Most preferred limiting their clothing to a single carry-on bag rather than being caught in Cheyenne or Edmonton because the airline shipped their suitcase to Atlanta.

Travel had some perquisites. The company's philosophy was that when staff was on the road, they were on duty twenty-four hours a day. So meals and drinks were on Markham. If things went wrong, support staff was expected to entertain the customers at dinner. Knowing the tradition, some customers admitted hoping the system would crash, so they could partake of the company's hospitality. For the staff member, that meant maintaining the company's reputation round the clock. If a colleague took ill or the schedules changed, you might disembark from one plane just to catch another. Supporting the team was paramount.

FAIR WARNING AT HIRING

However, unlimited free food and drink when consumed alone can be poor consolation for a minimal social life. Those involved in romantic relationships or who had family responsibilities were asked to consider these conditions carefully. It would be unfair both to the company and to the candidate, it was emphasized, if people were hired without knowing these things.

The tactic worked. More than once, job applicants phoned the company to withdraw voluntarily from the hiring process. Ironically, those who were self-aware and honest enough to bow out were probably the exact sorts it would have been good to have onboard.

With all those qualified graduates whose technical knowledge was similar, it became difficult to select new hires. It was often a team decision, and sometimes seemingly irrelevant personal details came into play. Employees on the road had to be able to converse effortlessly with everyone from junior clerks to CEOs, had to think their way out of technical difficulties, and always had to "keep their cool" when things went wrong as they frequently did with relatively untested hardware and software. This meant that when a recent Canadian MLS grad said she'd attended the University of Hawaii at Manoa, where the motto was reputedly "truth, knowledge, and a great tan," she scored extra points for initiative. When a young librarian from Beeville, Texas, explained she had a private pilot's license, she seemed a good fit. If she hadn't crashed her plane, she probably could be trusted with a couple million dollars' worth of computers. As a plus, Beeville was home to a naval air training station. Just as in the movie, at Geac they hired top guns.

Another common bit of wisdom is that most librarians are female, and most programmers male. The latter was not really the case at Geac, at any rate. A look at the roster on W. Christopher Martin's "Ex-Employees of Geac" Web site demonstrates as much.[6]

Was there a glass ceiling, above which female employees could not advance? Software companies tended to have flat hierarchies, and both programmers and librarians tended to love their jobs, aspiring to nothing higher than the middle management ranks. Over the years, many group leaders or supervisors were indeed female. Women headed the LAD and the Education Services training group, and occupied prominent positions in sales. At one point in its history, a woman vice president, Harriet Velasquez, headed the entire Library Systems Division (LSD). The same was true in other companies. Upon leaving Geac, Diane Koen would eventually become international VP of sales for the database company Ovid. And Jane Burke, one of the founders of NOTIS,[7] would become president of the ILS vendor Endeavor.

LIBRARIANS AS TRAINERS

Elizabeth Fenwick, hired during the early 1980s as an instructor-analyst, recalls training visits to Anchorage, Alaska; Miami-Dade County; the University of Wisconsin–Madison; the State University of New York (SUNY) at Albany; Brandeis; and the University of Rochester, among other sites. Until the contracts had been signed, customers had been dealing with salespeople who often told them things "that they themselves believed" about the system but that did not necessarily reflect operational and work-flow realities.

Often the trainers were the first wave of librarians the customers had actually met. We were librarians, or library-trained people, and we really knew libraries well. We knew how use the software. They had so many questions about the system. In many respects, our job wasn't to show them how to use the system, so much as how to get it to do what they wanted. The software [itself] wasn't that difficult to use.[8]

In 2008, Elizabeth Fenwick was chief executive officer of the Bradford-West Gwillimbury Public Library, which is located in the middle of the Holland Marsh, a fertile farming district north of Toronto, Ontario, where the soil is almost black in color. She held the same position in nearby East Gwillimbury for much of the 1990s but had spent much of the 1980s working in Geac's customer support section. Fewnick had grown up with computers.

My dad worked for IBM. He taught me how to count in binary. He thought it was important. He felt that this was the coming wave of the future, so we all learned to count in binary. In my high school, they went to automated class schedules, and everybody was up in arms about them, but I could see that they would be useful. I was all prepped and ready to go. I thought of computers as tools.[9]

Jessamyn West, librarian, pioneer blogger, and daughter of Tom West, the computing executive whose story is told in Tracy Kidder's Pulitzer Prize–winning book *The Soul of a New Machine*, says Fenwick was not alone.[10] She too learned to count in binary as a child growing up in a home with a terminal constantly dialed up to Data General. She used it to play the text-based game Zork. Attending a high school near Digital Equipment Corporation with access to a VAX meant learning about computers at an young age. "I learned to do 'computer stuff' when I was in high school, and I got along with the computer guys. . . . I think the biggest deal really is that I didn't see computers as a big deal. I saw them as (1) things to play video games on and (2) giant calculators."

Reflecting on the modern-day services available on the Internet, including library OPACs, West muses,

I think we [librarians] have the view, "Well, they're all just databases, right?" I think having that top-down view and not being cowed into not working with something just because I don't understand it (I can't program in PHP, but I know I can do pretty much anything a sophisticated end user can do with Wordpress [Blog software]) has helped me a lot. My dad and I both like gadgets and figuring things out, and this sort of approach has helped me, too. I think it would be hard to find a career nowadays that doesn't have computers as some part of it, but technology instruction, and running MetaFilter which is the job that pays the bulk of my bills, has really suited me. I presume knowing about technology from an early age and growing up in a culture where they were "normal" and where people who liked them were normal, was a big part of that.[11]

While a student at York University in north Toronto, Fenwick had come to know Mary Stevens, adjunct professor in the University of Toronto's downtown library school. Stevens held an MLS and an MBA, and was head of the York Library Systems Department. Stevens was looking for students who would be willing to try cataloguing maps using some new equipment: Texas Instruments bubble-memory terminals, which had been introduced to the market in 1976.[12] Bubble terminals looked like portable typewriters, topped with rubber cups into which a telephone receiver could be placed to transfer data to mainframe computers. These acoustically coupled modems operated at 300 baud, which was about the maximum achievable over ordinary telephone lines. What made them revolutionary was the fact that they contained enough local memory to store a few hundred records. Bubble memory terminals contained enough storage to record a few MARC descriptions of materials, and the TI machines were no bigger than portable typewriters, which made them ideal for "retrospective conversion" or "recon" operations. They gave cataloguers the mobility to work among the map cabinets or archival stacks instead of bringing cumbersome and fragile materials to some central point.

Stevens was using bubble memory terminals to catalogue the university's map library (along with Janet Allen, the map librarian) and portions of the university archives. The archivist, another University of Toronto adjunct professor named Hartwell Bowsfield, was an expert on Louis Riel, who had been hanged by the Canadian government for leading the Red River Rebellion. Bowsfield had written a book about Riel.[13] Bowsfield taught archives courses, and was skeptical about library-style cataloguing in general and especially about "putting things into this bubble of yours."[14]

So, while an undergraduate, Fenwick became familiar with MARC records with inventory control and with the internals of computers. At the time, the University of Toronto's Faculty of Library Science, now the Faculty of Information, offered courses in the BASIC, COBOL, or IBM 370 Assembler programming languages. All of them used 80-column punch cards to input instructions and data. "You did have to understand the workings of the computer, and hexadecimal numbers were sometimes useful too," she recalls. Fenwick chose Assembler.

The data was pretty limited, whereas, at York, we'd been looking at really large files of data. At York, we had been using the Plessey system, and it wasn't that much different from using punch cards, which we used at Toronto. I always was lucky at York because I had opportunities to use automation in ways which forced you to look at how it worked, and ways to get the information in and out." I couldn't relate to all those courses in the humanities and reference, and realized that I was more interested in cataloging, classification, and organizational theory.

Do certain sorts of librarians gravitate toward the computing side? Library school helped solidify Fenwick's plans.

I was lucky at York. I had ways of using automation that forced you to look at how it worked, how to get information in or out. What I really liked was the organizational things: cataloging, subject headings, the computer work. I realized pretty quickly that I wasn't born to be a reference librarian.

When she was offered a job as an instructor-analyst for Geac Computers, she took it. The job took her across the North American continent from Anchorage, Alaska, to Miami, Florida. She remembers spending many weeks in Madison, Wisconsin; at several at the SUNY sites, including Albany and Binghamton; and at Brandeis.

The trainers were the "first wave" of vendor-librarians that the customers actually met, and Fenwick believes that this shaped expectations on both sides. "They'd been talking to salespeople who will tell you anything and everything . . . and a lot of times it's because they believe in it, because they think it's true. But the trainers were all librarians, or library-trained people, and we really knew libraries well," she says.[15]

Instructor-analysts were hired because they were good communicators who actually understood how the software would be used in the workplace. Like most companies, Geac's philosophy was "train the trainers." So an onsite class would be held for each of the major system components: computer operations, circulation, cataloguing, and acquisitions. Those classes of eight or ten of the library's best communicators would then be tasked with training the rest of the staff. Fenwick's knowledge of MARC records led to a specialty: training cataloguers, circulation, and acquisitions staff.

They had so many questions about the system. In many respects, our job wasn't to train them in how to use the software, it was to help them explore what they really wanted to do with it, and then show them how to use the software. The software wasn't all that difficult. It was getting your mind around how you were going to adapt what you have been doing in your current environment, to what the system can help you do.

"The customers expected a lot about the software, but they didn't know much about its actual functions. Their questions were mainly of a professional nature," she says, "not about which buttons to push, especially among catalogers."

One site in Washington state in the United States stands out in Fenwick's memory. They were trying to determine how best to assign their barcodes to members of a large consortium. They had developed a complicated operational scheme for doing that, and the instructor managed to show them that it would involve much unnecessary overhead. "They needed a lot of organizational assistance. It didn't seem like training, more like consulting. There was a lot of 'hand holding.'" One director, she recalls, paid more heed to the Geac instructor than to her own internal experts. The trainer was able to tell her the same things but with the added credibility that comes from being a participant-observer rather than someone within the organization.

When asked about the lasting contributions made during the past few decades of library automation, Fenwick echoes the sentiments of Wade and Koen. She singles out the MARC cataloguing record. "The MARC record is unique to libraries, but will it be sustainable? We will be moving to metadata. At the time it was the most flexible, interesting, and innovative thing that could be developed as far as library data goes."[16]

For Fenwick, other library innovations are also of merit. The importance of standards, such as the Library of Congress Subject Headings, is important, she suggests, even though the lexicon changes. She gives the example of terms for native people used in the United States and Canada: "First Nations" or "First Peoples" in Canada, and "Native Americans" in the United States. Classification systems, like the Dewey Decimal Classification System and Library of Congress are also important contributions, she says. Though new mechanisms may emerge, she suggests an ongoing role for the profession:

The basic underlying thought process doesn't change, and we have done a great many interesting and innovative things in librarianship. The idea that we've got to get the information out there, but how we do it changes, gets superceded. But libraries do it better. You can assign more than one subject-term to a work.

The experience was not without its challenges and setbacks. Fenwick recalls arriving at the University of Rochester to do her MARC catalogue training. The systems manager, Roger Gifford, was in a quandary. He couldn't get the production system to work. Fenwick realized that the computer operations trainer who had preceded her had installed a demonstration system on the 8000. Training had to be postponed while a production system was couriered from Markham. She suggests that the company learned from the Rochester experience. Part of the problem had been the continual rush caused by the sudden influx of customers.[17]

We were moving really fast. We were out [in the field] all the time, and meanwhile trying to keep on top of the changes. It affected all different levels, training people at different levels. Engineering didn't think of it; they wanted us out there doing the job we did. But we were also trying to become a profit center, introducing additional courses like Fundamental GLUG and Advanced Operations.[18]

Like Elizabeth Fenwick, Linda Scott Zaleski remembers encountering computers at an early age. "I started programming FORTRAN in high school. I'm from the punch card and Teletype era."[19] Programming was not a universally taught subject, but a few students were given the option. As she recalls, the school's administrative computer was made available. In high school, she had volunteered in the library, and remembers doing serials check-in. She followed with a degree in computer science, but had wanted to be a librarian since the fifth grade. Upon graduating, Scott Zaleski remembers thinking that computing and librarianship could be merged in some fashion. She enrolled in the library program at the University of Illinois and remembers working with more punch cards, producing bibliographies.

"It was right at the beginning of library automation. CLSI was just starting, and Geac began its Waterloo University project soon after." She remembers her peers begin skeptical of her passion for libraries. "The library was the dark, dank place." There were courses in COBOL, but Scott Zaleski remembers that the "real" programmers in computer science were more interested in numerical analysis, operating systems, and other systems-level courses. ALGOL and similar languages were more of interest to her colleagues. She remembers being the only applications-oriented person.

However, one user-oriented system developed at the university during that time was Plato, an early online education system. She remembers a lot of collaboration among the Plato team, some of whom went on to develop Lotus Notes.

With her computing background, Scott took a job in the university's engineering library. Information retrieval was becoming important, and Scott Zaleski began working as a retrieval intermediary using systems like Dialog. At the time, library patrons filled in search request forms, and library staff entered them into the Dialog system using teletype keyboards. The resulting printouts would be made available for pickup.

Don Kaiser, a classmate who was working for OCLC at the time, suggested that Linda contact Michael Monahan, who was setting up the new Geac Library Systems Division. It consisted of less than a dozen people. Monahan, Erich Buss, and a few others had written a system for the University of Guelph system and then went on to write a system for Waterloo. These systems were customized, and, based on what the team learned, they became the prototypes for later releases. The next projects were to be the London, Ontario, public library and the University of Arizona. Wayne Mullin and Tom Owens, then Arizona employees, would later go on to work for systems vendors.

To make the system portable, it had to be parameterized. Hard-coded program routines to handle loans, renewals, holds, and fines for various types of materials and patrons had to be removed, and "policy tables" set up so that options could be chosen easily at different sites. She remembers programmer John Henshaw working all night on the London installation, and finding his car had been towed the next morning. As well, the crew found to their chagrin that the light switch in the computer room turned off power to the computer as well. At the time, a power failure meant a lengthy reboot and system restore, and could have meant costly "head crashes" for its disks. During a head crash, the recordable media on the disk's surfaces that contained the data could actually have been scraped away, and the disk ruined.

With systems running in Ontario, the crew, having lost a bid for the Chicago public library, moved on to Arizona. Eric Willis, who went on to work for California State University, Northridge, was also at Geac.

The system was being developed at a rapid pace, and bits of program code were being developed specifically for Arizona. Scott remembers working overnight on the "holds" logic for the circulation system, then training a customer the next day. "We did flowcharts on napkins," she recalls. "Sometimes, we actually documented them."

It was for Arizona that the team developed the GLUG report-writing language, documented by Tom Owens. Next came Yale University. The university had a very different view of the function of a "reserve book room," and its functions were sufficiently different from those of other customers that the team built a "conditional compile" option into its policy parameters tables. The option was labeled, "Are you Yale?"

Soon after Yale came Princeton University and two Connecticut consortia, the Capitol Region Library Consortium (the CRLC, whose system was dubbed "Circsess") and the South West Library Consortium (whose network was called "Bibliomation"). These consortia were "huge and big and hard" to automate, Scott recalls. The many institutions required interlibrary loan software, and those institutions had divergent loan policies. In the summer of 1982, the University of Michigan signed with Geac, as did Etobicoke, Mississauga, and a great many other sites in a short time frame. The online public access catalogue (OPAC) module was written in haste as well. Scott remembers designing its screen displays over a three-week period on graph paper, sequestered with Karen Trainer from New York University. They refused maid service and worked until the system was done.

LIBRARIANS AS PROJECT MANAGERS

In that year, Geac's office in Bristol, England, was being set up, and Bob Isserstedt, one of the company's founders, had transferred there. The Polytechnic of the South Bank was a new customer, and across the channel the University of Utrecht had signed with the Canadian company: a foreign purchase that, it was rumored, had required royal approval from the Netherlands' queen.

Scott and John Henshaw were posted to Utrecht. "The day we arrived, a circuit board failed on the disk processor." There were no FEs, so the programmers found themselves replacing the board with a new one shipped from Bristol. A small office had been set aside for them in what had been a palace during the Napoleonic era.

Because of the Dutch installation, Geac began working on multilingual circulation systems. For a time, versions of the system shipped back to Canada and the United States had their default languages set to Dutch. Working in the university, the programmers found themselves "subsumed" into the systems department. "You got to really learn and live the university library environment," Scott says. With no car at their disposal, the Geac team shared a bicycle. A quiet year of work followed at Utrecht, punctuated by occasional trips to Bristol.

Plans were underway for an Amsterdam office staffed originally by people from Bristol along with Dick Oudshorn from Holland and, eventually, his brother Menno. Several city libraries in the Netherlands followed, and shortly thereafter the U.S. Army, based in Heidelberg. David Murray, who had recently joined Geac from CLIS, and John Dilworth, who would head the Amsterdam office, signed the contract.

As part of the contract, Geac had to provide a Digital Equipment Corporation VAX minicomputer in addition to the Geac 8000 to be used for an unrelated information retrieval project. "The army was hard," Scott remembers. "We had never signed a government contract before." The army insisted that Geac staff the system from 7:30 a.m. until 4:30 p.m. Still in her early twenties, Scott found herself a manager, seconding Steve Knight from Bristol and hiring Tom Owens's assistant from Arizona to satisfy the army's staffing requirements. As well, when the Geac's Bristol representative was unable to attend a meeting with Digital Equipment Corporation, Scott found herself purchasing a VAX for the army.

Scott recalls one particularly difficult moment. The base commander, General Briggs, who was fond of cigars, attempted to smoke one in the machine room. Since the disk drives of the day were especially prone to dust and airborne particles, Scott and her youthful crew had to invite the general to leave. Another time, Scott forgot her briefcase in the army mess hall. She recalls how the military police "took great relish" in explaining how they had nearly blown it up.

Scott shuttled between Heidelberg and Utrecht on a biweekly basis, taking the "lovely" train route along the Rhine. Supply was at times difficult. Occasionally, paychecks from Canada would fail to appear, but the adventure was perhaps enough. "We had a close-knit team in Germany."

The Heidelberg group was mainly British, and dart matches with other expatriates were a favorite pastime. Scott remembers being asked to transfer to Australia where

CLANN, the Royal Melbourne Institute of Technology, and the Commonwealth Scientific and Industrial Research Association were new customers. However, Scott and Henshaw found themselves posted to Paris, where contracts with the National Library of France, the Vatican, and the Cité de Science et de l'Industrie de La Villette currently required attention; soon would follow the EU Economic Institute in Florence, Italy, and the city of Lyons, France.

The Cité de Science et de l'Industrie de La Villette was one of the first sites to implement robotics in the library. They were first used to retrieve videotapes. Back in the United States, special programming was being developed for The Smithsonian Institution.

"Too much custom code was being written," says Scott, and it created version problems. Development was being done in different regions, and the local development teams wanted control over their projects. To complicate matters, Geac had introduced its improved Concept 9000, a super-mini-computer that could run entirely new software and support functionality absent in the GLIS 8000 series. It was time to merge the products. "We called it the Bristol-Markham Wars," says Scott.

According to Scott, there were a few interesting challenges at the Vatican. The Vatican library staff was not used to MARC, and Scott found herself teaching them. "We couldn't wire the library. There was also no ladies' restroom near the library." Despite its long tradition, the library embraced the new technology. When Amsterdam's manager, Dick Oudshoorn, established an arbitrary date for closure of the Vatican card catalogue, Father Boyle, the Vatican librarian and a former University of Toronto professor, simply accepted the challenge.

Two years after returning to North America, Scott found herself working for NOTIS. Shortly thereafter, Northwestern University sold the company to Ameritech, a large telecommunications firm with no previous experience in the library market. After a time, Ameritech sold NOTIS to Dynix. In the process, the longtime NOTIS chief, Jane Burke, had departed, soon to become President of Endeavor. Several of the people mentioned in this book followed similar career paths, working at times for customers and at other times for rival vendors.

Looking back on the experience, Scott remembers both the challenges and the excitement. Scott recalled Oudshoorn groping for words while introducing her at a gathering. "This is Linda Scott," he said, "project manager of . . . difficult projects." As would most of her colleagues, Scott enjoyed the compliment.

NOTES

1. Geac Computer Corporation. *Geaction*. Markham, Canada: Author, 1972. p. v.

2. Westlake, Duncan R. *Geac : A Guide for Librarians and Systems Managers*. Aldershot: Gower, 1987.

3. Hudgins, Bill. "Thunder Bay: Circ's Up!" *Geac Library Newsletter* 7, no. 1 (1987): 2.

4. Various issues. *Computers in Libraries*. Westport, CT: Meckler, 1988.

5. Schick, Wendy. Interviewed August 2008.

6. Martin, W. Christopher. "Ex-Employees of Geac." http://www.exgeac.info.

7. The Northwestern Online Totally Integrated System, NOTIS, is described in "Northwestern University formally launches NOTIS." *Library Systems Newsletter* 3, no. 5 (May 1983): 33–34.

8. Fenwick, Elizabeth. Interviewed October 2008.

9. Fenwick, Elizabeth. Interviewed October 2008.

10. West, Jessamyn. Personal communication, September 2009.

11. West, Jessamyn. Personal communication, September 2009.

12. Flannigan, J. Steven and Texas Instruments Incorporated. "Bubble Memory Terminal: An Added Dimension to Data Entry." *Compcon Fall '77.* IEEE Computer Society, Institute of Electrical and Electronics Engineers. pp. 90–93.

13. Bowsfield, H. *Louis Riel: Rebel of the Western Frontier or Victim of Politics and Prejudice?* Toronto: Copp Clark, 1969.

14. The project referred to is described in Brown-Syed, C. "The CBC Television Drama Collection; Report of a Pilot Study." Unpublished manuscript. Toronto: Library Systems Department. York University Libraries, 1982.

15. For contemporary discussions of the impact of a systems installation upon staff, see Shaw, Deborah. "Human Aspects of Library Automation: Helping Staff and Patrons Cope." In *Clinic on Library Applications of Data Processing.* Urbana-Champaign: University of Illinois at Urbana-Champaign, 1985.

16. Fenwick, Elizabeth. Interviewed October 2008.

17. Bill Manson, interviewed in October 2008, another former Geac customer and employee, now CEO of a public library near Fenwick's, made the same observations about his time at Dynix, another vendor that experienced a sudden flurry of growth.

18. Fenwick, Elizabeth. Interviewed October 2008.

19. Scott Zaleski, Linda. Interviewed August 2008.

4

The Nature of the Vendors' Work

This book relies heavily upon in-person interviews, electronic correspondence, and postings to a special Wiki. However, those interviewed were apt to be senior librarians or computing professionals at the middle-management or executive levels. A more general description of workplace realities in the mini-computer industry could perhaps be done best by obtaining the perspectives of a few "front line" people who were directly involved in the development and implementation of interactive library systems (ILS). During 2008 and early 2009, several former employees and former customers of Geac were invited to respond to an online survey. The respondents were mainly technical staff, programmers, or field engineers (FEs) engaged in customer support or development, rather than librarians.

Because of the small numbers of respondents in the sample, the survey is merely informative rather than scientifically rigorous (17 started it, but only 7 completed every question). Nevertheless, it will suffice to provide an idea of the work environment and the expectations of its people. Moreover, the survey offered people, other than those directly interviewed and identified, a way of contributing while retaining some degree of anonymity. Many more contributed their memories through a Facebook group and using a specially devised Wiki, and their comments and anecdotes appear throughout this and subsequent chapters. Still other observations are the author's own.

AGE OF RESPONDENTS

It was widely presumed that programming and similar high-technology occupations were the province of the young. Indeed, 80 percent of the people who responded to the survey were 18–25 years old when they began to work in computing.

Of the 16 people who responded, 11 were male and five were female. Fourteen of them had begun working with computers when they were between the ages of 18 and 25, and ten of them were between 46 and 55 years old when they took the survey. While generalizing from such a small sample is dangerous, the results confirm what a casual observer might suppose upon walking into a computer firm during the mid-1980s. Most people there would be in their twenties, and a larger proportion would be male.

EDUCATION AND TRAINING OF RESPONDENTS

While seven had formal university training in computer science, three reported having no formal training whatsoever. Another three had taken only a few high school courses in computing before they found themselves working in the industry. Two had degrees in other, unrelated fields. The survey was open to people who had worked for vendors and customers alike, and though most respondents had some connection with a particular vendor, Geac, some had worked for various vendors over the course of the years.

However, after they began working with computers, five took more courses. Many computer companies, including Geac, offered free- or reduced-tuition benefits, and some of the company's American customer service technicians, or FEs, were eligible for similar benefits from the U.S. military since they had previously been members of the armed forces. Those who worked for colleges or universities would have enjoyed similar benefits. Most took college or university courses, and two were awarded degrees or diplomas after they had begun working in the industry.

Five reported working "for a vendor in a customer support, field engineering, sales, project management, or similar position involving contact with customers." Of the rest, three reported working "for a vendor in an internal position without much contact with customers." Only two described themselves primarily as "customers," but as we shall see, customers frequently worked for vendors as well, and vice versa.

Because it had been conjectured that respondents might have begun their careers at an early age and perhaps without college or university degrees in computing, they were asked, "Did you go on to improve your knowledge of computers?" Five said they had taken college or university courses, and six said they hadn't taken any other types of training courses. Of those who took courses, eight said they had taken advantage of courses available through their employer, the military, or some other funding source, and three said they had achieved degrees or diplomas specifically to assist in their work. None of the respondents had used free or reduced tuition to take degrees or diplomas in fields unrelated to their work. Many took courses or took additional training in programming languages like Java, or computing topics like networking and client-server architecture.

What did they do for the computer company? Ten had worked with the public in customer support, management, engineering, or similar positions. Five had internal jobs, which did not involve much customer contact. Four had been customers of computer vendors at one time or another.

TYPES OF WORK PERFORMED

Despite their official job descriptions, the responses given in Figure 4.1 demonstrate that jobs were largely interchangeable. Whether their primary responsibilities were for operating systems, applications programs, sales and marketing, or customer support, almost everyone ended up providing support to end users at some point.

What sorts of tasks did they perform? Five were involved in developing system software-operating systems, compilers or interpreters, communications software, and so forth. Eight worked on applications software, the end products used by customers. Three were involved in hardware manufacturing. Five had sales, marketing, or technical-writing positions, or had responded to bids for systems from customers, called requests for proposals (RFPs). All respondents said they had been involved in

Figure 4.1
Types of Work Performed

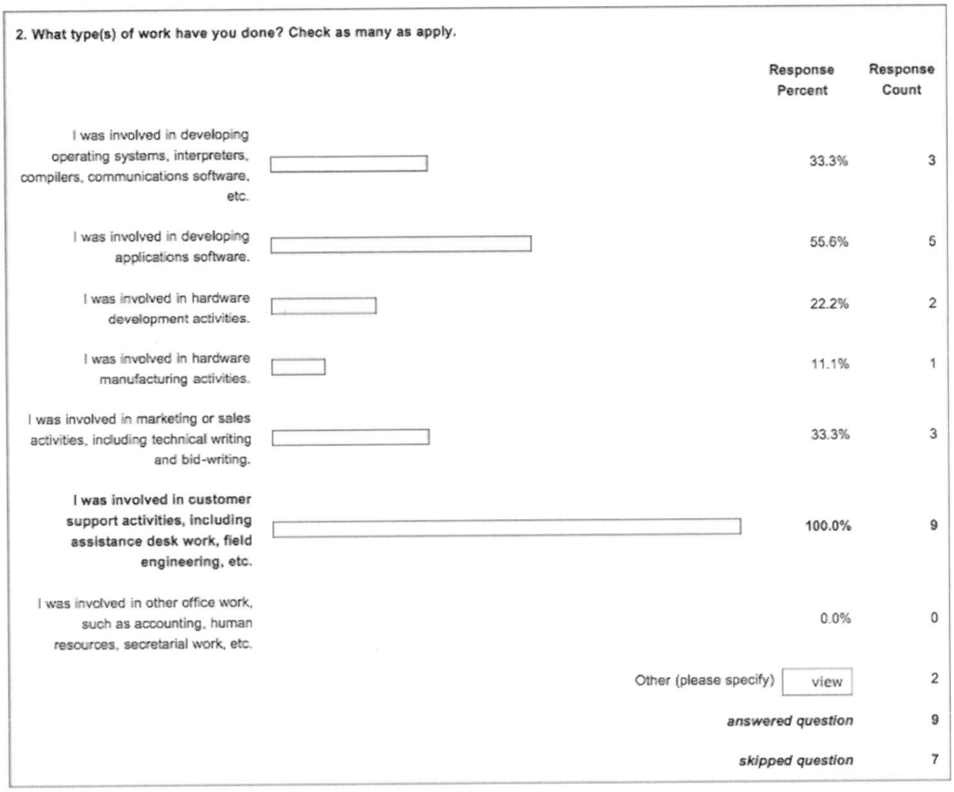

2. What type(s) of work have you done? Check as many as apply.

	Response Percent	Response Count
I was involved in developing operating systems, interpreters, compilers, communications software, etc.	33.3%	3
I was involved in developing applications software.	55.6%	5
I was involved in hardware development activities.	22.2%	2
I was involved in hardware manufacturing activities.	11.1%	1
I was involved in marketing or sales activities, including technical writing and bid-writing.	33.3%	3
I was involved in customer support activities, including assistance desk work, field engineering, etc.	100.0%	9
I was involved in other office work, such as accounting, human resources, secretarial work, etc.	0.0%	0
Other (please specify) view		2
answered question		9
skipped question		7

customer support in some fashion, whether working on the Library Assistance Desk (LAD), doing field engineering (installing and maintaining equipment at a customer site), or performing similar roles.

JOB SATISFACTION

Which aspects of the work produced the most job satisfaction? Overwhelmingly, "the people I worked with" drew the most frequent response. Next, respondents most often cited "solving problems," "the customers," and "the corporate culture or atmosphere," with "the chance to travel," "the technical challenges of the work itself," and "the ability to work independently" frequently ranked as "somewhat important" or "very important."

Financial rewards, and other rewards often considered important in the workplace, received a more interesting response. Compensation and benefits were considered "somewhat important" by six of the respondents and "very important" by another six. Status symbols, such as company cars or corner offices, received less enthusiastic responses. Half of the respondents considered them "somewhat" or "very" important; the other half thought them "unimportant," "not very important," or "neither important nor unimportant." However, one of the prose responses was quite telling. From a more mature perspective, one person wrote, "To clarify, some of those things would be important to me now, but I was too naive then."

For this small group of former employees and customers, human factors were clearly the main motivators, as other prose comments revealed. "The work itself and job satisfaction are always number one." Another person listed "money, bonuses, a nice lunch, and a feeling of satisfaction" as important, while others mentioned "office parties" and "overtime, days off, and free beer" as favorites. One customer service staffer remarks, "I worked out of my home for about ten years as a remote FE [field engineer], so the big reward was control of my schedule."

Strikingly, traditional measures of advancement such as being made a group leader or middle manager were not always seen as benefits. "Sometimes moving to an office, [being provided with] a company car, [or the opportunity to] travel was a given part of the job and not always a perquisite. Working on the project that you wanted, that was important." One person mentioned being given supervisory duties, but with a qualification: "Managing one person or three (which as techies we had no idea how to do)."

The chance to travel, on the company's expense, was considered somewhat important by nine, but twelve thought the company's customers were very important to their own satisfaction. Four considered travel entirely unimportant.

By contrast, "compensation and benefits" ranked low on the scale. Five thought them very important, another five thought them somewhat important, two did not consider these factors important, and two thought them definitely not important at all. However, other perquisites like company cars, corner offices, and so forth drew an even flatter response. Fifty percent considered them either somewhat or very important, four considered them not very important, and two thought them inconsequential or completely unimportant. However, eight thought employee stock options were very important, and five thought them somewhat important. The chance for career advancement was considered somewhat important by ten of these respondents. However, only two thought actual "career paths" were very important. As one respondent put it, "Those things were not important then, but I was naive." So what exactly did employees value the most? What corporate rewards were the most attractive? The survey allowed people to expand in their own words, and these are some responses, in no particular order:

- The work itself and job satisfaction are always #1.
- The money - the bonuses, a nice lunch, and feeling of satisfaction.
- Office Parties.
- Overtime, days off, and free beer.
- Sometimes moving to an office, company car, travel was a given part of the job and not always a perquisite. The project that you wanted, that was important, sometimes managing one person or three (which as techies we had no idea how to do). I worked out my home for about ten years as a remote FE (field engineer), so the big reward was control of my schedule.
- The work, advancement, and compensation.
- Customer feedback. Pay raises and bonuses.

WORK ENVIRONMENT

Wendy Schick, for many years the chief executive officer of the Burlington Public Library and one of Geac's first customers, recalls her first visit to the Steelcase Road office. "It looked like any computer company. Obviously, they were all geniuses and very smart people." But could a casual observer tell which of them held the more important rungs on the corporate ladder?

If one were to walk into Follett, Plessey, Geac, or any number of computer companies of the era, the scene would not have been that much different from the Data General company so aptly described by Tracy Kidder throughout his book, *The Soul of a New Machine*.[1] Physically, one would find oneself amidst a forest of cubicles, gray or pink or mauve, with oak-veneered contoured workstation desks, and the occasional potted plant or *Ficus benjamini*. Middle managers were largely indistinguishable from junior programmers. "No uniforms! There were management offices or partitions though." The secretaries were few, powerful gatekeepers and sources of crucial corporate memory.

The dress code evolved by example. Chuck Williams, Geac's president for many years, wore an open-collared white shirt, with rolled-up sleeves, almost every day. The same was true in other companies, like Plessey or Follett. If you saw someone in a suit, there were probably dressed that way for one of two reasons: either they were in sales, or they were support personnel going to a customer site for the first time. "Always wear a tie on the first day," went the rule, "So they know you own one." After that, the protocol was to dress like the customers, who were used to campus or library attire. One customer remarked at a trade show that he preferred dealing with people who looked like his fellow librarians, and distrusted "slick" salespeople.

Mike Sweet, chief scientist and vice president for Advanced Development, also continued to dress casually, as did most employees who had come from academic institutions. For a while, shoes were optional in the advanced development group. One respondent writes,

"Dress code?" "No way. What was nice was that the software engineers were always pretty equal. I guess though you could tell the guru by lack of shoes."

This comment was a reference to Sweet. His most conspicuous trait was his disdain for footwear. As the principal inventor behind the company's hardware, he was highly regarded—and the people who worked for or near him often emulated him.

Finally, according to company legend, the safety committee had to legislate shoes because people in the computer assembly areas ran the risk of stepping on sharp components and injuring themselves. Given the odd hours people spent at work, comfortable attire was important. Again, according to company legend, Geac's programmers at the relatively isolated Bristol office were known to appear in the middle of the night, still clad in pajamas. If a brilliant idea struck or if a customer had a problem, you either dialed in or simply went into work and wrote the requisite code.

This is not to say that there were no attempts at greater formality. During the early 1980s, a manager of field engineering decreed that all FEs should wear proper shirts with ties. At the University of Arizona in Tucson, where daytime summer temperatures rarely dip below 100° Fahrenheit, that would have been quite uncomfortable. Tom Owens, then the Arizona systems administrator and a man given to loose-fitting Hawaiian shirts, told the local FE to disregard his orders. When his manager called to ask if the FE was properly clad, Owens responded truthfully. At the height of a Tucson summer, jeans and a T-shirt were indeed proper campus attire.[2]

During the hippy era of the 1960s and early 1970s, when long hair was in vogue, there was a popular saying: "It's not what's on your head that counts, but what's in it."

Figuratively, this amply describes the atmosphere prevalent in the engineering groups, both long-established companies like Plessey and the many start-up companies that furnished library hardware and software. While nicely coifed, most computer people chose casual clothes. The quickest way to achieve prestige was to write an elegant piece of program code, or to develop an innovative "fix" to a customer's problem. These could acquire legendary status. For example, a programming solution to a problem in the London Borough of Hillingdon was referred to for years as "The Hillingdon Fix."

FINANCIAL BENEFITS

Jack Sennett, who worked in corporate communications for Geac during the early 1980s, once observed, "Most of our employees are under 25. They voted down a pension plan, in favor of free tuition."[3] In the vendors' work environment, like those of its library customers, intellect and innovation counted for much more than salaries, offices, numbers of direct reports, or being invited to the annual corporate fishing trip. However, in Geac's case, employee stock plans and bonuses were also quite popular. Perhaps these "windfall" financial benefits were more popular because of the youthful workforce.

By the end of the microcomputer era, when corporate takeovers were becoming common, fueled by infusions of venture capital, that situation changed. "I wonder what characterizes that phase in a company's development, when you can't explain what you're doing, but everyone just gets it?" muses Diane Koen, who held increasingly senior positions in Geac, Southam News, and Ovid. "If you could just bottle it"[4]

Michel Vulpe, then a programmer and now a successful CEO, suggests, intriguingly, that the corporate atmosphere might not be so much a sign of a company's age but, rather, a sign of its owners' ages. Arguably, the engine driving the vendor companies of the early 1980s was their junior programmers and engineers. Again arguably, small companies geared to one or two markets only, and especially those markets that were esoteric themselves, are more apt to share the domain knowledge of their customers. "The venture capitalists who bought these companies were all in their forties, and they did not know the industry," Vulpe observes.[5]

Most computer companies of the day had fairly "flat" organizational hierarchies. A few had vice presidents of divisions, some group leaders, and a huge and somewhat interchangeable remainder of ordinary folk. What mattered most to the average employee? Were position titles, compensation, and opportunities for advancement important? How important was an impressive desk or office, a company car, or other typical status symbols? In the Soft Systems Methodology developed by Peter Checkland , such symbols, whether overt and visible, or less obvious when encountered out of context, are referred to as "commodities of power."[6] "Examples of such commodities are the formal authorities associated with particular roles within the organisation, intellectual authority, and authority arising from reputation or special expertise."[7]

In the high-technology companies of the day, those commodities were sometimes less than obvious. Most people worked in open areas, often divided into cubicles, and scattered around the peripheries were a few offices, but those did not always have a bearing on rank. Some, but not all, had one of the most coveted offices with windows. So how important were these things to respondents at the time? Five said their cubicle, office, furniture, or décor held no importance whatever.

"There were no uniforms," says one respondent. "There were management offices or partitions though." Others agreed. "The managers had offices but otherwise our department was fairly equal," says one. "Managers had their own offices, right? The more important, the better the office as well," says another.

However, seven valued the opportunity to work independently most of all. The commodities of power must be sought in less obvious places. All said that the people they worked with were very important sources of job satisfaction, and nine said the corporate culture and work atmosphere were very important. Respondents said they worked with programmers and operating system developers, field engineering managers, technical writers, bid writers, and, above all, customers.

When it came to the technical challenges involved, eight said they were somewhat important, and the other eight thought them very important. As well, 14 listed the opportunity for "solving problems" as the most important source of satisfaction.

Among the duties listed were designing, installing, maintaining, and supporting software and networks; providing sales support; testing products; field engineering; reviewing specifications and technical documentation; writing code; and configuring and maintaining systems in the field. One response in particular illustrates the many roles expected of employees in startup companies:

Development, design, installation (occasionally), training, systems analysis, project management, some sales and sales support, more project management, configurations, help desk, testing. I did everything except write the actual code. But, hey, those were the early days and we had to do it all.[8]

Installation duties involved configuring systems and, often, migrating data from old to new ones. One respondent "[c]onfigured UNIX systems, ported their data from their old systems; went to various sites to do customer training (i.e., training librarians how to take care of UNIX systems, how to query their database, etc)." Another worked on "[t]ransaction processing and throughput, the introduction of multi-threaded circulation / multiprocessor hardware," adding, "Multithreaded processing is now commonplace." Some responses were fairly technical, but even to those unfamiliar with the terminology, they demonstrate how memorable the work was.

In library circles, reduced/changed InterMARC to be more compatible with USMARC (indicators), fixed little things like the right time to beep at the circulation desk (answer when something is amiss). We collaborated always over the network. Things like standards for library interoperability (OSI), started then, and today that work can be seen in Z39.50, NCIP, SIP, and the ability for the WorldCat to place a hold on a book anywhere and ship it. Standards for library functions were created then and today the systems have sometimes not come too far from that time.[9]

Were the required resources available? "Work-arounds were the order of the day," says one person. "But essential funding was generally available." Another says, "Our work-arounds were that we just worked more."

Urgent problems were given carte blanche. "The faster the repair the better," says a field engineer. "Field engineering had all the resources it ever needed if it was an emergency situation. 'Fix the problem first then figure out who pays for it' seemed to be the motto." However, "Spare parts were sometimes an issue," notes an engineer. "Especially during Geac's period of bankruptcy."

Did people remember any special challenges? "Trying to debug the crazy Informer terminals and come up with modifications for them," says one. "We were asked to develop an bank terminal application on an Intel 286 PC driving 4 or more terminals," says someone else. Given the capacities of those early personal computers, that would have indeed been challenging. Another respondent sums things up nicely, "Nothing lasted long—developments tended to render yesterday's solutions irrelevant."

"There were no uniforms," says one respondent. "There were management offices or partitions though." Others agreed. "The managers had offices but otherwise our department was fairly equal," says one. "Managers had their own offices, right? The more important, the better the office as well," says another. Another is more emphatic. "No way—what was nice was that the engineers were always pretty equal."

Several survey respondents elaborated on the workplace atmosphere. "There were lots of home-grown facilities; atmospheres variable, empires and fiefdoms proliferated as the company grew," one observes. "[We had] very basic facilities (no fancy offices). The group we worked with were relaxed, funny, entertaining and brilliant. Everyone helped each other out and fed off of each other's ideas / solutions," says another. A third characterizes the atmosphere as follows: "Basic, very basic cube-land, but it was a fun atmosphere especially after hours when we got the most work done (well that was in the 80's)."

Socializing after hours was important. One respondent recalled "fun interaction between people," socializing after hours, and annual camping trips for members of Geac's Lakeside facility, a busy office with administrators, field engineering and a data centre. "The facilities were satisfactory and we usually had a rather gung-ho atmosphere," says another, and yet another sums it up: "I made life-long friends at Geac." All in all, the concerns, sentiments, and aspirations of these people seem fairly typical of people in their twenties and, to some extent, of computer people of all ages and at all times.

This workplace atmosphere had some drawbacks, as one respondent points out: "Maybe we should have allowed or taught more balance, because burnout, divorce, and even some serious breakdowns were not uncommon."

Despite the isolation, especially among FEs stationed alone in remote areas, there was considerable contact, electronic or in person, with colleagues in the larger offices. "I worked quite a bit with (senior field engineers) in Markham," says an engineer. "Mainly, the management decided the life and death of the projects. At times, I did become the expert as I had always worked in very small groups and lots of research was required to solve problems encountered."

SUMMARY

Looking beyond the surfaces of these statements, an overall picture emerges of a workplace in which intellectual activities and technical feats along with the opportunity to work with others of related minds figure highly. Along with comments garnered from the Wiki and Facebook pages, this small survey also underscores the narratives of librarians provided in the previous chapter: roles within this particular vendor company were to a large extent interchangeable, and regardless of official titles, people undertook whatever work was required to complete particular tasks.

However, it also becomes apparent that senior managers were indeed deciding the overall directions and strategies of which junior employees were either unaware or unconcerned. As one might expect of a primarily technical group, corporate strategy appears less important to them than the actual work and the other people involved. It should be mentioned that Geac and the other ILS vendors were not unionized. It is doubtful that they could have operated successfully had employees not been willing to work long hours, to set and keep their own schedules, and to travel so widely when required to do so. In this respect, ILS vendors resembled ILS clients. Though possibly unionized, academic, public, and special libraries probably operate with similar values; library work is highly intellectual in nature, and library workers are probably not motivated primarily by the external attributes of success.

Did former employees remember particular things as sources of pride or feelings of accomplishment? One remembers "[t]he bank of computers at Bibliotheque Nationale, Paris"; another remembers the Riviera office, with its sign "the caGe" made from the scrambled letters of the company name. Another remembers the size of computer rooms, and how that has largely changed. Another thinks fondly of the Geac 8000 computer itself. For another, particular places and people stand out, and notably:

This one is easy, Yale University Library Circulation Desk and all the Geac originals plus Fred Martz and Audrey [Novak] would be in the picture. Can I have a second? It is the office on the Herrengracht in Amsterdam.[10]

On the more personal side, a respondent notes, "Probably the library system installation at P.L.A.N. in San Mateo California; I met my wife there." But the final word must go to a respondent whose fondest memory was "[o]ur team and the little system we developed."

Looking back at the conjectures informing this book, are we closer to determining where the spirit of innovation came from and how the process was enabled? It seems clear from the previous chapters that customers and designers worked together closely and that the designers enjoyed working with their customers. As we said in the introduction, quoting Paul Nixon, "It is really about discerning what the customer *wants* . . . not what they are asking for. Design follows." This may be challenging since users can only partially articulate their needs and the technical solutions have not been anticipated. However, since librarians and programmers worked together so closely during this period, and since development was, of necessity, undertaken quickly, the fundamental logic and structures that would be incorporated into the ILS process were expedited. We have seen this from a customer's viewpoint in the narratives of Wade and Harris and from a designer's viewpoint in the European narratives of Scott Zaleski. Our confidence that their stories are not atypical is confirmed in the narratives of the survey respondents. Both designers and customers were working collaboratively, sometimes frenetically, on real-world solutions, in a segment of the computing industry about which, at the time, only they were principally concerned. In subsequent chapters, we will examine just what it is that they accomplished, and suggest some lasting benefits.

NOTES

1. Kidder, Tracy. *The Soul of a New Machine.* New York: Modern Library, 1997.
2. Survey response, 2009.
3. Sennett, Jack. Personal communication, 1982.
4. Koen, Diane. Interviewed June 2008.

5. Vulpe, Michel. Interviewed January 2009.

6. Checkland. *Soft Systems Methodology : A 30-Year Retrospective*. New ed. Chichester, UK: Wiley, 1999. Passim.

7. Staker, R. J. "An Application of Checkland's Soft Systems Methodology to the Development of a Military Information Operations Capability for the Australian Defence Force. DSTO–TN–0183." Electronic article. Salisbury, South Australia: Defence Science and Technology Organisation, 1999. http://dspace.dsto.defence.gov.au/dspace/bitstream/1947/3503/1/DSTO-TN-0183.pdf

8. Survey response, 2009.

9. Survey response, 2009.

10. Survey response, 2009.

$$\overline{}$$

5

On Company Time

One of the advantages of the flat administrative hierarchies that most computer companies maintained was that certain jobs were more or less interchangeable. For example, sales support persons whose normal tasks involved responding to requests for proposals (RFPs) might find themselves asked to work with a technical writer; and instructors might find themselves acting as project managers. Next day, someone from sales or marketing might wander by and ask if anyone had any photographs of company installations abroad.

Trade shows, notably the American Library Association's midwinter conferences, usually held in January, were always the occasions of frantic preparations. The exhibit booth would have to be done up with the latest products and glossy brochures, first-level marketing pieces designed to attract the eye. Longer "functions and features" documents would be drawn up, but technical manuals and training material would be reserved for sites that had actually signed contracts.

If you worked long enough with companies like Follett, Geac, Dynix, or CLSI, you probably found yourself on the road. Booth duty at trade shows, long-term project management assignments, one-day troubleshooting and handholding expeditions to customer sites, and even development conferences with programmers or marketing staff from far afield were among your responsibilities, and all these had to be done in person. This was long before the global Internet made it possible to demonstrate systems, conduct teleconferences, or transmit and install software updates remotely. So newly hired programmers, or seasoned veterans, known not by their job titles but by their spheres of expertise, might find themselves in Alaska, Amsterdam, Los Angeles, Bristol, Sydney, or other cities far from their home bases.

While employees were on the road, companies usually took good care of them. When many employees were likely to be called upon for lengthy stints abroad, some companies entered into long-term leases or engaged property management companies putting up employees in suites or sublet condominiums.

One such residence used by Geac lay on the shores of Sydney's Lavender Bay. With its splendid view of the Sydney Opera House framed in the arch of the Harbor Bridge, this was one of the most expensive pieces of real estate in Australia. Brochures left by real estate agents were full of pictures of nearby properties selling in the AUS$200,000 range.

Lavender Bay is rimmed by jacaranda trees, and in the Australian spring, they bloom rosy purple. The huge grinning face that marked the gate of Luna Park, an amusement park whose music and midway loudspeakers blared late into the night; the Milson's Point terminus of the Hornsby railway line; and the Sail Australia school with its orderly rows of tethered sloops bobbing in the gentle swells were all visible from the balconies of flats the company rented for ordinary rank-and-file employees. The company philosophy was as follows: "While you are on the road, you are on company time 24 hours a day."

That meant little scrutiny of restaurant bills, gas refills, car rental costs, and even occasionally first-class airfare upgrades. If it was necessary to be somewhere on short notice, normal concerns over getting the best rates would be waived, sometimes on the sole authority of the employee doing the traveling. Later, of course, the accountants might have questions, but timeliness trumped most routine concerns.

In December 1987, Geac's Australian presence was well established. From an expensive suite at the MLC Centre in the heart of Sydney's business district, the company had relocated to the high-tech enclave of St. Leonard's not far from companies such as Wang and Sun. There, field engineering, headed by Ian Williams; the overall chief-of-station, Ced Bradbury; the local software resident specialist, Mike Himelfarb; and sundry visitors from Stockholm, Amsterdam, Bristol, and Markham shared an open desk space with a consulting firm called The Peripheral People.

SOCIAL: COHESION AND GROUP IDENTITY

Softball was a popular after-work pastime for employees of many organizations during the 1980s. University departments, banks, and almost any institution's employees could be found playing coeducational softball in the evening, and computer companies were no different. In the nonunionized environment of high-tech companies, you might even get off work early if it was time for the playoffs. The teams were frequently organized by work unit, and team names were expressions of group identity.

Sports teams were popular in all sorts of companies, as well as among the different divisions of a university's campus. Within York University's in-house league, for instance, employees of Scott Library chose the name Scotty's Little Softies, a gently self-effacing reference to a type of facial tissue. One of Geac's teams called itself the Fuschia Sox, in contrast to major-league ball teams like the Boston Red Sox.

Geac's Library Assistance Desk (LAD) was a part of the customer support tasked with listening to customer problems and ironing out software problems as they arose. Their team, The Bug Busters, had purchased state-of-the-art baseball jerseys, printed with a custom logo depicting an insect wearing a baseball glove. In the mid- to late 1980s, when the company was in receivership, administrative employees chose the team name Corporate Receivers.

Many of the company's technical core employees, who had a reputation for eccentricity and brilliance, were tucked away in an unmarked office building. They were free to keep their own hours, smoke cigarettes, drink beer, and, like most high-tech gurus, come to work in jeans. They were known around the company as The Hosers. The name was a reference to a popular comedy show featuring a couple of archetypal Canadian backwoods bumpkin characters called Bob and Doug Mackenzie. The Mackenzies wore "grunge" clothes before that term came into fashion: lumberjack shirts, jeans, and stocking-caps called "tuques." They ended most sentences with "Eh?" a Canadian expression equivalent to the American "Huh?"

The Hosers softball team was just one aspect of group cohesion. They also played a popular online trivia game in the pubs on Tuesdays, much like the popular television show *Jeopardy!* which pitted individual tables of people at bars around North America for prizes like T-shirts. The people who invented computing did not have degrees in computing, and in those high-tech boom years, people drifted into computing from other fields. Computer company employees might include marine biologists, sports experts, even the occasional poet or medievalist. The Hosers were no exception, and with all that knowledge covered, the Hosers usually won at trivia.

By the end of the 1980s, companies were going "smoke free," and Geac was the same. While smoking, the moderate consumption of alcohol, and blue jeans and T-shirts at work had been traditional parts of high-tech culture, all that began to change as the company emerged from receivership. The Personnel Department purchased a smoking cessation training package, and the president issued an order intended to phase in a company-wide ban. As a first step, there would be no smoking except in the cafeteria.

Later, smokers would be banished to the outdoors. This posed a problem for the Hosers, whose entire workspace was confined to one room in an industrial strip mall. As a consequence, they declared their lone coffee table "the cafeteria" and left a huge ashtray upon it filled with a heap of cigarette butts.

It took a brave executive to breach the Riviera. In about 1988, when Stephan Bothe became president, he took it upon himself to visit each of the company's Markham offices. The Library Systems Division (LSD) still occupied a one-story red brick edifice on Steelcase Road, with the accountants and personnel people up the road on John Street.

Computers were manufactured at the company's purpose-built research and development facility on Valleywood Road. The Hosers had their own rented space on Riviera Drive, a good five-minute drive from Steelcase. The building had no sign, and the front door was permanently locked. As mentioned in Chapter 1, to get in, you had to find the unmarked loading dock. "The Riv" became a haven for the company's most innovative research and development projects, ones that occasionally ran counter to the work being done at Steelcase and Valleywood.

Much of the work at the Riv dealt with banking, pharmaceutical, office automation, and similar systems. By the end of the decade, the Hosers were quietly working on ways to migrate the company's software away from the proprietary hardware that had been its main source of revenue.

RECREATION OR LEARNING

The mini-computers of the day had no graphics capabilities. Only letters, numbers, and the special symbols appearing on a keyboard could be stored in the machine or displayed on a screen. The classic computer game Adventure, by Will Crowther and Don Woods, is the "character-mode" computer game par excellence. Its popularity among programmers was noted by Tracy Kidder. The objects of the game were to explore Colossal Cave, picking up useful or costly objects; to fend off attackers; and to escape with your life, Reincarnation was available on a limited basis. "It is now pitch dark. If you proceed, you will likely fall into a pit."

During the 1980s, programmers young and old filled countless spare hours lost in the Colossal Cave. Some of us wrote scripts to play the first hundred moves or so automatically. This did not always work, because the knife-throwing dwarfs appeared at unpredictable intervals. Of course, if you knew how to get to the source code, you could figure out the ending too, but that would have been cheating. In computer operations sessions, trainers used games like this to familiarize new systems librarians with the notion that computers would only do exactly what you told them. For this reason, some customer trainers liked to use it in introductory computing classes. Some of the more enterprising players developed computer "shell scripts" to play the first fifty or so moves of the game automatically. Adventure illustrated to computing neophytes how literal-minded machines were.

```
$ advent
Welcome to adventure!! Would you like instructions?
N
You are standing at the end of a road before a small brick building. Around you is a forest.
A small stream flows out of the building and down a gully.
east
You are inside a building, a well house for a large spring. There are some keys on the
ground here. There is a shiny brass lamp nearby. There is food here. There is a bottle of
water here.
take lamp
OK
```

Adventure was full of campy humor, such as the large "barren room, with its warning, 'Caution: Bear in Room,'" or the "Troll Bridge" with its sign "Stop: Pay Troll." Geac's programmers developed some games in ZOPL, and its trainers had used one of them in particular to acquaint novices with computer behavior. It was a "20 Questions" game that, the more people played, they learned new objects and questions to ask. When first installed, it knew only one question, "Are you thinking of a computer?" The player thought of an object, and the computer guessed what it was. For instance, if the machine guessed "frog" but you were thinking "tadpole," it would ask for a question that could be used to distinguish a tadpole from a frog in future. Microsoft's Windows systems have traditionally been shipped with games like Solitaire, and one might conjecture that playing cards on a PC might have served many neophytes as a way of learning how to use a mouse. Teaching customers about the ways computers behaved presumably improved communication with vendor technical staff, facilitated problem solving, and had the secondary effect of increasing social cohesion among vendors and their customers.

Arguably, social cohesion was enhanced though informal groups like sports teams, or crafting merchandise and logos to help employees identify with particular automation projects. Again arguably, team spirit might have had the effect of increasing collaboration while promoting friendly rivalry among divisions of a company at least among members of its junior and middle ranks. Game playing, used as a teaching device, might have had some positive learning outcomes, but it reveals a fondness for the process of automation projects that might have been lost on some customers. One might argue that customers are more interested in the positive outcomes and benefits to their organizations that computing solutions can provide than their intricacies and their esoteric capabilities. However, getting junior- and middle-rank employees to "buy into" automation projects is critical to their success. If library employees, especially systems operators, felt confident with the systems for which they would be responsible, ongoing operations might flow more smoothly. On the vendor side, establishing informal workplaces and allowing people to set their own work schedules, dress codes, and so forth was and perhaps remains a way of compensating and rewarding highly creative people in nonmonetary ways.

Michel Vulpe, CEO of Toronto-based i4i Inc., observes,

> It's the same with every computer company. If you visit Google's campus, or Sun's, or Microsoft's campus, you'll find the lava lamps. You expect these people to work fourteen hours a day—to give you their lives—and they do it, because they think it's "groovy" or "cool."[1]

The denims and campy T-shirts that comprise the "official computer geek uniform" are part of the corporate culture of the computer industry, what Vulpe calls its "manufactured aura." He observes that every organization or community of similar ones, whether the military intelligence community, the bankers, or the denizens of Silicon Valley, has its own "official way of dressing, eating, behaving, and even partying."[2] His comments are borne out in whimsical publications like *The Official Silicon Valley Guy Handbook*.[3] Whether or not these activities and environments had any demonstrable effects on productivity or inventiveness, they certainly existed, and formed part of the work environment for both customers and vendors. Despite the limits imposed by contractual obligations the cohesiveness that can come from sharing a common terminology and through informal socializing probably contributed to the "spirit of cooperation" extolled by Rona Wade as one of the most important characteristics of the era.

NOTES

1. Vulpe, Michel. Interviewed January 2009.
2. Vulpe, Michel. Interviewed January 2009.
3. Bell, Patty, and Doug Myrland. *The Official Silicon Valley Guy Handbook*. New York: Avon Books, 1983.

6

Transformations

In Soft Systems Methodology, the term "transformation" refers to the work being done by a social or computational system to the conversion of some input to some output.[1] The central change that was taking place during the mini-computer era was the transformation of a large number of libraries from manual and batch-automated paper-based workplaces to workplaces whose essential processes were electronic.

Since the computer industry had been largely unaware of the needs of libraries as customers, this involved, in a less obvious fashion, the transformation of a segment of that industry. This industry became one concerned, not so much with general business or scientific functions, but with the specific demands of online transaction processing and enterprises with large databases. Management information is critical to any business, but libraries were in the actual business of *managing information*. This meant an attitudinal shift for software and hardware engineers. Management information usually describes and helps control the process of producing and delivering some product or service. In the case of libraries, it was the information itself that constituted the "product."

The transformation of the library to an automated workplace and the shift in design logic required to accomplish that involved a high degree of collaboration among customers and designers. In the case of Geac Computers, the library division was an "internal customer" of the company's engineering division and needed to convey its requirements to them as well. The process was simplified, to a degree, by the fact that the major players in the Library Systems Division (LSD) and Advanced Development had been with the company almost since its inception and could simply speak to one another. In companies that sourced their hardware from major manufacturers, that process would have involved traditional sorts of business negotiations.

A similar process had taken place at the onset of the era at the pioneering circulation vendor, Plessey. While the other major ILS vendors accomplished the same sorts of things, and arguably did them better in various respects, the Geac and Plessey stories provide a unique glimpse of the challenges faced industry-wide.

Portions of this chapter appeared in a modified form in Brown-Syed, C. "From CLANN to UNILINC: An Automated Library Consortium from a Soft Systems Perspective." PhD thesis, University of Toronto, 1996.

By the late 1970s, libraries had been using automation-like processes to manage circulation functions for several years. The McBee Keysort System is an example. McBee cards were similar to the punch cards once used by newspaper delivery carriers. Each week, once the customer paid, the paper carrier used a paper punch to cut a circle or notch in the place on the card that represented the week in question. City bus drivers used a similar idea, punching bus transfer slips to indicate boarding times or bus routes. The McBee cards placed in book pockets could be notched along their edges to identify books that should be returned on certain dates, and copies kept in a drawer on the circulation desk could be sorted easily by running a long needle-like tool through the hole that represented a certain date. Since the McBees were notched, those matching the condition would simply fall out of the deck and onto the table, while the others would remain impaled upon the needle.[2] Systems like this had been available at least since World War II.

With the advent of more readily available general-purpose mainframe computers, and languages like FORTRAN and COBOL, it became possible to switch to Hollerith Cards, also called IBM cards. These were 80-column cards that could also be inserted into book pockets. Unlike McBees, Hollerith cards could be punched to represent the characters in IBM's Extended Binary Coded Decimal Interchange Code (EBCDIC), or the 128 American National Standards Institute's ASCII characters, which are even today the basic codes transmitted by computer keyboards when users touch the letters or numbers. The Control, Alternate, and similar function keys alter those basic values to allow things like accents, called "diacritics," and so forth. The IBM cards in books were read and stored on tapes for processing on mainframe computers, and the day's transactions could be added to or subtracted from the list of books on loan in a "batch process" overnight.

CAMPUS MAINFRAMES

During the late 1960s and early 1970s, ordinary users had no access to computing centers. Computers occupied a great deal of floor space and produced a great deal of heat. A modest-sized disk drive with a capacity of, say, 650 megabytes could well be the size of a washing machine. Other components, like tape drives and the computer's central processing unit (CPU), could occupy several cabinets the size of refrigerators.

Printers were as big as office desks. All this equipment needed to be air conditioned, and was prone to dust and power fluctuations. Computers were housed in special rooms, with raised flooring filled with cables connecting all these components. Air conditioning ducts under the floor blew cold air up under the components, and huge power conditioners made sure that no sudden spikes or drops in the AC power harmed the sensitive machines. At some centers, computer operators went about in white lab coats because disk drives, especially, were sensitive to dust.

Since dust could be lethal to disk drives, the bigger university computer rooms had exhaust fans that ensured that the air pressure was higher in the computer room than outside. When someone opened the door, the higher pressure would keep the dust out.

It suffices to say that few libraries in the world could afford their own mainframe computers given the cost of not only the machines but also the associated labor and environmental requirements. That meant that the library would be one of many of the campus computing center's clients, and that their "jobs," like the nightly circulation list, would be placed in a queue vying for computer time with the astronomers, chemists, biologists, and payroll office.

Like several other large libraries of the time, York University in Toronto had been using 80-column punch cards (Hollerith cards, or IBM cards), inserted in book pockets, and plastic library cards punched with IBM codes. Transactions like the issue, renewal, and return of items were completed by inserting the patron's library card, followed by the string of book cards, into a machine on the circulation desk called a C-Dek. The company that supplied these was Mohawk Data Systems. The first C-Deks were "static readers." That meant there was a slot on the top, and you lowered the punch card horizontally into the slot until the machine scanned the punched holes, then responded with a "clunk" and a light went on. The next-generation machines were "dynamic." You slid the card into an aperture on the side of the machine, and it scanned them as they rolled past a sensor, much like swiping the magnetic strip on a credit card. The sequence of library card reads and book card reads was written to a half-inch computer tape, and after closing time, the data were processed on an IBM 360 or 370 mainframe computer in the campus computing center.

By this time, libraries were performing online searches of indexing and abstracting databases such as Lockheed's Dialog system. Because the only way to talk to a computer was through punch cards or teletypewriters, "search intermediaries," or library staffers, would accept patrons' requests submitted on paper forms, develop a search strategy, and submit the request. That night, the search results would be printed on continuous-form paper and be left in the patron's inbox, a physical cardboard box or paper-tray, for pickup the next day.

Coincident with the development of smaller mini-computers, the next generation of library automation systems would operate in "real time," providing results immediately rather than overnight. Some of the forerunners in this emerging market niche were companies like CLIS, Plessey, Data Phase, DOBIS, NOTIS, DRA, III, Dynix, and Geac. A useful timeline depicting the origins and the ongoing development of library automation vendors has been maintained for some years by Marshall Breeding, and is available online.[3] The effort was geographically dispersed. For instance, Geac's headquarters were located in Canada, CLSI's in Massachusetts, Dynix's in Utah, and Plessey's in the United Kingdom. This chapter deals mostly with Plessey and Geac to illustrate the ranges of problems addressed by all of the major vendors of the period, and includes references to CLSI and NOTIS.

PLESSEY DATA SYSTEMS

Headquartered at Soper's Lane in Poole, United Kingdom, Plessey Data Systems is seldom mentioned in the library literature written in North America, probably because it had only installed a few sites over the course of the 1970s. By the middle of the next decade, the company name had dissolved. However, its subtle influence on the course of library automation far outweighs its physical presence on the continent.

Its library systems division carries on under the name of DS Limited. However, its North American presence was strong enough to merit setting up an office in the North Toronto area not far from the Canadian Forces base at Downsview. Library systems were a small part of Plessey's enterprise, which included landing systems for airports.

Plessey's choice of a location in the northwest of what is now Toronto was probably due more to the existence of Downsview Air Force Base than of the new university. Many high-technology companies were locating at the northern end of the city. Another cluster, which would eventually include Pure Data, Geac, and similar companies, was growing to the northeast of the city.

But Downsview was also the home of DeHavilland, makers of the DASH-7 and DASH-8 commuter planes, and had been the home of A. V. Roe, builders of the famous Avro Arrow supersonic interceptor, which was coveted by several of the world's air forces but never deployed. The National Research Council's Defense and Civilian Institute for Environmental Medicine (DCIEM) was also there. They had developed pressure suits, and future member of the Canadian astronaut corps, Dr. Ken Money, was actively engaged in space-sickness experiments at DCIEM. Money and his colleagues recruited York student volunteers, put them in a dark spherical chamber, and spun them around in a centrifuge to see how soon they would vomit and to figure out how to stop it. Money once explained that he'd done the experiment so many times himself that he was no longer susceptible to motion sickness, so he needed a supply of student volunteers. It was natural that Plessey, with its lengthy history of aerospace connections, should find a home nearby.

The early library systems created by Plessey were written in a programming language called CORAL 66. The name is a contraction of "Core-Reducing ALGOL," another language from which it had descended, and over which it offered the advantage of taking up less space in memory.[4] At one time, computer memory was based on ferrite rings, called "cores." Collectively, memory was thus called "core."[5]

CORAL had received approval by the North Atlantic Treaty Organization (NATO), which is perhaps why its first U.S. customer was the U.S. Air Force Academy at Colorado Springs. In the early 1970s, Toronto's York University purchased a Plessey Module 1B system but passed the company over during a system upgrade in 1982, selecting the Geac Library Information System (GLIS).

Plessey's major contributions included their solution to the problem of multiple terminals and the introduction of the "Plessey" barcode format. For many years, companies like Geac were still required to read Plessey barcodes even though the Codabar label format invented by CLSI had become almost universally accepted. In theory libraries with the older format wished to avoid converting to the new.

The Plessey Module1B was a "batch mode" system in the main, collecting circulation transactions much like the older C-Deks and writing them to tape; but it offered a major advantage. It had an online "trapping store," of blocked patrons and requested books, and before each transaction was processed, it checked to see if patrons and books were eligible. Plessey had hoped to upgrade York to its new Module 4 system, which offered online circulation and used DEC VT-100 video terminals to view the circulation lists along with purpose-designed checkout stations that incorporated barcode readers and displayed the status of each transaction.

BATCH MODE CIRCULATION SYSTEMS: YORK UNIVERSITY

In order to illustrate the sea change that took place in library circulation systems during thee early 1980s, let us examine the case of Toronto's York University Libraries in more detail. A copy of the system description and the initial purchase agreement between York and Plessey is still available in the university archives together with a cover letter written by Robert Berman, Plessey's marketing manager, who was based in Downsview.

York was a new university established in 1959 as a spin-off of the University of Toronto. It was first housed in a former private estate called Glendon College. For the first few years and as a parting gift from its parent institution, York faculty and students would enjoy access to the University of Toronto's extensive library system, which at one point included about 50 component libraries. As the fledgling university spread its wings, a new library system would be established just for York. In 1965, York opened its new main campus located north of the city in Downsview, Ontario, on what had been a family farm.

During that period of explosive growth, other universities across North America and around the world were buying up farmland for new campuses. The University at Buffalo's North Campus in Amherst, New York, is another example. Like the American land grant universities of a previous era, these new institutions were typically located outside of the already developed areas of major cities.

Administrators of such institutions were faced with both challenges and opportunities to build things from scratch unburdened by the physical constraints of city centers. The library services were gradually moved to a new main library, which opened in 1971. Being new, it was in a good position to benefit from the latest innovations in computing.

The Steacie Science Library on the new campus was a candidate for an architectural award and now housed most of the fifteen staff whose ranks had grown from an original seven professional librarians and four support staff. It also housed the university administration, and would become the home of the York-Ryerson Computing Centre (YRCC), which processed all the administrative and academic computing requests. In those days, all computing was done by means of either using 80-column IBM Hollerith punch cards or using teletypewriters-typewriters connected by wires to a mainframe computer.

Punched paper tape was still being used to boot computers as well. In 1971, the new main library, Scott Library, was officially opened. It had space for a million books, and was to be endowed with an automated circulation system. There are statistical analyses of transactions made with the Mohawk C-Dek system done by the Library Systems Department from 1970.

Most of the library's collection was still housed miles away at the Frost Library on the Glendon campus. From the outset, Glendon College had been conceived of as a bilingual institution providing instruction in Canada's two official languages, English and French. The other component colleges of the "new" York University would offer instruction only in English, and would be housed on the new, somewhat rural campus. Here and elsewhere, there would eventually be a need for computer systems that could handle French accents and that would contain bilingual subject headings. Of course, once computer companies figured out how to handle French, they would be able to build Spanish, Dutch, or German systems as well.

Most equipment then in use worked only with the 128-bit American Standard Code for Information Interchange (ASCII), which allowed only the numbers, letters, and special symbols found on today's keyboards. Campus mainframe computers were apt to be supplied by International Business Machines (IBM) and to use the company's more extensive, but still not really multilingual, Extended Binary Coded Decimal Interchange Code (EBCDIC).

This was the case at York. Regardless of whether ASCII or EBCDIC coding schemes were used, non-Latin character sets like Greek, Russian, Japanese, Korean, and Chinese would not be feasible until the adoption of Unicode, which would really come only with the adoption of Graphical User Interfaces (GUI) during the 1990s.

From the outset, York's libraries would employ computers in a variety of ways. Catalogue cards would be produced from the UTLAS consortium's CATSS database, one of the bibliographic utilities that, along with WLN and RLIN, then vied with OCLC for supremacy in the shared or union catalogue market. When the new Scott Library opened for use during the early 1970s, online searches of indexing and abstracting databases were offered on an overnight basis. At designated tables in the campus libraries, community members could fill out search query forms, and staff from the university's Survey Research Centre in the Institute for Behavioral Research would enter the queries using teletypewriters. Printouts of the search results would be left at the tables in the libraries, often by the next morning. A cooperative union serials system (CUSS) allowed patrons to see which of a number of regional libraries held copies of magazines and journals. All of these systems operated in batch rather than in online modes as far as the users and front-desk library staff were concerned.

By 1977, committees had been formed at York to discuss closing the card catalogue. This was not because it would be replaced by an online public access catalogue (OPAC) but because computer output microform (COM), especially COM microfiche, had been in use for some time.

To begin with, York performed its circulation using McBee keysort cards, then IBM Hollerith cards. These 80-column punch cards contained just room enough for an identifying number, the first few words of a title, and a copy number. They were read by Mohawk Data Systems C-Dek punch card readers and written on IBM 029 Keypunch machines. Transactions were recorded on reel-to-reel computer tape drives housed in the campus computing center, and they were processed at night in batches on the campus mainframe computer. Sometimes, because of the physical limitations of the wiring between the terminals and the tape drive, "length and parity errors," "cyclical redundancy check errors," and similar data integrity problems could occur. The signal could simply arrive at the tape machine in a corrupted state, and the transaction would have to be performed again. The new system, negotiated in 1975, would provide better data security and increased functionality.

The first of the library's daily processes to be automated was circulation. In fact, in 1976, Plessey Canada Limited had only one operational system in the country at Ottawa's Carleton University. A similar system would be installed at the U.S. Air Force Academy in Colorado Springs. Plessey was a time-honored company with major defense contracts in the United Kingdom and with NATO.

By 1978, the company's Module 4 system was a truly online system offering real-time query and display of circulation transactions. It also had brief author and title information for books and personal information about patrons. It would be ready to be offered for installation at the Calgary Public Library. Calgary is located far to the west of Toronto, at the foot of the Rocky Mountains, and far from the Downsview and Dorset offices. To ensure timely support, Plessey stationed an engineer and operations staff at the library. The Module 4 was among the first of a new generation of commercially available mini-computer-based systems and could truly claim to be an online circulation system in the modern sense. However the system that Plessey initially offered Toronto's York University was primarily a batch mode system. Transactions were collected during the day, and the library processed them in batches each night on the campus mainframe computers.

In 1976, Plessey Canada Limited (an overseas branch of Plessey Data Systems) offered York an improved way of working. This was Plessey's Module 1B, to be called the YUL Circulation System, described by Marketing Manager Robert Berman as a "turnkey system." The 1976 contract is a total of 30 pages in length. By later standards, the document's language and the language of Berman's cover letter seem remarkably informal and vague. When it comes to the amount of money to be charged for maintenance, the document merely states that Plessey would negotiate a reasonable fee. It is difficult to imagine university lawyers agreeing to such a wording today.[6]

The system's specifications reveal much about the capacity of mini-computer-based systems, and about customer expectations. From it, we can also form an appreciation of the work flow involved. While the university's three main libraries would be equipped with "composite terminals" for checkout and return of items, administrative actions like blocking borrowers, placing holds on items, or even querying the system to see which patrons or items were blocked would only be done from the teletypewriter that acted as a system console. All the major processing would take place on the university's mainframe computers. The Module 1B would act a collection device for circulation transactions, and nightly tapes would be taken physically to the York-Ryerson Computing Centre for processing. In fact, the Plessey system would not even contain the authors, titles, or subjects of books, or the patrons' names and addresses. The only "online" data in the system would be 14-digit barcode numbers. It would serve the new main Scott Library, the Steacie Science Library on the new campus, and the Frost Library back at the Glendon site.

This is how it worked. When a patron wished to check out books or other materials, the circulation staff would scan a control barcode, putting the terminal into checkout mode. Next, they would scan the patron's library card and then the barcodes on the books. That sequence, patron barcode followed by one or more item barcodes, would be written simultaneously to the system disk and to a half-inch reel-to-reel magnetic tape. When items were returned, their barcode numbers would also be written to the tape prefixed by a discharge code. Each night, the tape would be read on the mainframe computer. Next morning, when the Plessey system was brought up, the previous day's transactions would be forgotten. However, the "trapping store," which contained the barcodes of requested items and what Plessey liked to call the "trapped," that is, sanctioned borrowers, would remain intact to block any loans that ought not to occur.

The front-desk staff had no way to see, in real time, any bibliographic or patron information on the system or even to find out which items were on the shelf or out in circulation. For that, one would consult printouts made during the overnight processing runs. Those printouts would be delivered to the two main campus libraries by a staff member who retrieved them each day from the computing center. The Frost Library, located miles away at Glendon College, would have to wait for its daily circulation list. It would arrive on the library van along with the boxes of books that every library system sends back and forth daily among its branches, ones returned at a different branch or requested by readers at the branches.

The Plessey system, officially called the SPC Module 1B for "stored program control," incorporated a small disk drive, a tape drive, and a paper-tape reader for booting the CPU. The CPU itself was an Interdata (later Perkin-Elmer) 7/16 mini-computer, about the size of an early PC. All of these components were rack-mounted in a single cabinet, about the size of a refrigerator. Unlike the campus mainframes, the Plessey system did not require special air conditioning and dust control, and was housed in the Scott Library Circulation Department.

The total system cost for the YUL Circulation System would be $117,589.60.[7] However, the company offered $1,000 off the price if York agreed to construct about 1,500 feet of conduits for data cables. Full payment was due 30 days from shipment of the major components. As well, the company offered a special $1,200 printer to create

Plessey-style barcodes, a $4,000 portable data capture unit (PDCU) to be used for backup and inventory, and a supply of blank labels at $30.50 per thousand.

Appended to the contract were the design specifications for the system, amounting to about 30 pages of text plus the appendices. A decade later, a similar proposal would typically occupy five or six archival transfer boxes, as customers demanded more stringent specifications, documentation, and performance criteria of commercial ILS vendors.

At this early juncture, Plessey had every incentive to live up to its word, as Berman's letter explains. This was to be the first 1B system, replacing the earlier 1A.

I would also like to point out that this is only the second system in Canada for Plessey and that York University is the first of its type. Plessey Canada has made a large commitment to be in the Library circulation control business. If we wish (and we do) to gain more business, it would definitely not be to our advantage to let York University down. I would also like to point out that I believe Carleton University will back me up on saying that Plessey has a good regulation [*sic*] in support.[8]

With the company's headquarters a ten-minute drive away, response time for customer support would certainly never become an issue. While it performed only one function, circulation, this was indeed a "turnkey" system, because Plessey supplied both the hardware and the software and would provide the programming and field engineering support. Berman's letter concludes, "Your biggest bargaining power is definitely not money. If Plessey does not support York University, I would not hesitate to make the statement that we would not sell another system in Canada."

One big advantage of the Plessey system had to do with data integrity and security. Because the company offered York the option of writing each transaction simultaneously to disk and to tape, the transmission problems that occasionally plagued the old Mohawk and mainframe computer system could be circumvented. The library would always have a "checkpoint" backup of the tape on the 1B system disk. However, that image would be overwritten each morning because there wasn't enough space on the disk to keep multiple backups. On page 31 of the specifications, there is a note about security:

Transaction tape security options. (Item 8). The data contained on the transaction tape is vital if the total system (including any main frame) is not to lose touch with the real world, in particular loss of discharge data could lead to the production of unnecessary and annoying overdue notices.

Tape image on disk. (Item 9). On these systems sufficient spare disc capacity is made available and an exact image of the transaction tape is written concurrently to the disc area. At the end of the day when transactions have finished copies of the monitor can be produced at will by dumping the entire disc area to fresh magnetic tapes. The copy on disc will be lost immediately the next day's operation begins.

The Plessey proposal, which was reputedly discovered and used by rival companies to create "targeted" requests for proposals (RFPs), consisted of a rather informal memo from then sales chief Robert Berman, entitled "DESIGN SPECIFICATION FOR THE YORK UNIVERSITY AUTOMATED LIBRARY CIRCULATION SYSTEM #2YU61175.67" It begins, "The system shall be known as YUL CIRCULATION SYSTEM. System module number is 1B. Size of the borrowers trap file is: 50,000 borrowers. Size of the item trap file is: 100,000 items."[9]

In lay terms, a computer could hold only about as much information as one finds in a standard graduate term paper of ten or 12 pages of text. Because the tape would be processed on the campus mainframe, the encoding scheme and tape format selected would be IBM EBCDIC. The local system would include a "9-track 1600 CPI phase encoded read after write" tape drive. Plessey provided one magnetic tape with the machine. The system was expected to operate in an office environment, and to run off standard 115VAC/60Hz wall outlets. The CPU came with 32 kilobytes of memory. The specification notes, "An additional 32K of core memory will be supplied for a total of 64K in the system."

For backup and inventory purposes, Plessey would supply a PDCU, the sort of hand-held device used in supermarkets to check food stocks. To simplify arm and wrist movements and to speed checkout, Plessey's light pens (barcode wands) were equipped with ingenious self-inking date-due stamps affixed to the shafts of the pen. Several stamps were necessary in practice, because not everything went out for the same length of time. Because self-inking date stamps were attached to the barcode wands, circulation staff could read the book labels and stamp the date-due sheets with one arm movement and a flick of the wrist. The labels themselves were 14 digits long, but the barcode symbology was a proprietary one, developed by Plessey.

The document outlines the Plessey Patron Barcode Structure in detail. For example, a Plessey patron barcode might contain a "type identifier," borrower status, a borrower number, privilege and replacement codes, and a trailing checksum, and the number of bytes required for each element was described in the proposal. Perhaps this is because barcodes were relatively new in library usage, and perhaps too because disk and tape storage space was at such a premium. By comparison, a 14-digit CLSI format barcode typically contains a type identifier (2 for patron, 3 for book), a four-digit agency prefix, a unique number to identify the patron or book, and a trailing checksum.

The Plessey composite terminals had keypads for entering dates or changes to the default checkout and return parameters. However, not all functions would be permitted at all terminals. For instance, putting blocks on borrowers, or erasing their records, could be suppressed at certain stations. Borrowers and requested items were to be blocked using "trap codes," and the online log of requested books and blocked borrowers came to be known as the "trapping store."

Among the equipment would be a control teletype through which the system operator communicated with the computer and that could double as a printer for creating reminder, overdue, or fines notices. Patron and item enquiries would also be done on the teletype machine, meaning that searches of the database and the resulting hits would appear on continuous-form, pin-feed printer paper. York's main Scott Library would receive two composite terminals, one issue terminal and one terminal for discharge, while the Steacie Science Library and the Leslie Frost Library, located miles away on the Glendon Campus, would each receive one composite terminal. The system would allow variable loan periods, and with authorization it would allow staff to override the defaults.

As noted, the Plessey contract, dated June 17, mentioned security provisions, "including transaction tape security option of simultaneous recording on tape and disk." This meant that transactions written to the tape for later mainframe processing could also be written to the Plessey system's disk drive as a precaution. If something were to happen to the tape, another copy could be made. Communications among the branches were also described. The Scott, Frost, and Stacie libraries would be connected by "dedicated voice grade communication lines," meaning ordinary telephone lines that, in those days, operated at 300 baud. Internal connections between the circulation desk and the CPU should be limited to 1,500 feet of cabling. As far as the actual processing of data was concerned, York agreed to write the requisite mainframe programs. The company also provided a special label printer for creation of barcode labels.

By 1978, when the Plessey Module 4 was being installed at the Calgary Public Library, these limited capacities had been circumvented. Inquiries and transactions could be done online and in real time, and the new branch control units allowed multiple terminals at service points. However, telephony had not improved significantly over the course of the decade. Individual modems were needed for each incoming line from a branch, and actual customer dial-up to the OPAC, though already envisaged, would place more load on the system and require more modems.

Geac Library Information System

Geac's world headquarters were in Markham, Ontario, a high-tech enclave north of Toronto colloquially know as "Silicon Hill." Throughout much of the period, Geac specialized in two "vertical markets": libraries and banks. Some of its library systems development was done in Bristol and London in the United Kingdom, and it had sales and support offices in Alexandria, Virginia; Amsterdam; and Sydney, Australia, along with manufacturing and support offices in a dozen other locations. Geac built its own mini-computers, because its clients needed machines that could talk to many terminals quickly and accurately. Geac's machines excelled in the online transaction-processing environments of its banking and library customers.

As early as 1984, Geac strategists had seen the need for simpler, less costly, and more useful systems. With its major technical problems solved or circumvented, the computing industry switched its attention to the customer, and the customers were librarians who graduated from programs rapidly changing into schools of library and information science. These schools were introducing computers and their capabilities to the students. Some of the professors in these expanding programs held degrees in computer science.

Then, as now, if you took a diploma or degree in computer science, you probably were taught nothing about library automation. It was simply too small a market niche to even appear on the radar. But libraries had needs that few other industries of the time had considered. They processed materials in many languages, and they wanted online transaction processing; accounting in foreign currencies; lengthy, variable-length data records; and guaranteed response times of less than two seconds, from terminals hundreds of miles from central computing sites. Vendors responded by developing faster machines, and software with more library-specific functionality. Geac's solution had been the development of an even faster mini-computer, the Concept 9000, which went into production with the name System 9000.

By the end of the 1980s, Dynix, a Provo, Utah–based rival, introduced a computer it called the 9000 Killer with reference to the top-of-the-line Geac machine, the System 9000.[10] The 9000 had outperformed Digital Equipment Corporation's VAX computers in benchmarking experiments that in those days compared the number of "megaflops" and "dhrystones" a computer could perform. The term "dhrystone" is a pun on "whetstone." Instead of measuring the number of floating point operations (flops) a computer can perform, this metric is meant as a more general measure of processor speed.[11] The 9000 could talk to over 512 "dumb" computer terminals that were just keyboards and screens with little or no processing power, something libraries and banks both needed to do. Today's fastest computers are measured for their performance of "giga" or even "peta" flops.[12]

UPGRADES AND MIGRATIONS

Requests for Information

Installing or upgrading a library system could be a lengthy and involved process. First, budget approval for a new system had to be justified to the university or the municipal library board. This meant that someone had to do preliminary research and produce a report. Then, requests for information (RFIs) might be sent to dozens of vendors to determine which systems suited the scale and functionality of the project.

RFIs were not issued in all cases. When they were, it was as the first step in a lengthy process of vendor identification and selection, contract negotiation, system implementation, and final acceptance of the new hardware and software. An extant example of an early implementation cycle describes the process followed at the U.S. Military Academy at West Point.[13]

The RFP Process

Requests for proposals were lengthy documents, often prepared by committees within the library and mailed to several vendors for competitive bids. Typically RFPs, which included more detail about the library's collection size, growth rate, patron base, and special concerns, would be sent to half a dozen vendors whose systems seemed likely to fit the site's requirements. The RFP had to be specific regarding desired functions and features of the system, because it, together with the subsequent contract, could be legally binding. For example, if a vendor promised that the catalogue screens would be multilingual, when responding to the RFP the library could withhold payments until that feature was implemented. Task forces and committees took months to finalize the RFPs.

Once the RFP had been mailed to vendors, their bids departments needed a certain amount of time to respond, typically measured in months. Since documentation and sample reports were often requested along with the bid, the vendors might ship several archival transfer boxes of papers with their responses. Reading the proposals from half a dozen vendors would take the library's task force members more weeks or months of time before a short list, typically of three vendors, could be agreed upon. Vendors usually prepared several sorts of marketing literature. Short brochures, sometimes called "glossies," would accompany RFIs. Detailed technical descriptions, called "functions and features" documents, had to be sent with the RFPs. As well, configuring a system might mean filling out lengthy specifications tables, like the Geac *Policy Parameters* described by Linda Scott Zaleski.[14]

What is more, during the explosive growth phase of the early 1980s, vendors were deluged with RFPs and had to be selective in responding to them. Some had obviously been mistargeted, sent to vendors of large systems when smaller ones were required or vice versa. According to a popular account, one repeated request a distant overseas customer asked for a bid on several hundred Geac 9000 computers. Since the cheapest

9000 cost roughly a million dollars, the bid department had ignored the request. Finally, sales staff faxed back a reply, asking an enormous sum, and the matter was dropped. Then, as now, it is incumbent upon libraries to research the products available, and to direct their requests for proposals to vendors having systems of suitable size and cost to fit their needs. It must be noted that unlike retail items, library systems are rarely advertised by price. This is because each site represents different configuration challenges. This may be true even in the case of site licenses for software, with pricing based on ranges of workstations, numbers of simultaneous users, or similar factors taken into account.

In some cases, the library or its task force might engage a consultant to manage the selection process and present the short list. Rob McGee, founder of RMG Consultants Inc. with offices in the United States and Australia, is a pioneering and still-active library automation consultant. Joseph Matthews, who served as editor of *Library Technology Reports* for many years, is another. Perhaps the definitive text on preparing RFPs was penned by McGee.[15]

Some vendors tended to treat consultants with caution. Experience taught that some were difficult to please, and more than once, bids prepared by specific consultants were rejected out of hand and more likely prospects pursued. When weighing the pros and cons of replying to RFPs, vendors had to consider the costs of supporting customer sites, so geography played a part. While software support could be managed centrally using voice and dial-up telephone connections, field engineering had to be done onsite. It was not always possible to ship a mini-computer to a regional depot for maintenance, and few libraries could afford duplicate systems for "hot" backup purposes, so field-engineering response time was a major concern to libraries and vendors alike. Libraries, like banks, could not afford downtime.

However, various backup systems existed, some the forerunners of today's palmtop devices. For instance, Plessey's contract with York University Libraries mentions a PDCU that could be supplied as an option. Geac would later supply a personal digital assistant, the Psion Organiser, for the same purpose, and other vendors used various handheld machines made by Telxon. Such units could be used to keep libraries functioning while service personnel were en route. They could also be used for taking inventories, or on bookmobiles.

Geography was a major factor, but not necessarily a limiting one. For instance, when Geac received an RFP from Miami-Dade County in Florida, the chance of a sale was almost overlooked. "We hadn't even considered that part of the country," says Michael Monahan, who was then head of Geac's library sales force. However, upon examining the specifications, the sales team realized that their GLIS system matched the site's requirements almost exactly. "The bid was accepted with absolutely no revisions," Monahan recalls. "It was astounding and unique."[16]

If there was no regional field engineering office and little chance of acquiring enough customers in the library's vicinity, a promising sales opportunity might have to be skipped. In Geac's case the same engineers could maintain systems for the company's library and banking customers, so the chances of providing regional support were somewhat better for all concerned. Vendors who did not manufacture their own hardware could contract with more computer service companies or with the equipment manufacturers themselves (e.g., DEC or IBM). An example of an independent service company was Computer Professionals Unlimited (CPU), which served the Michigan area out of its base in Detroit.

Once vendors had been allowed enough time to respond to a library's RFPs, it would take weeks or months for the library to evaluate competing offers, and to arrive at a short list of vendors. While this may seem like a long time, it must be remembered that while plain text files were routinely being transmitted over computer networks, the ability to transmit publications that contained graphic elements like charts, diagrams, or photographs, was years away. If the library's task force was made up of a dozen staff members, twelve copies of the proposal, along with accompanying manuals and "functions and features" documents, would have to be assembled by the vendor. A vendor's proposal might fill several shipping boxes, and it would take the library some time to compare and evaluate proposals submitted by three or four vendors.

Add a month or more for the short-listed vendors to travel to the library site for demonstrations and sales presentations and a few weeks for the library to arrive at and announce its decision, and time to receive board approval or the go-ahead from the university. Online demonstrations were difficult before the global Internet, and demonstrations systems were typically too large to fit on CD-ROMs. It was far better to send sales and sales support staff to the site and to conduct a demonstration under controlled circumstances. Such presentations were jokingly referred to as "dog and pony shows."

Then the serious part of the negotiations would begin. Sales staff from the vendor would meet with library staff and/or their consultants to iron out the fine points of the contract and the implementation schedule. After months or even years had elapsed since the project's inception, the library would be in position to make a purchase. It was considered "good form" to announce the final decision in the trade literature; and commonly the library and vendor would issue a joint press release. This was useful to the vendor as it enhanced the company's reputation, reassured existing customers, and encouraged stockholders and investors. It was also useful to the library, because it usually staved off sales calls from other vendors.

However, vendors who had lost bids were not always acquiescent. At the very least, they might consider phoning the chief librarian and asking for elaboration on the reasons for their rejection. Ostensibly, this was to improve their future dealings; but in extreme cases, information gleaned from such calls could be used to prepare for litigation. In "low-bid" jurisdictions, a losing vendor whose system was inadequate but less expensive than the winner's could launch a lawsuit.

Another strategy might involve interviewing the systems librarian, noting weaknesses in the library task force's selection logic, and then contacting the library's CEO, library board members, or university administrators with claims that the system librarian was inept, and that the contract should be reexamined. One does not equate the library world with this sort of competitive behavior, but there are documented cases of its having happened.

Sales staff had good reason to be aggressive, because they typically received a base salary plus commission. Even 3 percent of a million-dollar sale represented a tidy sum. Some vendors also provided yearly bonuses and extended commission for sales support staff or for everyone in the company. Add-on sales of items such as additional disk drives or printers might be handed off from the sales force to an assigned project manager in the support team, so an additional incentive to maintain good customer relations might be felt throughout the company.

Performance bonds might have been posted as part of the contract, and the sum owing was often made in "milestone" payments that would be made once specific implementation targets had been reached. Librarians generally planned on keeping a system for five to seven years; and given the lead time required for subsequent purchases or upgrades, the cycle might begin again within a few years. After a relatively short hiatus, library systems staff, in addition to performing their normal duties, might find themselves continually planning for systems upgrades, enhancements, or replacements.

Why were RFP documents complicated? New programmers and people who worked in computing but not in library automation often wondered just that. After all, circulation systems for libraries looked, at first glance, much like inventory systems for hardware stores. The main differences probably lay in the complexity of bibliographic data and the necessity of accommodating the behavior of library patrons, and those of internal staff.

Library data is complicated from the outset. As part of the function known as "acquisitions," librarians buy materials—videos, books, sound recordings, and computer software—from a variety of vendors in many different languages and from many different countries. They must pay for them in many different currencies. Sometimes, the books are written in non-Roman alphabets. Moreover, materials in library catalogues must be described consistently both internally within a library system and in conformity with established external standards. The integrity of the bibliographic data in a library's catalogue is of great concern to technical services staff. The catalogue represents many hours of labor. It facilitates the retrieval of information only if its contents are consistent, or so librarians have traditionally believed.

Libraries are service organizations often tax or tuition supported, and their automated systems are used directly by their patrons. Those patrons are individuals, and each one has a different set of expectations. Fortunately, most fall into recognizable groups whose expectations can be more or less predictable.

However, ILS customers each think of themselves as having unique needs, because of their sizes, the types of institutions they serve, the demographics of their service areas, their hours of operation, peak service periods, and above all because of their membership, lending and fines policies. Unlike word-processing systems, ILS must be highly configurable to meet the needs of each customer but still similar enough to make their maintenance and upgrades economically and practically feasible.

TRANSFORMATIONS: THE TECHNOLOGIES

Keith Thomas had joined Geac early in 1984. Thomas says, "The original GLIS transaction model was based on someone's reading of a classic IBM paper on transaction processing. It was entirely serial. It was based on IBM's BiSync protocol." Thomas began working with Jacob Slonim, Avi Schonbach, Erich Buss, and others, in a fourth-generation product group called 4G, in whose group the vision was an "information utility" that would greatly exceed the functionality of simple library systems. Slonim, Schonbach, and Thomas all published material on the International Standards Organizations' Open Systems Interconnection (ISO/OSI) concept and its applications.[17]

While we have seen some of the perspectives of customers, and those who installed systems and trained them, Thomas presents another picture of collaboration from the point of view of the Library Systems Division, which constituted an "internal customer" for the company's engineering and Advanced Development groups.

I was managing the GLIS 9000 group in Toronto. I was responsible for those people in the UK who were working on the Bibliothec Nationale de France. The other people in the UK reported to Philip Drew. We did a presentation in the Geac boardroom. We described how the multi-threading system could work without locking. We two things: we had a good transaction processing model and the multi-processor framework that allowed multiple threads without locking. With the 9000, if you needed more throughput, you just added more processors. Mike Sweet was there, and at the end, he said, "You know, that sounds kind of sweet." That was the thing that got the 9000 past the benchmark test in Dublin for the University of Essex. Our results were better than anything you could crank out on a mini-computer in those days.[18]

Sweet was sufficiently intrigued by what the Library Systems Division was doing that he developed routines within the microcode, the very low-level instructions a machine acts upon, to allow faster OPAC searching. But faster speeds, essential to winning contracts like Essex and the Bibliothèque Nationale de France (BN), were only part of the challenge. Thomas remembers the security concerns put forward by the Bibliothèque:

The BN had a security model that would have made the CIA proud. It was so secure that certain operations could only be performed by the National Librarian. That may be apocryphal, but nobody could prove that there weren't lockouts, and occasionally, people encountered them.[19]

Like the Sigma, the 9000 microcode had instructions that were interruptible. Without such a feature, the longer the instructions the machine had to act upon, the more the concern that one instruction might mask another.

In terms of its architecture that whole scale of multiprocessor, dense, chip-level multiprocessors was not necessary in the 1980s with the chips that were coming out then. But now, they are back in fashion, with companies like Intel, and machines like the IBM Roadrunner [supercomputer]. The 9000 was a bit-sliced computer, the individual components being 4 bits wide, with a 16 bit word-length throughout. What we're seeing now is a 9000 on a chip. It can simulate nuclear explosions. Like most technological ideas, the 9000 was both advanced, and there was something behind the curve about it.[20]

In ordinary language, what this means is that if you take a great many small machines, and get them to work together, they can outperform a big machine many times over. There is something democratic and philosophically satisfying about this notion, that the power of coordinated teamwork can outperform raw power.

Along similar lines, Sweet's Advanced Development team experimented with redundant array of inexpensive disks (RAID). Today, when disks are all inexpensive, the "I" in RAID stands for "independent." The reason for RAID is data protection: if you write data in several places at once, nothing is lost should one component fail. At one point, Sweet's team built a prototype of a machine called the MF-100 that had 100 small disk drives.[21]

As one of the first Geac employees to work on library projects, Michael Monahan presents a different perspective on the development of proprietary machines designed for high-volume transaction processing. His explanation deals with the demands of the company's library and banking systems clients for high-speed fault-tolerant machinery.

The 8000s were first delivered to libraries, but the company wanted to sell them to banks . . . credit unions, then Canada Permanent Trust. The competitor was Tandem because it solved the banking problem. Tandem had technology such that if almost any component failed, you could replace it while running on a backup and then bring it back online. The 9000 was never completely fault tolerant. But Tandem was expensive. Truly duplexing everything is expensive, the disks, the channels, the power supplies, the clock, IBM faced that with some of their multiprocessors. If the clock failed, the whole system was gone; reducing the probability of failure means increasing the cost.[22]

However desirable it was, fault tolerance was not the essential selling factor behind Geac's successful library sales. In fact, its 8000 series hardware was already delivering an impressive degree of reliability.

We never tried to sell the 9000 to libraries on the basis of fault tolerance. Libraries needed large amounts of up-time, and significant amounts of performance, but were unwilling to incur the costs that would have made the difference between 99.5 and 99.8% availability. You could turn the machine off and on and it would re-start.[23]

Monahan recalls how Princeton University had phoned during the middle of a lightning storm. The campus computer center was down, but the 8000 kept restarting. The library wanted to know how often and how many times the system would recover on its own. "We told them to shut the 8000 down. It wasn't intended to go up and down like a yo-yo."

Sometimes, older components made better technical and business sense. For example, before the industry switched to complementary metal-oxide semiconductor (CMOS) memory chips, a computer memory had been based on magnetic "ferrite" cores resembling small metal doughnuts with electrical wires passing through them. Taking advantage of the basic relationship between electricity and magnetism, you could control the polarity of each ferrite ring by passing voltages along the wires. Once polarized, the cores did not destabilize for a long time. Each core could hold one bit of information, a zero or a one. In order to have any useable amount of memory, one needed many banks of magnetic cores. Some of Geac's early machines used core memory.

Companies making core memory were making it cheaper and cheaper. The first time we attended an Association of College and Research Libraries conference in Boston, we took a whole machine. It had been running diagnostics at the factory. The memory boards had been taken out for shipping, and when the system was powered up again in Boston, it began running the diagnostics. The switch-over from one technology to another isn't always obvious, in terms of the cost-benefits involved.[24]

Addressing the development of standards, Monahan reminds us that while most were the result of deliberate committee activities, some happened more or less by accident. He cites the case of the library automation industry's adoption of the 14-digit Codabar barcode label format, which CLSI had pioneered. While some of Plessey's former customers such as the U.S. Air Force Academy would make any new system's ability to read Plessey barcodes a sale condition, Plessey, and its successor DS Limited, were no longer active in the North American library systems marketplace, so there was a supply problem. Monahan says that though Geac could read the Plessey labels, in practice they were never used. Everyone replaced them.

In Geac's case, adoption of the standard had come about with the active participation of the universities of Guelph and Waterloo, the first of the company's academic library sales. Librarians had suggested that the Codabar format with its leading codes of 2 for patrons, 3 for books, an identifying number, and a trailing check digit was becoming a library standard. However, before the patron or book number, the CLSI format included a four-digit "agency prefix" to identify each unique library customer. It would be necessary to call CLSI and ask for a range of agency numbers that would not conflict with theirs. At first, CLSI was reluctant.

CLSI suggested this violated copyright. They wanted to come to Toronto to see the system. Finally, we said, "Your only choice is to give us two numbers, or we'll pick them." Following the path of least resistance is a wonderful example of creating an overnight standard, which has served the library industry well. If you changed vendors, your labels would still work.[25]

TRANSFORMATIONS: TECHNICAL ASPECTS

As stated earlier, libraries buy materials—videos, books, sound recordings, and computer software—from a variety of vendors, in many different languages, and from many different countries. They must pay for them in many different currencies. Sometimes, the books are written in non-Roman alphabets. Moreover, materials in library catalogue must be described consistently, both internally within a library system and in conformity with established external standards. They have different categories of patrons and different loans, fines, and renewals policies. The hours of service and, consequently, the due dates may vary among the branches of the same library system, and most certainly will vary among the different libraries in a consortium.

Libraries are service organizations, often tax or tuition supported, and today their automated systems are used directly by their patrons. Those patrons are individuals, and each one has a different set of expectations. Fortunately, most fall into recognizable groups, whose expectations can be more or less predictable.

As well, ILS customers think of themselves as having unique needs. Unlike word-processing systems, ILS must be highly configurable so as to meet the needs of each customer, but still similar enough to make their maintenance and upgrades economically and practically feasible.

Librarians have specific needs, which systems designers strive to fulfill. Librarians needed rapid transaction processing and user verification and accurate sequencing of messages (lest a book appear to be returned before it was charged out). They also need systems that protect the privacy and confidentiality of transactions. Because branches of libraries or different libraries in a regional consortium may be geographically disparate, libraries need to communicate over considerable distances in short amounts of time. They must pass fairly large amounts of data back and forth, at least descriptions of materials, and at most the actual texts or images. Some of that data may be written in non-Roman alphabets. Libraries need systems that can remain in operation over relatively long workdays, and that can recover from failures quickly. Today, data-encoding standards that allow multilingual records, relational databases like SQL, and telecommunications infrastructures and communications protocols like the Internet's TCP/IP have addressed most of these concerns. However, during the period covered in this book, such challenges were still being addressed.

Work flows in libraries and the demands placed upon ILS vary considerably with time of day, day of the week, and month of the year. For instance, a university library in the Northern Hemisphere will be busier between September and May. A public library may be busier during semester breaks and over the summer. Urban libraries may see rush hour traffic at noon, when people visit over their lunch breaks. College libraries may be busiest just before scheduled classes, when students rush to catch up on their assignments. System throughput and the ability to handle sudden spikes in the numbers of queries and circulation transactions were tested severely by these varied patterns of use. In the days before the Internet, when telephone lines were used for data communication, achieving a two-second response time across a network even in peak periods was a common performance target.

In order to minimize delays, local automation systems used bibliographic indexes of authors, titles, call numbers, and so forth and performed initial lookups against these indexes instead of against the full-text records. But this meant a trade-off. During the night, operators had to build the indexes.

No matter what the demands, any computer spends much of its time idling because humans function slower than machines. Eventually computing capacity grew to the point that it became possible for the continuous "background" index-builds while the system was functioning. The circulation and catalogue systems would run in the foreground with the system updating the indexes during slack moments between transactions—what programmers would call unused machine cycles or "idle time."

However, there were other functions to be performed at night when the library was closed. When people still expected printed overdue notices and fines statements, for example, someone had to be there to load the paper and special forms into the printers. Jobs like these took precious machine cycles, so they were put off until night. Management reports, financial reconciliations, automated check production for book orders, and other acquisitions functions would probably be run as part of the "overnight" processing.

For libraries, this meant hiring a staff of operators to work the midnight-to-dawn shift. The main job of the overnight staff was to perform the backups, in those days done on half-inch reel-to-reel computer tape. Each vendor's system addressed these issues in different ways, but every ILS had to deal with them.

This sort of processing activity had additional management benefits. An ILS is a treasure trove of management information. While library planners may rely upon user surveys and demographic information obtained from local government authorities, circulation and OPAC search logs can provide actual pictures of usage down to the branch or even the work station levels. If all the Italian books are stored at the central branch, but 80 percent of their readers now live near a suburban branch, the circulation statistics will tell you at a glance that it is time to move that collection. If most weekend patrons use the library between noon and 4:00 p.m., you can consider closing at 6:00 p.m. While sampling methods used in survey research can only describe subsets of a population, system logs can show you exactly what is happening across a system perhaps down to the individual keystroke and to the microsecond. Oddly, though ILS have been capable of generating such reports for decades, they are sometimes overlooked as sources of management information.

CHARACTERISTICS OF THE BIBLIOGRAPHIC DATA

Several of those interviewed mentioned the importance of standards like MAchine Readable Cataloguing (MARC). What exactly is it, and why was it so important not just in the development of bibliographic utilities or consortia that exchanged records but also in the development of IL? This is what a MARC record looks like to the computer:

```
2200145
45000200015000000900009000151300027000242450018
0005126000500006950000370011952000890015660000320
024565100420027770000260031 9 a0141439947 c3d3
aDoomsday BooklEnglsih aDoomsday book aHarmonds-
worth, MiddlesexbPenguin Booksc2004 asample record
aNew English translation of all volumes of Doomsday
Bookuhttp://www.penguinbooks.com aWilliam the
Conquererd1066 aUnited KingdomxEnglandy11th
Century aWilliams, AnneEditor00558[26]
```

After the record number, 2200145, comes a "leader" made up of a long string of numbers that define the fixed and variable fields within the record proper, called "tags." Next come the tags themselves, if present.

One can probably discern certain fields easily, for example, "Doomsday book" would be the 245 "title." "Harmondsworth, Middlesex" would be the place of publication, and the string of characters "sample record" would be a 500 "note" field. The 6xx subject fields appear toward the end of the record. This record describes a book with no single author, so there is no 100 "author" tag. However, there is a 700 "additional author" tag for the editor, whose name is "Williams, Anne."

The record is passed from one machine to another or from one applications program to another as a "bit stream," a series of letters and numbers; and the program acts upon the header and the data in the fields to create online displays and so on. Nowadays, the raw MARC data are translated into HTML or XML for display on catalogue screens or Internet browsers, with suitable headings and punctuation inserted. In the 1980s, special display programs that were part of the library automation system itself had to be written to accomplish this task. For example, the publication information in the 260 tag could be displayed on the catalogue screen as "Published: Harmondsworth, Middlesex: Penguin Books, 2004." To the catalogue, it looks like this: "260 $a Harmondsworth, Middlesex $bPenguin Books$c2004."

The variable-length MARC tags contain subfields that are prefixed by letters (a,b,c) and that have meanings that vary in different contexts. Some tags and subfields can be repeated if necessary. For instance, books rarely cover only one subject, so the 6xx "subject" tags may occur more than once in a record. Books may be published in two locations, so the $a and $b subfields in the 260 "place of publication" tag may be repeated. The pamphlet *Understanding MARC Bibliographic*[27] offers a rapid overview of the scheme.

As can be seen from the example above, it is quite possible to include the URL for an online copy, a photo of the book's cover, or, in this case, directions to the publisher's Web site within a MARC record. The actual contents of the various tags and the rules for their usage are defined in the *Anglo-American Cataloguing Rules*, 2nd edition (revised), commonly called AACR2R.[28]

The data representation scheme called MARC, ISO standard 2709, is often criticized today as being unsuited for describing digital documents, but from a technical standpoint, data stored in one format can easily be translated into another. In fact, this happens each time you view a MARC record using a Web browser or on a catalogue screen in the library. MARC is routinely translated into HTML, the display language of the Web. The cataloguing rules themselves may be insufficient for today's varieties of data. This is why AACR2R may eventually be replaced by a new manual called *Resource Description and Access* (RDA), which is currently being discussed by the Joint Steering Committee for Development of RDA (JSC).[29] This committee includes representatives from the American and Canadian library associations, and CILIP, and was previously responsible for maintaining AACR2. RDA is being developed with a view to describing both printed material and material that is "born digital."

According to the JSC Web site, "RDA provides a set of guidelines and instructions on formulating data to support resource discovery. RDA provides a comprehensive set of guidelines and instructions covering all types of content and media."[30]

While the AACR2 cataloguing rules are often associated with the MARC record format, cataloguing rules are about ensuring consistent content in a database. MARC is a data representation format. A given MARC record is as good as its content, or as inadequate. AACR2 or RDA tells cataloguers what to put into a bibliographic description. MARC provides a consistent format for storing the data, that is understandable by machines running different software.

Over the years, MARC has fulfilled its initial function of providing an exchange format that is "platform independent," that is, it can be exchanged among and incorporated into local automation systems around the world. Today, regardless of the underlying software, ILS systems use Web browsers to display their contents to staff and to patrons. However, during the 1980s, another clever use for MARC had been discovered. Since MARC allows one to identify the major components of bibliographic records easily, the identifying tags and subfields could be used by programmers to drive screen displays. Before Hypertext Markup Language (HTML) and the World Wide Web, OPAC vendors needed to write software to translate MARC records from their internal storage format into something the public could understand. Fortunately, most of the necessary information was already contained in the records themselves. The software could determine from a MARC record's leader what type of material it represented: book, journal, video or film, sound recording, and so forth. The MARC fields, or tags, and their subfields could be "parsed" or deconstructed by the software, and appropriate headings displayed on the users' screens. For instance, if a record represented a book, the system could display headings like "Author," "Title," "Publisher," and so forth on the screen. If it represented a film, those headings could read "Director," "Title," and "Producer." Instead of displaying "Pages," the screen could say "Running Time," and so on with other types of material.

SMALL CAPACITIES AND COMPACT COMPUTER CODE

By the 1980s, with increased computing capacity came increasing complexity. Because memory and disk space were still severely limited by today's standards, the quest for economy and elegance was continuous. Microsoft's filenames were limited to eight characters, followed by a three-character extension, for example "readme.txt."

The extension indicated the type of file—program, Word document, plain text, etc. Filenames were limited to six characters on the Geac 8000 system, and names beginning with the letter "U" caused program execution. For instance, commands like "ULARG!" and "UZERO" (pronounced "you large bang" and "you zero") would create a large file and initialize it to millions of zeros. Wherever possible, run-time responses from operators were limited to two characters. "Run" became "RU," and "Yes" became "YE." The program code itself would be as elegant and efficient as possible. To ask a question and obtain an answer from the system operator, only this program statement would have been necessary:

```
ANS_(YESNO,"Continue?",STRLEN,ye/no);
```

Because confirmation would be something often required, programmers had written a special routine called "yesno," thereby compressing several statements into one. It asked the question in quotes and assigned the reply to the variable on the left, in this case named "ANS" for "answer." It was based on the more general "ITOY 3" call, which asked for input from operators and assigned the response to a variable. In turn, "IOTY" meant "input and output from teletypewriter." What is interesting is that esoteric programming jargon like this was shared with the company's customers. Since the source code and manuals for Geac's system were distributed to all its customers. Their systems administrators were encouraged to take programming courses and to develop local modifications—within defined contractual limits.

It should be noted that Geac's library system was actually written in HUGO, a "superset" of ZOPL, in which groups of frequently used programming routines could be called using single statements. On the banking side, which used the company's Applications Building Language and Environment (ABLE), the same was true. Nevertheless, if anyone wished to write special programs in the underlying ZOPL language, one could.

Since ZOPL manuals were shipped with all new systems and customers could take courses in ZOPL and GLUG, many systems administrators at library sites would have had no problem understanding much of this jargon. HUGO, which was a superset of ZOPL, contained many program routines that were designed especially for library applications. System administrators at customer sites were never trained in HUGO, which was considered "dangerous." Instead, those who wished to program the machine to retrieve special management reports would take courses in the GLUG language that allowed them to read from, but not alter, the library's circulation, acquisitions, and catalogue databases.

In allowing its users even that much latitude, Geac was somewhat atypical. Competing companies like CLSI did not rely so much upon the operators at sites. As well, Geac delivered the source code for its system to the customer sites, not a "compiled" version that only the computer could understand and run. There were trade-offs. Customers could and did come up with enhancements to the system. However, they might also write "site-specific modifications," about which the company could be unaware. This could lead to version control problems and could perplex help-desk staff if problems arose at particularly innovative sites. Needless to say, running a large automation system regardless of the vendor demanded that someone onsite be fully conversant with the system and the processes and work flows associated with it. For instance, even ordinary transactions like issuing a book to a patron, receiving one back, involved several underlying steps for the machine.

CIRCULATION TRANSACTIONS

In some ways, a book that is being returned to a library presents a more complicated problem for an automated system than one that is being borrowed. When a patron wants to take something out, the staff member or the computer system must simply determine whether the patron is eligible to borrow and whether the book can go out to this sort of patron. We can express the logic in Pseudocode, plain language statements that could be translated into some programming language. For example, here are only some of the steps involved in a "charge" or "checkout" transaction.

1. Read the next barcode.
2. If it is an item barcode, charge it out to the current patron.
3. If it is not an item barcode, look it up in the patron database.
   - If the barcode is not in the patron database, return an error message and quit.
   - Display the patron's name for verification.
   - If the patron has been blocked, return an error message, and allow the operator to override.
   - Determine the type of patron: adult, child, or other.
4. If it is not a patron barcode, look it up in the materials database.
5. Determine the type of material: two-week loan, reference, or other.
6. If it is not allowed to circulate, return an error message, and allow the operator to override.
7. Calculate and display the due date.
8. Make a record of the transaction.
9. Update the item's "times checked out" counter.
10. Update the borrower's "activity" counter.

By contrast, when a book is returned, the logic can be even more complicated. The book could have been requested by someone else, could have been returned at a different branch, could be overdue, and so forth. A library calculates the amount owing on overdue items the moment they are returned, so a return or "discharge" transaction may involve creating a new "fines" transaction. While fines might seem straightforward, there is always the possibility of an exception to the general rule, for example, a library might charge no additional overdue fines for books returned after hours, on closed days or holidays or for other reasons.

1. Read the next barcode.
2. If it is not an item barcode, return an error message and quit.
3. Look up the item in the transaction file.
4. If it was not checked out, update its "times returned counter," to show it was used in-house, quit.
5. If the due date and time in the transaction file are earlier than "today" and "now," check the hours of operation, schedule of holidays and closed days for this branch, or any special fines rules.
6. calculate fines, generate fines transaction.
7. If the item is on hold for someone else, generate a "hold available" message to alert the operator to keep the book.

8. If the item is not at its home branch, generate a "ship to" message, and alert the operator.
9. Remove the book from the circulation transaction list.
10. Remove the borrower from the circulation transaction list.
11. Update the book's circulation count.
12. Update the borrower's usage count.

The fascinating thing about online transaction processing is that steps like these (and the above is a simplification) were all meant to take place within a few seconds. A two-second response time was expected by many librarians across a system that might have run over telephone lines. Software engineers had to solve problems like this with the early circulation systems.

CATALOGUING AND AUTHORITIES

Even more complicated challenges awaited them once OPACs displayed the full MARC bibliographic records. Catalogue input software could verify authors' names and subject headings against the Library of Congress "authorities" files in real time, and acquisitions systems that could keep track of multiple book vendors and foreign exchange rates, and do double-entry bookkeeping, came into the mix. Only once those major functions were part of the same ILS could it truly be considered "integrated."

Library of Congress authorities files contain lists of conventional ways of writing authors' names and a standardized, or "controlled," vocabulary for subject headings. All the works by authors who wrote under pseudonyms or who sometimes went only by their initials and at other times by their full given names could be retrieved and displayed together for the patron, making multiple searches unnecessary. For example, Mark Twain's books, and those of Samuel Clemens, could be retrieved and displayed at once.

Outdated subject headings, like "Indians of North America," or "American Indians," could be replaced "globally" by comparing a catalogue to the authority files, and having the software accept later and more appropriate headings such as the usual Canadian term "First Nations" or the term used in the United States, "Native Americans." This capacity is very important, since groups of people frequently change the ways in which they self-identify. As well, geographic place names tend to change over time. With good authorities software, an ILS system could "flip" the headings overnight and could also validate input as cataloguers typed in new records. According to a Library of Congress representative, the authorities service was phased in over a number of years.

LC began inputting name authority records on April 1, 1977 [and] began distributing name authority records in 1977, or, more likely, 1978. Initially, transaction records were distributed, i.e., records containing only what had been corrected or changed. This proved to be unsatisfactory. Beginning April 1, 1984, changes and deletions were issued as full records (the manner in which they are issued today). [Subject] authority records were not issued at the same time. Name authority records came first."[31]

While the dates are uncertain, it is safe to say that by the mid-1980s, it would have been possible to perform authorities maintenance of a library's OPAC, using data provided by the Library of Congress. Libraries began requesting that their automation vendors facilitate the process.

OVERNIGHT PROCESSING

Even though the systems of the 1980s were thought of as online because transactions appeared on screens in real time, maintenance processes were associated with them that demanded considerable computing resources. Today it would be possible to run as these as background jobs during the day, at lower priorities than the main ILS. Given computer capacities, these jobs were typically run as "overnights" so as not to impact system response time. That often meant hiring a staff of computer operators to work at night. Since magnetic reel-to-reel tapes were typically used as backup and recovery devices, someone would at least have to mount a series of tapes each night and to initiate the overnights.

By 1992, when systems like the Geac Library Information System for the 9000 computer (GLIS 9000) had become rather complex, incorporating circulation, acquisitions, and catalogue functions, the overnights could literally take all night. Their proper execution would be important, since the ILS might not function as expected the next morning if the files had not been fully updated.

LOCAL INITIATIVES AND A TYPICAL OFFLINE-PROCESSING CYCLE

This section is intended to provide some notion of the offline computer processing that was performed nightly to support ongoing system operations, notice production, management reports, and database security and updating activities. It will contribute to an understanding of the types and amounts of activities performed by operations staff at the UNILINC central site in Australia, as well as provide some indication of the complexity of maintaining a multisite integrated library system of the period.

UNILINC had given the author access to its system logs during a research visit in 1992. While some of the processes described here must still be conducted, others have been rendered obsolete because of the industry-wide adoption of relational databases like SQL. As well, due to vastly increased computing capacities, others can be done as background jobs while the library system continues to operate normally. However, the basic maintenance activities—the actual updating of the library's records and the production of management reports—must still happen in one way or another. The logic of doing those tasks was largely worked out during the era we are discussing. As well, we shall see how UNILINC's operations staff streamlined the processes, wrote code, and developed work-arounds that demanded they know a great deal about the system's internal workings. This in turn supports the hypothesis that cooperation among vendors and clients was very important.

Sources consulted include the site's actual overnight processing batch control files as well as entries contained in the system's output monitor log. The latter was a file that recorded the start and stop times of processes on the system as well as other events required for security or scheduling purposes.

The Bibliographic Processing System (BPS), which maintained the cataloguing database; the Circulation System (Circ); and the Acquisitions and Serials System (Acq) each had its own nightly and weekend batch-processing schedules. Typically, the weeknight batches were less complicated than the weekend processing schedules. Examples are given here of the types of jobs performed in each system on a Monday night representing the typical weekday job stream. Many other processes were conducted through overnight batch processing done either on other nights of the week or periodically in the background while the ILS was running. Examples include end-of-month and end-of-year processing, uploading lists of students at the beginning of a term, and so forth. This outline is representative rather than comprehensive.

While the processes described here were specific to the GLIS 9000, many of the functions performed would have be "platform independent." That is, they represent data manipulation that would be required to maintain other ILS of this generation; however, the task breakdown and the terminology used to describe it are vendor specific. Each vendor's system came with its own verbal shorthand and jargon. Where Geac pronunciations might be confusing, representative pronunciations have been given phonetically. For ease in pronunciation, the metasymbol "*" should be voiced "Star," the metasymbol "!" as "Bang," and the "^" metasymbol should be rendered "Up." Operators would have had to learn this jargon in order to communicate with the vendor's support staff or even to remain relatively sane while reading the user manuals.

A system user interacted with the Series 9000 computer through a program called Session Manager. This process was part of the Operating System's communications subsystem, and governed what was referred to in the Open Systems Interconnection model as the "presentation layer."

Because the Series 9000's Session Manager (PORKER) allowed each user including the console operator to run up to nine interactive sessions simultaneously from one terminal, many of the processes described below actually ran concurrently in different interactive (KQ) sessions. Cleverly, the UNILINC operations staff had written batch programs that called other batch programs so that the whole operation could be started by one person but would mimic the actions of several staff members over the course of the night.

It is noteworthy that operations staff at the customer site had developed these computer scripts themselves. They were leveraging the existing system's features to make the machine exceed its designers' expectations. In order to explain the complexity of the task, and the ingenuity of the solution, we must now introduce some esoteric jargon. Learning that jargon was part of the operator's duty. It facilitated communications with customer support staff, and arguably, gave one a sense of belonging to a community wider than one's own library. At library conferences, members of different vendors' User Groups bandied about terms that were specific to their particular systems. The following section includes a great deal of Geac jargon, and describes processes that take place today in a matter of seconds or minutes. During the time in question, an "overnight" process truly might take all night.

Through "multithreading" techniques, some active jobs were capable of spawning other jobs without operator intervention. For instance, a process whose duty it was to manipulate index files could automatically clone itself if the workload became too heavy and divide up the duties. As a result, processing that could not possibly be completed in one night if handled sequentially could in fact be completed in time for the 7:30 a.m. system runup.

Here is a simplified version of a typical weekday overnight processing session, based on UNILINC's Monday night procedures. The Monday circulation overnight batch (LBMON, pronounced "El Bee Mun") began by running a job called CPRVAL ("See Pea R-Val") to check that any in-process records had been closed properly, that is, to make sure that when the online system was brought down, no transactions were partially processed. Next, a complete disk-to-disk backup of the circulation files was performed, the transaction recovery file (TCP file) was reset to its empty state, and a full file-sized checker (LPFCHK, pronounced "El Pea F-check") was run to determine the sizes and numbers of records in each of the various circulation system files.

The system was now in the proper state to begin the overnight processing batch (LBOVER) itself. This job's principal duty was to maintain the transaction file (**TRAN, pronounced "Star Star Tran"), which contained the information linking items on loan with the patrons who had borrowed them. This involved deleting "historical" transactions, and rebuilding the transaction file so that only current ones were contained and took between three and four hours. System integrity checks, terminal activity analyses, and other statistical and operational reports were created during this process.

Once the transaction file had been tidied up (i.e., the garbage collected), the next step was to generate various printed forms such as overdue and fine notices (run nightly) and special reports required by the various member libraries (some done nightly, others on particular nights). The Remote Spooling Subsystem ZQSQRL (pronounced "Zed Q Squirrel") automatically routed some of these reports to workstations at the various libraries, where an online menu-driven program allowed branch librarians to view, print locally, or discard individual reports without printing them. In keeping with the "squirrel" motif, the file containing these reports was called "**NUTS."

On Monday night, the forms production batch was followed by a daily picking list for the certain university libraries run every night, which took about 30 minutes to complete. Next, a nightly "holds availability" report (about 10 minutes of processing) was run especially for one campus of one of the member universities.

Next, the Circ system was backed up in full to an Exabyte high-density cartridge tape drive, and the system was prepared for the next day of running. The Communications Subsystem of the GEOS operating system was then reinitialized using a process called "COMUP." This restarted the Fault Tolerant Applications Manager (FATMAN) and brought up the online jobs.

On the BPS side, more processing was being performed. This batch process FBNITE (Eff Bee Nite) remained more or less constant during each week night. The FBNITE batch made use of four concurrent interactive KQ sessions by placing operator commands in chunks of memory called "type-ahead buffers," greatly reducing the time of completion. In other words, the operations staff had rigged the system to imitate four live human beings by passing commands back and forth to various programs within the computer. When one program needed operator instructions, it would find them waiting in a type-ahead buffer.

Normally, the OPAC would be brought down when the library closed, and the file time would be set to midnight of the previous day. However, if there were a tape to be loaded containing newly received catalogue records from the Australian Bibliographic Network (ABN), this processing then took place first and the system's recovery files would have to be checked for in-process records so that more detailed or more current work done by local cataloguers would not be overwritten by the incoming records requested previously from the national library.

The OPAC was brought down by sending a command to a second KQ session. For insurance, this command was actually issued twice, once in the master KQ session using the normal online control program FPMISC with the command "DOWN CAT." A program called UP2DAT made sure that the catalogue was up-to-date or would continue to "invoke" or "call" itself until this was the case.

Next, the BPS used by cataloguers was brought down and the recovery files (RECO files) were backed up to disk. The down batch for the BPS system (BPSDW) started by terminating the BPS from KQ session number 3. This ensured that the BPS would be brought down even if there had been a communications (COMS) system malfunction. When this was finished, the system tables were loaded into memory. Because of the Series 9000's paged memory management techniques, these tables that describe the system parameters could be held in main memory for quick access no matter how large they were. Examples of systems parameters included loan lengths for different classes of books, borrower statistical and patron privilege tables, terminal and branch locations, and so forth.

In preparation for spine label production, the labels file (**LABS) was reset. The system's internal electronic mail file (**UGBR, pronounced "Star Star Ugh B-R") was zeroed as well. The UCHECK program was then run to unlock any "in-process" records. If the system had come down at the normal time, there should theoretically be no "in process" records as the data manipulator subprograms should have processed any outstanding cataloguing by the time the batch was started. At this point, the in-process record file (**INPR) file could be zeroed. Next, the GORESQ (Go Res-Q) process was run to sequence any holdings records added since the previous night.

Data protection measures were then undertaken. The job FBZBAC (Eff Bee Zed-Back) was run to backup the recovery files (RECO files) to duplicate "Zed-set" files on another disk drive. Next, the record sequence numbers (RSNs) were manipulated using the batch job FBLREC (El Bee Rec-El). This preparatory processing concluded with the job MBMARK, a MARC record update program.

Always careful to ensure the collection's integrity, cataloguers demanded that new records be put into temporary holding or work files until they could be verified by supervisors. At this point in the overnight, the BPS system was brought up again so that new cataloguing records could be loaded from the Work file to the main catalogue or "Core" file.

Because the cataloguers' input system, BPS, and the OPAC were normally run simultaneously, it was then necessary to bring down the public query part of the system by issuing a "terminate job" (TJ) command from another KQ session. This brought the CAT down. Meanwhile, the main session issued the command to begin the work-to-core transfer program, FBLMST, which was the major job undertaken on the BPS system during the night. To speed processing, the index update (OIU) can be given higher priority using the priority change command for the job ZQMUPD.

Once the work to core transfer had been completed, any incoming tapes from the ABN could be loaded into the work file using the job ABNLOD. Any work generated from the ABN tape load could then be processed, and valid records loaded from the Work to the Core files as the night progresses.

Finally, the BPS overnight waited until the system clock reached 7:15 a.m. (a preprogrammed alarm point set by the job LPTIME) and issued the commands to put the CAT up for the next day's public query activities. This was accomplished by issuing the FPMISC command "UP CAT." As well, the Acquisitions System's up batch (ABUP) was executed from the BPS overnight as soon as the CAT came up.

The Acquisitions overnight began with an LPTIME instruction to take down the ACQ system at 18:00 hours using ABKILL since all the cataloguers would have gone home at 6:00 p.m. File size checkers (ABFCHK) were run, followed by a full backup (ABBACK). Next, the serial receipts were sorted, and jobs were run to create and produce daily purchase orders. Requests for checks were then produced for transmission to the appropriate accounting departments to pay for purchased materials.

With the day's reporting completed, the ACQ overnight processing began. The first step was to garbage collect the Overnight file (**OVNT). Because long records posed problems in a mainly fixed-length-field database environment, some files had associated "spill" files to handle the excess text. Each Monday, the acquisitions bibliographic record spill file (**ASPL) was garbage collected, and its percentage of use noted. Next, all relevant index files were rebuilt or rebalanced. A note in the batch advised, "CBINDX runs CBS.32 which runs NERD32 which runs CBCHKS," referring to ancillary or secondary processes.

Monday was also the night designated for running the claims report. This generated form letters to be sent to publishers requesting they send any journals that should have arrived but were more than a given number of weeks late in arriving. The actual number of days or weeks could be set for each journal or publisher. That concluded the Monday acquisitions overnight batches.

GENERAL INDICATIONS OF SYSTEM ACTIVITY AND DATABASE CONTENTS

As well as checking the integrity of a database, overnight processing could be a source of management information for the library. Knowing which service points were being used heavily or lightly, at which hours, and at what branches could assist with staffing. Knowing which materials, books, videos, and so forth were in high or low demand, by what sorts of patrons, and at which branches could assist with collections development. Daily, monthly, and annual activity indicators could prove useful in formulating library budgets and in supporting them before library boards or university administrators.

The Circulation file size checker program LPFCHK was run each time the system was initialized and before and after any offline processing that might modify the database. The output demonstrates many things about circulation transaction activity, but for our purposes, the number of bibliographic records and transactions is of particular note. A few representative lines of actual output will illustrate the sorts of data available for management and system security purposes.

```
Geac.REL20.0 LPFCHK - Fri 22 May 1992 12:10
FILE TRKS ST RS RECRDS LRECRDS MRECRDS DATE TIME PCT
[lines omitted]
**BNUM - 1,350 30 384 2,071,680 2,071,680 2,071,680
21-05-92 22:10 100% *
**CALL - 18,000 30 19 1,097,234 1,097,234 1,367,905 21-05-92
22:10 80% *
**ITEM - 31,000 24 38 4,711,848 4,711,848 4,711,848 22-05-92 3:14
100% *
**TCP1 - 3,000 0 0 0 0 0 00-00-00 0:00 0% *
**TRAN - 3,000 6 70 283,318 588,172 8,751,970 22-05-92
2:05 70% *
```
Source: Program LPFCHK, run by the author on May 22, 1992.

The **CALL and **ITEM file totals indicated the number of bibliographic records in the circulation system. Each **CALL record represented a unique title, while each **ITEM record indicated a particular copy of a book. The **STUD file (originally meaning "student") contained a record for each borrower, the **TRAN file indicated the number of current transactions, and the backup file **TRA2 indicated system activity on the previous day. On the day in question, there were 1,097,234 bibliographic records in the system, pointing to 4,711,848 individual items.

Some selected figures output from the Terminal Line Analysis program (LPTRSH) will demonstrate system activity during the time period from 08:04:32 to 22:10:52 on May 25, 1992. The system's GODO count, corresponding roughly to the number of times users touched their "send" buttons on network terminals, came to 147,309. The first user logged on at 08:05:14 that morning, and the last message posted came at 22:04:56 that night. That day, users performed 147,309 operations on the circulation system alone, transmitting a total of 2,875,687 characters. The "busiest" of 325 active circulation terminals that day was terminal 818, located at the University of New England's Northern Rivers campus in Lismore, Australia.

```
TERMINAL DETAILS FOR ACTIVE TERMINALS
TERMINAL SENDS CHARACTERS WANDS WAND ERRORS RESETS
818 3,755 79,772 1,265 0 5
TOTALS 147,309 2,875,687 38,296 0 291
```
Source: Excerpt from report *Terminal Line Analysis from File *ZTCP1*, May 25, 1992.

At this particular terminal, staff wanded 1,265 barcodes either on borrower cards or on library books during charge, discharge, renewal, or fines transactions. The system totals refer to all network circulation activity for that day. At least 2.96 percent of the day's activity at Lismore involved wanding standard 14-digit Codabar labels on patron badges or books. In fact, the average is 21.24 characters per send, so on average, about one third of the day's work involved wanding barcodes. This pattern of great exchanges of comparatively brief messages is typical of a circulation system. As each transaction results in database update activity, it becomes evident that the circulation files are indeed volatile.

Statistical reports like those excerpted assist network operations managers in scheduling and allocating resources. Collections management and other management information reports, either predesigned or custom designed using Geac's GLUG language, are also of interest. Some "snapshot" details ware normally included in the "message of the day" broadcast over the system news utility, called SHNEWS. Here is part of a typical news message:

```
WEDNESDAY 27th MAY 1.00PM
BANKSTOWN STOCK-TAKE ==================== Today, Wed
27 May, the above library will be doing a stock-take. In
order to facilitate this operation, the message "Book
was not charged out" will be temporarily turned off. It
will be reinstated on completion of the stock-take.
```
Source: File SHNEWS, May 27, 1992.

The news entry continues, giving weekend hours for closed-reserve collections, upcoming training courses, and a quick summary of new bibliographic records added the previous day with an indication of some common errors followed by a timetable giving hours of operation. The last time new records were added to the circulation database (on May 24), they included 2,399 new records representing 4,246 items. This means an average of about 1.8 copies per title were added.

For a consortium like UNILINC, another important indicator of network activity from the point of view of cooperation and resource sharing was the interagency activity report generated by the program LPIAR. This "on-demand" report broke down loans from each agency within the network by the library of origin of the borrowers. The interagency report produced figures that appeared in the UNILINC annual report and helped planners understand interagency borrowing patterns as well as the demand for specific sorts of materials within the consortium.

The average borrower and even the average staffer in a library probably had no idea of the complexity of the computing processes that happened overnight so that the catalogue was working the next day and patron accounts were accurate. The work stressed the resources of existing machines and human operators nearly to the limit. On some days, the overnight processing took longer than expected, and, as a consequence, the library system simply came up late the next day.

All this was part of a normal Monday overnight. When the academic year began in all those member universities or when it ended and entire lists of students had to be updated, there would have been much more work to do. Patrons would have been loaded by tape, and no patron with outstanding transactions such as loans or fines could have been deleted. If students were going home for the summer vacation, mailing programs would have been updated automatically, so that they continued to receive notices from the library at their permanent home addresses rather than their campus residences. People who were no longer members would have been deleted from the system providing they owed no money or had no materials on loan.

Typically, libraries used two or three types of overdue notices, issued for a week, three weeks, or a month after items were due. The first notice was often a gentle reminder, the second a sterner warning, and the final one a bill for accrued fines, the price of the book, and a service charge. Fines would accrue until the final notice, at which point the library considered the item lost forever and billed the patron for its replacement.

Most vendors allowed their sites to customize the wordings on these notices. This is where programmers and technical writers had to be careful in wording the generic notices shipped with the system. It is also where programmers' humor sometimes caused unintended results. At one point, Geac's programmers had come up with a bizarre set of wordings, so offbeat that they were certain any new customer would alter them to suit the site. But what if the new customer was unaware of the option? The sample wordings ran like this: "First notice of overdue items. Bring them back, or we will nail your fingers to the circ desk with a light pen." The next was worse: "Second notice of overdue items. We are sending Luigi and the boys to break both of your legs." Chaos could ensue if a library accidentally mailed out such notices.

Even onscreen messages sometimes caused difficulties. Any word in thousands of different displays could be misinterpreted by staff or, worse, the public. When lag time caused delays at the staff and public terminals, Geac's system flashed the rather confusing message "No recognizable poll from host."

RAT 40K

A computer is like an onion because it has many layers. At the outside, one finds the user interfaces or "shells" and the "applications" programs that actually do things for people like Microsoft Word. Beneath them lie layers of communications programs and the operating system, which tells the computer how to perform basic tasks such as obtaining commands from users or programs and providing the requested information. Sometimes called the "kernel," the OS can be addressed by operators using "shell" commands. Those are now seldom used, except by specialists; but before Graphical User Interfaces (GUIs), all operating instructions were issued from the UNIX shell or the Microsoft "DOS Prompt," now called the "command" program (CMD). In the Geac environment, it was called the "KQ prompt" and run by a ZOPL program called "!^KQ" (pronounced "bang up kay cue" or, more often, just "KQ"). UNIX shells have more imaginative names; the Korn shell and the Bourne shell were named after their writers. The C shell (csh, pronounced "seashell") was written for people who use the programming language C and the revised and improved Bourne-Again shell (bash).

In the UNIX world, the OS is often likened to a nut with the OS located in the Kernel, and the programmers talking to it through the Shell. Several "flavors" of shells were invented to make communication easier. As stated above, some were named after their inventors; some had more humorous names, like the C-Shell (pronounced "seashell") designed to help writers of C-language programs easier, or the improved Bourne-Again Shell (bash), which is still one of the most popular.

The whole structure exists to support applications programs such as word processors or library automation systems that end users actually use in day-to-day life. But still further inside than the kernel is the native instruction set of the computer's CPU chip itself, Reduced Instruction Set Chips (RISCs). RISCs have fewer, more commonly used instructions built into them, being optimized so that frequently used routines will run faster. The alternative is to build in every possible instruction just in case it might be needed. Librarians are familiar with this sort of "just in time" versus "just in case" rationale.

Computer languages that are optimized for system performance can also differ from ones designed for the benefit of users. Languages like COBOL encouraged programmers to think about what the end user would like and to work backward from the end products, which were most often printed forms or reports. This method of designing software is called "top-down development," and in principle it is a perfectly good approach to customer satisfaction. However, languages like COBOL were developed for general business uses, not for online transaction processing, manipulating large strings of text, or unpredictable field sizes like those used in describing library materials. A book or film's title could be one word or a few dozen words long, and the same book could have one subject or half a dozen.

The MARC record was designed to handle the various contingencies, and on average, according to Geac's analysis, MARC records were about 768 bytes long. That is almost a thousand bytes, or a kilobyte. In those days, disk and memory sizes were measured in megabytes. It would not take many thousands of MARC records to use up a megabyte, probably about 1,400 descriptions of books unless you used some sort of data compression. The large university libraries of the 1980s typically had collections of a million, or perhaps even 10 million, books.

Geac measured memory in 16-bit words. Normally, you could put two 8-bit bytes of data into a word, but Geac also had an "A3" format, which allowed programmers to squeeze three bytes into two words (32 bits). Languages like C, Perl, Java, and so forth are conducive to "bottom-up" development principles. The idea is to figure out how to do simple things, like sorting numbers or handling input and output to a computer terminal, and to write just enough program code to do those things well. Put the small programs into a shared "library," and you can use them over and over in different programs, as required. This not only speeds program development but also makes things run faster. Of course, this does not obviate thinking of the user's needs and designing systems around them. However, it can result in the production of many reusable pieces of program code that may mean less time spent on future projects.

The more things you can implement at the lower levels, the faster the system will perform. However, routines that have been hard-coded into the system are usually harder to change or improve upon. Since Geac owned the operating system, it could change it on the fly, optimizing routines that its customers discovered they would be needing frequently, at lower levels of the nut.

Modern computer operating systems do many things for users automatically, like figuring out how much memory the applications programs need in order to run properly. Sometimes, they still run out of memory, but with most home computers holding at least 2 gigabytes of this digital workspace, that happens less and less frequently. The early mini-computers had tiny amounts of memory by comparison. The Geac 8000 allowed programmers only 64 kilobytes of RAM or core space for any given program. Of course, using techniques like "overlay" programming, there were ways of increasing that size. Subroutines that would be used frequently but then left idling could be rolled in and out of memory as needed. Digital Equipment Corporation (DEC) made virtual memory a foundation of its VAX series of mini-computers, and the technique is still used. It means treating a chunk of disk as an extension of RAM or core memory.

Geac's library systems went by names like GLIS, but the programmers always called the mainline program HUGO, after the language in which it was written. HUGO made extensive use of overlay programming. Like a good librarian, HUGO didn't always remember everything it had to do; it knew where to find things when needed. There were hundreds of tiny HUGO overlays to perform simple tasks that would be needed often but not continually. It simply called or invoked the appropriate overlay. HUGO can be thought of as a superset of ZOPL, the company's basic language. Modern systems like the open source Koha library system make use of hundreds of tiny programs written in the Perl language to do much the same thing, but for its time HUGO worked at blinding speed. The UNIX and Linux family of operating systems also make much use of libraries of programs written in the C language. The subtle difference is that the HUGO overlays were written to take roughly the same amounts of space so they could roll in and out without causing memory exceptions. Nowadays, with dynamic memory allocation, that doesn't much matter.

The requirements for an ideal operating system were laid out in books like *The Fundamentals of Operating Systems* by Lister.[32] The 9000 was like a realization of Lister's book. It had multiple full function processors (FFPs). The largest library version, probably the one at Australia's UNILINC, had seven processors. That, plus the dynamic paged memory, allowed sophisticated techniques like multithreading. If a program like the library catalogue became too busy, another copy could be spawned, or cloned, to take on the extra work; and since Geac had complete control over the operating system, the hardware, the firmware, and the applications, even more optimization was possible.

The 9000's microcode (the tiny instructions that the operating system relied upon to perform simple functions) was fully downloadable. New routines for things like sorting numbers or letters swiftly could be written and incorporated into the microcode as required. That all gave the 9000 the transaction processing speed to outperform even Digital's "VAXen" on benchmark tests, and other library vendors, like Dynix, began searching for "9000-killer" machines.

Memory exceptions occur when a program accidentally overreaches the workspace it has been allowed and begins writing into the workspace of another program. This feature of memory can be exploited by hackers; and computers are especially vulnerable to it while performing communications with users. This "buffer overflow" vulnerability is commonly exploited in Distributed Denial of Service (DDoS) attacks that hackers use to bring down servers on the Internet; but back in the 1980s, an operator could encounter them simply by not asking for enough memory to begin with. When those computers were shut down with programs running, the contents of memory could become confused.

Library system administrators who used the Geac 8000 or 6000 grew quite conversant with memory limitations because before they ran programs, they had to issue "reattach" or "RAT" commands asking the OS to allocate memory for the program. Typically, they wrote scripts, or batches that contained the memory requests and then the request to run the program. A page of shorthand instructions for restoring and recovering a failed system reads,

```
System booted with HUGO up?
Backup **TCP1, **TCP2, **LOOG and **HGEV
RAT,40K
RU,LPRCVR
Do a full backup and an LPTSCN if possible.
```

The transaction files, TCP1, and so forth kept track of communications with terminals. They contained keystroke logs. Backing them up was key to restoring the system after a failure. The instructions mean to "request 40 kilobytes of workspace, then run the recovery program LPRCVR" (pronounced "el pea recover"). Then, run an integrity scan on the transaction files.

If a transaction log becomes corrupted, bizarre situations can occur. A book may appear to have been returned before it was taken out, or, worse, the wrong patron may be billed for an overdue or missing item, or credited with someone else's payments. A short recovery program could be run to reprocess just the transactions that had happened between system startup and system failure; but if that didn't work, you had to restore the system to a state of known quality, for instance using a backup made the previous night at closing time. In the worst cases, those tapes did not read properly, so you would have to go back to the previous "complete" backup, usually made once a week. Mike Himelfarb, former head of the Library Assistance Desk in Markham, remembers just such a situation:

When I took over as Supervisor of the LAD (Library Assistance Desk) in 1984 no one told me about the all-nighters. One memorable occasion occurred when Scarborough Public Library had a drive 0 crash on their 8000 without a readable tape backup. Of course, it all happened at

3:00 pm on a Friday afternoon. The most recent backup we could read was 48 hours old and the only way to get the system back up was to run "long recovery." Trouble was the recovery files had errors in them because of bad data being written while the disk was failing.

I recruited Anna Marcon who was Project Leader for Circulation and Terry Cohen who was on pager that night to help fix the database. We spent hours running T-scans and every database checker known to man followed by 18 hours manually patching the hundreds of errors. Many jokes were told, most of which wouldn't have been the slightest bit funny had they seen the light of day; and we drank way too much Coke and coffee but not enough beer. It was a slow and painful process, but by late Saturday afternoon SPL was up and running. The site was eternally grateful and Anna and I have been friends ever since.[33]

With the advent of the Geac 9000, many of the earlier limitations were circumvented and much more computing power was put into the librarians' hands. Memory was allocated in "pages" of 1,024 words each, a word being 16 bits, which normally held two bytes (letters or numbers) each. The compressed A3 format packed three letters into the space of two. Memory could be assigned dynamically. The 9000 offered yet another advantage. If a power fail was detected in progress and an uninterruptible power supply (UPS) was connected to the computer, it could write the contents of memory off to a protected place on the master system disk. When the power came back on, the system would access the disk and remember what it had been doing. This sort of "fault tolerance" made the 9000 attractive to Geac's primary customers: libraries and banks and credit unions. However, there were other computers, especially those made by a company called Tandem, that were much more fault-tolerant.

Since their inception, electronic digital computers have contained nothing but combinations of binary digits—zeroes and ones. This is as true today as it was in the period we are dealing with in this book. All the pictures, videos, audio recordings, and text documents we see on our computer screens are made up of or represented by combinations of zeroes and ones. Also since its inception, data processing has involved inputting data, manipulating or processing the data, and outputting it. If the output does not meet the intended need, it is fed back into the process so that the desired results can be obtained. This pattern of input, process, output, and feedback characterizes the fundamental method of computing.

Information that is never communicated is of limited use. We hold a great deal of information and knowledge in our brains or minds, but unless we act upon it or tell others about it, its usefulness remains local. Computers too need to be able to communicate in order to be optimally useful; but before the Internet was adopted as a standard, this could be complicated. Librarians are all about sharing knowledge, and most of them do so at no direct charge to the users of that knowledge.

This makes libraries and their computing systems natural communicators. In order to communicate, humans and computers must share certain standards: languages and their grammars for humans, and data communications protocols for computers. The 1978 book *The Network Nation* describes dozens of popular computer communications networks, almost all of which relied upon ordinary telephone lines.

The Advanced Research Projects Agency Network (ARPANET), whose standards became those of the modern Internet, warranted just a few paragraphs in this 528-page tome. Essentially, all those different networks spoke different languages, and messages passed between and among them had to be interpreted and translated. We will have more to say about this Babel-like situation later.

Over the last four decades of the 20th century and particularly in the period that most concerns this book, the 1980s, people's expectations of computing, communications, and the types of data that are interesting and useful changed dramatically. Some concerns, such as the provision of financial information, have remained fairly constant and predictable. Balancing your accounts may be more complicated today than it was years ago, but it still involves keeping track of numbers and performing operations upon those numbers.

Libraries, however, contain a huge variety of things other than tables of numbers, including literary works, scientific reports, novels and poetry, and so forth. The descriptions of these items can become quite lengthy, especially if they include archival materials like folders of personal correspondence. It should come as no surprise, then, that libraries, which contain so many different types of information, might have broader computing requirements. We will explore librarians' expectations of computing more fully in this chapter, and we will see how those expectations helped shape the development of library automation systems during the 1980s.

COMPUTERS AND PERIPHERALS

Tony Gunton's general-purpose dictionary of computing, first published in 1990, provides some insight into the technical capabilities of computers and the expectations users had of them at the time with regard to data representation, communications, and processing, and with regard to the industry standards then in use. Data representation standards mentioned included EBCDIC and ASCII; communications standards included RS-232 and TCP/IP; and the ISO's reference model was ISO/OSI. Structured Query Language (SQL) is one of the report-generating methods mentioned. When it comes to computer memory, various types appear in the dictionary: magnetic core, RAM, EPROM, PROM, and so forth. For portable memory devices, one finds half-inch magnetic tape, magnetic disks, and optical disks mentioned.

MAINFRAMES, MINIS, SUPERMINIS, AND MICROS

Mainframe computers had been dominant during the 1960s. The 1970s saw the rise of mini-computers, but by the mid-1980s, their hegemony was beginning to diminish. As library professor Bernt Frohman astutely observed,

[T]he shift toward end-user computing had begun with the introduction of the microcomputer, better known as the personal computer (PC). However, when compared to their lumbering cousins the minis and mainframes, PCs were still in their infancy, small in capacities as well as in size. To be sure, they soon came to replace dedicated "dumb" terminals as workstations in libraries attached to mini-computers that performed the major duties; but the first PCs on the market did not even contain hard or fixed disks, only "floppies," and their memory limitations were severe, even by mini-computer standards. Moreover, they were truly personal, designed for single users not hundreds of customers at once.

What could library buyers expect of microcomputers at the beginning of the 1980s? Not much if you were looking for bibliographic management or circulation systems "out of the box." Given the amount of disk space available, this is hardly surprising. If you wanted to maintain a bibliographic database, you still had to rely upon a mainframe computer, though a PC with a user-friendly interface could enhance the experience. To store the amounts of data needed by even a small library catalogue, you had three options: magnetic tape (reel to reel or cassette), floppy disks, or a mainframe computer with its ranges of peripheral disks that were then the size of washing machines.

The first microcomputers did not come with hard disk drives at all. Every time you booted them, you had to insert the operating system disk into Drive A, because there was no place inside the computer to store it when you turned off the machine at night. One 1983 guide to purchasing microcomputers explains the processes that users had to follow in order to boot the system from floppy disks and to run applications programs.[34]

```
insert os into drive a
```

Walton's manual lists a handful of operating systems, including the CP/M system (which powered the Osborne computers) and several proprietary varieties of DOS along with Xenix, a scaled-down version of UNIX developed by Intel. With the exception of Xenix, which came from a multiuser lineage, none of these systems even asked users for user names and passwords at startup. They were truly personal systems designed for small computers and single users. If you wanted to exchange information with another PC or with a mainframe, you had only one real-time option, a dial-up telephone line that probably operated at 300 baud. Alternatively, you could write the information to a floppy disk and mail it to them by ordinary post.

By the end of the 20th century, available operating systems belonged to one of two software families, tracing their ancestries either to DOS (e.g., Microsoft Windows) or to UNIX (e.g., Linux, IBM's AIX, and Macintosh OS X). During the intervening years, systems like IBM's OS-II were born and passed into extinction. OS-II addressed government security concerns but never enjoyed wide deployment for home use. It was soon eclipsed by Apple's Macintosh line and Microsoft's Windows.

By today's standards, Walton's list of desirable operating system functions seems humble. Make sure, he says, that the system has these important file management capabilities:

To create, update, and delete files
To rename files
To maintain a directory or index of what files exist on a particular diskette
To examine a diskette in order to calculate the size of each file and the amount of storage still available for use on the diskette
To copy individual files or entire diskettes
To reconstruct files from damaged diskettes (This feature is still relatively new and may not be available on many popular operating systems.)

With expectations of microcomputers so modest, it is hardly surprising that they were thought of as toys by some who worked with mainframe and mini-computers. However, those basic functions must be there. The functional specifications laid out in the 1975 book *The Fundamentals of Operating Systems* are no less valid today.

Of the high-level languages then available—COBOL, BASIC, and so forth—little can be said except that they were useful in most organizational settings but not designed to manipulate the odd and unpredictable sorts of information that libraries need to describe their holdings. Most languages required fixed-length data fields, but library information was almost always of unpredictable lengths. Even the compilers for the best of these languages (COBOL and Fortran) posed space problems. For the first few years, BASIC was the commonest language in the personal computer world.

Beyond all this were the data storage problem and the problem of speed. PCs were slower than minis and mainframes, and bibliographic records for anything but the smallest collection were too big to fit on them. The average MARC record was calcu-lated at 768 bytes, and when floppy disks contained only about 1000 bytes, automating a university library with even a few hundred thousand books in its collection was sim-ply impossible until the microcomputer matured in the 1990s. Interim solutions like writing the catalogue onto microfiche had been in use throughout the 1970s; and during the 1980s, CD-ROMs had also become available.

The decade of the 1980s saw the beginning of a shift toward end-user computing. By the end of that decade, personal bibliographic systems for microcomputers, like Refer-ence Manager and Endnote, had become available. For much of the decade, the machines that met librarians' needs both for rapid transaction processing and for large amounts of disk storage continued to be mini-computers. As far as library-specific software goes, Walton's manual names none. Instead, it lists programming languages, ranging from assembler languages to several varieties of BASIC. Assembler or assembly languages are considered low level, close in their outward appearances to the actual procedure calls used by the computer.

DATA STRUCTURES AND TRANSACTIONS—THE CASE OF NOTIS

The Northwestern University Totally Integrated System (NOTIS) was built upon the IBM mainframe environment. Better known to the public as LUIS, it ran under IBM's CICS operating system and survived many years of service. Some NOTIS systems originally installed in the 1980s were still in operation well into the first decade of the 21st century, but the earliest LUIS systems were far from "totally integrated."

The data structure is defined in two documents dating from the early 1980s, which explain the data structure used in keeping track of public access to the system, the user transaction journal file.[35] "Each record in the file represents either a user input event or a program output event," says the LI700 document.[36]

Most records can be paired up: an input event followed by an output event. There are two known exceptions to this rule: 1) when the user requests a transfer from LUIS to LCUS or vice versa, two Input events are recorded, followed by one output event; and 2) some records may be lost when CICS crashes.

Each system terminal was identified by a four-byte Terminal ID number. Bytes 5–9 recorded the date on which the transaction occurred, in "Julian date" format: YYDDD, where YY refers to some arbitrary date in the past (say, January 1, 4713 BCE) and DDD to the number of days that had elapsed since this date. Using Julian dates means that you never have to worry about things like new centuries or new millennia, and many systems developed during this time, including Geac, used Julian dates almost exclusively. When much of the business world, especially companies whose systems were written in COBOL, forecast dire consequences for computing at the turn of the year 2000, library systems programmers had little to fear. The DDD component of the Julian date would simply keep incrementing.

Bytes 5–9 of the record contained the time, down to the tenth of a second, and using a 24-hour clock. The writer cautions.

Note that at midnight, CICS updates its clock several seconds before its date. During this interval, journal records are created with the correct time, but with yesterday's date. If the file is checked for constantly increasing date and time fields, these records will appear to be out of order.[37]

Next came the transaction ID, the task number used by CICS, an Attention ID (AID) that signified either an input or an output, a code to indicate the type of display being sent to a screen, an error code, a command code, the number of hits in the database, and the number of lines displayed. Additional fields recorded the MARC format; the LCUS responses "A" and "B" referred to the message displayed to the user; and, finally, in bytes 45–120 of the transaction record were the text of the input. "For each input event, this is the exact data entered by the user," says the description. Evidently, some of the NOTIS-related code was written in PL-1, a high-level language that some programmers referred to disparagingly as IBM's Suicide Language. During the late 1970s and early 1980s, PL-1 was taught widely in colleges and universities as it was comparatively easy to learn and suited to a wide variety of applications.

OPACS, which provided full bibliographic details of works, were distant dreams during the 1960s and for much of the 1970s. The circulation systems of the time used "brief records," and even "dumb" terminals or cathode-ray tube (CRT) terminals were prohibitively expensive for all but the largest university libraries, priced in the neighborhood of $2,000–3,000 apiece. Moreover, disk space was incredibly limited by today's standards. An average MARC record is about 768 bytes long, but the libraries that were being automated often contained millions of records. With disks costing about $50,000 for a 650 megabyte drive, local storage was also beyond the reach of many independent smaller libraries.

Jean Dickson, who worked with the NOTIS system, writes,

The 1983 NOTIS screen display resembled the layout of traditional catalogue cards. No other local or distant databases were available through LUIS, nor was there any remote access. [T]here was no keyword search capability, and subject searching required input of exact LC subject headings (with automatic right truncation, as today).

Already, librarians were exploring ways of mining data from circulation systems, data that could be used in collections management and provide crucial ammunition at budget and planning sessions. Transaction logs are of course essential in determining who has which books, who owes what fines, and who brought things back to the library. They can also be sources of management information. Since every message to and from every terminal in a system is recorded, it is possible to determine which service points in a system are busy at what times of day, which sorts of material are most frequently called for, and which sorts of people are using them. Geac provided a "terminal line analysis" program that used the **TCP files for this purpose, and they were essential for system recovery after a crash. Circulation transactions provide much of this information, but logs of OPAC use can be illuminating too. Writing in the early 1990s, Jean Dickson used OPAC transaction logs to explore the failure of searches conducted by end users.

LIBRARY REQUIREMENTS, DATA REPRESENTATION, AND TRANSACTIONS

In the early 21st century, talking to many users at once is not much of a problem; you use the Internet. In the 1970s and 1980s, you needed telephone lines, modems, and some way of distinguishing the messages from one another or from simply becoming garbled. Even within the same building, signals would degrade. Running many dedicated telephone lines between a library's branches and the computer room was costly Plessey solved this problem using branch controller units (BCUs) that were multiplexers, small boxes that allowed four terminals to talk along one line.

Sir Timothy Berners-Lee, inventor of the World Wide Web, worked on the BCUs while a young programmer at Plessey's facility in Soper's Lane, England. He also worked on another essential library program to make sure the barcodes would read properly. It was called SPLAT.

Half a decade later, Geac wrestled with the same problem—getting many terminals to talk to a mini-computer—and opted for "polled" terminals. That meant hooking up several terminals at a service point into a "daisy chain," the wires leading from one to another. Each machine had a poll code that could be set manually using tiny dip switches. Messages to all terminals were passed down the wire but were delivered only to terminals with certain poll codes. For somewhat obscure reasons, the first poll code in a group was always set to 41, the next 42, and so on. In the ASCII character set, the letter A is represented in Hexadecimal (base 16) notation by the number 41, B by 42, and so forth.

If the system slowed or failed, terminals displayed the ominous warning "No recognizable poll from host." Initially, and for many years, the limit was 512 polled terminals on a Geac system. Breaking that barrier would have to wait until the advent of the System 9000.

The quest for speed and for fault tolerance was something the customers promoted; but library budgets meant that large capital outlays for things like automation systems had to be introduced carefully. Librarians bought systems hoping that they would last five to seven years. Some librarians sought to prolong system life by upgrading existing equipment and software, postponing the lengthy and intensive cycle of issuing new requests for proposals and seeking funding from administrations.

Other vendors wrestled with transaction throughput and multiple terminals as well. Marlene Harris, a veteran of successive system upgrades from both the vendor and customer sides, recalls how a limping CLSI system caused long lineups at the circulation desk. At busy times, the queue wound past the service desk and up the stairs to the stacks. She recounts the series of events that led to this situation and the course taken to rectify it. The story is fairly typical of a "migration" from one system to another, and deserves to be told in her words.

Our system basically croaked. We did not do an RFP. We couldn't. It had gotten to 30 seconds for a single circulation transaction. To scan a card, to scan a book . . . was the next 30 seconds . . . in a busy Chicago suburb, on a typical Saturday afternoon, there would be a lineup of moms with stacks of 20 books.

The CLSI system was so old, it was not running MARC records. Granny was slow, and she was old. It was a PDP 11-73. It continued to run, physically. CLSI couldn't determine exactly what went wrong. They kept trying to analyze it and couldn't actually pinpoint the nature of the problem.

As they tried to determine what was causing the slowdown and the lines on Saturday and Sunday afternoon got longer and longer: the line would go down the circ desk and down the stacks and start curling up the end of the next stacks. We did a software upgrade over Christmas, and afterwards everything went to Hades in a hand basket. There was some functionality in it that we wanted but it wasn't worth it. We hadn't added agencies or terminals. The only real difference was that we'd done the software upgrade. Obviously, they didn't know what was going to happen.

The library had been planning a move to a new building for 1993, and had planned a system upgrade to coincide with the move. In the event, money was obtained from the building fund to cover the emergency system replacement. The physical move went ahead in 1991, Harris recalls.

The replacement system was built by DRA. Harris remembers calling Innovative Interfaces, and learning that for the time being, the company was not pursuing new customers. "People who had [Innovative Interfaces systems] were always terribly happy and impressed with them," Harris says. Perhaps one reason for its level of customer satisfaction was the company's sense of pacing. By not taking on new customers for a time, they could make sure that pending installations went well.

How did the major vendors deal with migrations away from their systems, to those of competitors? Probably for the most part without rancor. The sales cycle would give them another chance to win back the customer five years hence, and in the near term, the loss might not be total. There was still money to be made in exporting the data from the old system and "converting" it for the new. Harris explains the physical process of migrating the data from one system to another:

CLSI was a bit funny about [our migration to DRA], but they didn't want us to get any unhappier than we were. It went well, all things considered. The head operator, which was all you could say someone did on the old CLSI system, retired, during the whole long drawn-out nightmare. The system used 300 Megabyte disks. They couldn't store MARC records which we got from OCLC. There were cables snaking across the floor. There was a cable with a terminal in the middle. We had to figure out the optimal number of cables to make the transfer work overnight because we had no tape backup. This was one of the old-fashioned migrations . . . it involved the physical process of getting the records from the PDP into the VAX. It hid behind the PDP; somebody went down looking for it and literally couldn't find it, it was so much smaller.

What was the optimal number of cables to make the transfer overnight? Seven was too many, three was too few . . . was it five? Somebody had to look after, did have to babysit kicking the process off, or it would slow down our whole operation, and it ran all night. Only so many records could go through in a night.

OCLC had been storing our MARC records. The CLSS records had the OCLC codes, and once everything was in, we had to get our OCLC dump on tape, and have DRA do the overlay on the VAX. One thing that nobody remembers is that OCLC was no respecter of anyone's schedules, though they do high quality work,

We also had to send the whole thing out for authority records. It took the whole summer. We also had to train everybody.

The DRA system had OPAC, circulation, acquisitions, and a serials module that we did not set up. This was the first acquisitions module we'd ever had.[38]

How else could designers increase the speed and reliability of mini-computers? Aside from adding more processors or computers to the system to rectify the speed problem, you could add more disks to the system, to relieve throughput "bottlenecks" caused when many programs were writing data to or reading it from the same disk. Increasing the number of disks could also help ensure that critical data got written in several places at once. Don Bagshaw recalls how Geac's cofounders, Gus German and Ted Grunau, promoted what today is called a RAID as a solution.

I was in California with Gus German when he came up with the idea for the MF-100. It was 100 disks in a big array. Of course this is now known as RAID. I couldn't say if Gus invented the idea or not, but he was definitely the first I heard speaking about it. Ted Grunau started pushing it at Valleywood, and a prototype was built by Dave Steacie. Probably Mike Sweet was involved in it as well.[39]

Given that the smallest disk enclosures of the day were roughly the size of a shoe-box, a 100-disk array would have been large. Then, as now, computers spend much of their time reading and writing to disks, because, being mechanisms with moving parts, they take longer to perform input and output. Magnetic or optical heads that do the reading and writing must line up with the proper places on spinning disks, and must do so with great accuracy. So, while Geac added more processors to the 9000, the old disk-input/output (I/O) problem persisted. In practice, the 8000 arrangement, whereby processors were dedicated to particular functions, communications, disk input and output, and program execution, was carried forward with greatly increased flexibility to the multiprocessor 9000.

Dedicating an FFP to communications or to disk was useful because the timing of disk I/O operations was such that characters would be missed at higher baud rates if communications and disk I/O were occurring on the same FFP. The communications board itself would buffer some characters, maybe eight. However once you start a disk I/O, the FFP can't do anything else until the disk I/O completed, and that would take longer than eight character times to complete, so there could be dropped characters.

At the applications level, the library and banking systems of the time and modern-day relational databases such as MySQL or Microsoft Access make use of indexes. When a search of the database is requested by a user, the system first scans a list of authors, titles, or subjects and then retrieves the full records that match the search criteria. Bagshaw remembers applying this technique to the banking software.

For Canada Permanent, I wrote a "phone book" name index. Nowadays you would just put it all in memory, but memory was expensive back then. There were 26**3 buckets (AAA, AAB, etc), actually I think maybe 28**3, and some of the more common names were specially encoded (ie WONG, CHARLIE might be in the W@C bucket). This made the name lookups mighty fast, but of course the index was useful only for names.[40]

A Circulation Scenario

Writing in 1981, John Corbin describes the major components of a library automation system, suggesting four levels at which they might apply.[41] At the top level (level 0) comes the library as a whole, and at the next (level 1) come the four major modules of the overall system, namely acquisitions, cataloguing, circulation, and reference. He then proposes two further subdivisions of the circulation system. Level 2 contains borrower registration, checkout, checkin, and overdue items systems. The checkout system is further divided into Level 3 functions, which include regular checkout, reserve, and special checkout functions.

The fact that Corbin describes circulation on three levels suggests that the process is a bit complicated. We will explain why by means of a couple of scenarios. There is an essential difference between circulation and the other major functions: acquisitions, cataloguing, and reference. The data structures used to describe books are complicated and are based on rules and procedures that we will talk about later. However, bibliographic data and its retrieval pose different sorts of problems from the contingencies involved in merely circulating a book or DVD. Circulation systems are a species of online transaction processing, and they involve a series of logical steps that must all be performed within seconds, hopefully without burdening patrons and staff with esoteric information.

In practice, several of these functions overlap, and to see why, let us imagine a scenario. A patron approaches the circulation desk of an academic library carrying an armload of books, CDs, and journals. To avoid confusion, we'll say this is taking place at York University's Scott Library. We'll call the patron Professor Wilson. In the patron's mind, they are simply materials that are needed for research or recreational reading. To the library, and therefore to its computer system, they represent a potentially large number of states of affairs, each of which the system must deal with.

Before we begin, it should be noted that different rules might apply to different copies of each book, or to different libraries within a system. In one library, a CD might circulate for two days to undergraduates, while in another the same CD might go out for a week. If staff or faculty members took out the same CD, they might get it for 100 days at one branch, but only a week at another. If a graduate student was writing a thesis, or acting as a teaching assistant, she might be allowed a 100-day loan as well, but during the rest of her studies, she might have the same privileges as any other student. In other words, circulation systems had to be as flexible as a library clerk with a rubber date-due stamp and the authority to make loan, renewal, or fines decisions.

The year is roughly 1982, and it is 11:45 p.m. when Professor Wilson arrives at the circulation desk. The library closes at midnight. The clerk asks the patron for her library card, and scans its barcode. The system performs a check on the card, which might have been reported lost or stolen, or the patron herself might owe fines or have withdrawn from the university. Or, there may simply be informational messages for this user, like "A book this patron ordered has arrived and is on the shelf in back." Assuming that there are no special conditions, the system responds with a beep and displays the patron's information on a screen, but to safeguard privacy, it must display only as much as is needed.

The clerk then scans the first book barcode. It is a type of book that normally circulates for three weeks to undergraduates, but this patron is a faculty member. The system matches the patron's category with the material's category, and automatically changes the loan period to "100-day loan." However, the system determines that this would make the book due on Easter Sunday—a closed day for Scott Library. It automatically alters the due date to Easter Monday.

The next book is a noncirculating reference book, so the system rejects the attempt to charge it out. However, since it is nearly midnight, the circulation supervisor overrides the block and allows the charge to proceed, setting the loan period manually to

09:00 hours the next day. To do this, he has to enter a password, which means that the circulation system must incorporate different levels of authorization for different functions.

The next items turn out to be a magazine issue and a two-hour loan reserve reading room item; the system refuses to let them out. Again, the clerk asks the supervisor to authorize a special loan. After all, nobody will be reading these things between midnight and opening time, so the patron might as well have them.

The next item was apparently checked out to a different borrower. This is meaningful information for the library, but not for the professor. Professor Wilson merely wishes to check out a book that one of her students had been reading, and there is no point in troubling the patron with meaningless information. So, the system beeps, and flashes a message saying that the book had been on loan to another borrower and updates the records to show that Professor Wilson now has the book. Since the book was overdue by four days, the system calculates the amount owing and adds $2.00 to the student's fines account.

To Professor Wilson, it doesn't matter that the last book in her armful is really a renewal. She has been reading it and wants it for a second time. However, this book has been requested by another borrower. The system beeps, and the clerk politely tells Professor Wilson that she cannot have it again. The clerk then puts the book on the holds shelf, and the system generates an e-mail and/or an automated telephone message to the requesting patron advising that the book has become available at Scott Library Circulation Desk and will be held there for pickup for three days. If three days go by, it will be released for others to borrow.

Professor Wilson asks if she can have the book back once the other person returns it, so the clerk places a hold on the book in Professor Wilson's name. Professor Wilson then says that she normally visits the Frost Library, which is miles away. The clerk alters the "hold pickup location" to Frost. Wherever the book is returned, it will be rerouted to Frost Library and kept there for three days so Professor Wilson can claim it.

Relatively happy, Professor Wilson now tells the clerk that when she has finished reading one book, she would like it to go onto two-hour loan for her students. The clerk calls up the book's record, and places a "reserve room request" on it. When the first circulating copy of this book is returned, it will automatically be flagged for the reserve reading room and its loan period will be altered to "two-hour loan." Since another copy appears to be on the shelf upstairs, the system generates a "picking slip" for the shelvers.

As each item is checked out, Professor Wilson's activity count and the "charge" counts of the books are incremented by one. When the books come back, their "discharge" counts will be incremented by one. Managers will use these activity counts when making collections management decisions later on. The system can identify classes of patrons who use the library the most or the least, and the books that people actually borrow, by generating lists of patrons or items with high activity counts. This can also be useful for marketing and outreach activities, as well as for budget planning.

As this scenario demonstrates, the modules described by Corbin must interact with one another. A checkout transaction implies several other transactions, including borrower and item availability checks. With online circulation systems, there is a lot of work being done behind the scenes, and ideally neither the patron nor the clerk needs to be aware of most of them. However, each of these contingencies presents challenges for designers, and all of them were dealt with during the mini-computer era.

Next afternoon, the phone rings at Professor Wilson's home. The Markham Public Library's voice-messaging system is ringing to tell Wilson's daughter that a book she has ordered is ready for pickup. We'll call her Alison. For privacy reasons, the computer does not mention the book's name. Wilson and her daughter arrive at the library, and before claiming the requested book, the girl finds another she would like. It is about sex and has been assigned a "material type" that normally prevents it from being loaned to minors.

At the circulation desk, the clerk scans Alison's card, and the system beeps. It says that the book *Mark Twain's Missouri* is waiting for Alison on the holds shelf. The clerk then scans the second book. Does Alison, who is 12 years old, have permission to borrow an adult book? A flag in Alison's record shows that Professor Wilson has indeed given her permission to borrow whatever she likes, so the transaction proceeds.

ACCOMMODATING LIBRARY POLICIES

Public, academic, and special libraries, sometimes operating in the same automated consortium, may have different policies and concerns. Automation vendors had to build a great many options into their systems at a very early stage, or be faced with many incompatible versions of the basic software—creating a nightmare for customers and support staff alike.

This was true of bibliographic data as well as circulation, holds, renews, and fines policies. Many public libraries, for instance, used the Dewey Decimal Classification System and Sears subject headings, while their academic counterparts used the Library of Congress (LC) Classification and LC Subject Headings. While most humans can tell a Dewey number from an LC number at a glance, they are just strings of letters and numbers to a computer. The machine had to be taught how to distinguish them and how to sort them properly. This was a problem that was typically not addressed in computer science class, so programmers had to figure out the logic as they went along. We will discuss bibliographic data momentarily.

By 1985, when Corbin wrote another book about implementing local automation systems, his own University of Houston libraries had become a Geac site.[42] However, while Corbin's 1981 book was fresh from the presses, Geac had come up with a way of incorporating many of the contingencies encountered above into a system implementation guide book called *Policy Parameters*.[43]

The major part of the policy parameters document was a series of tables that, when taken together, formed a matrix of logical contingencies. For example, a "patron privilege class" table contained different types of borrowers, with different loan, renewal, and fines privileges. A "material types" table contained different sorts of materials, each associated with loans, fines, and renewal periods. At checkout time, the system could match a patron privilege class with a material type and generate conditions such as the loan period for each transaction.

Each bibliographic, copy-level, item-level, and patron record contained six optional fields that could be used for anything the library wanted. They were intended to provide statistics for management purposes.

Each site could choose from a set of conditional compile options (CCPs) that configured system-wide options like date formats, special handling of various contingencies, and so forth. The final CCP in the book had been written to handle the exchange of fines information between Yale University's bursar's office and libraries. It read, "Are you Yale?" and caused occasional confusion.

Beyond all of those options, Geac allowed each customer a certain number of "special rules," generally six per site. They would require original programming code to handle situations that were unique to a customer's site and not covered in the wide range of standard configuration options. An example of a special rule would be program code to implement an unusual library policy such as allowing users to borrow two-hour loan books on reserve for a course until 9:00 the next morning, if the time was near midnight. In pseudo-code, that could be written like this:

```
If time > 23:45, and if material-type = 2 hour loan,
then due date = today + 1, and due-time = 09:00.
```

It is possible to implement the most unusual of library policies as long as you can specify them clearly and as long as the system contains the required information to begin with. If so, then code can be written to implement almost any policy. One can imagine all sorts of strange contingencies: "If the patron has red hair and if the day of the week is Sunday, then the patron gets no fines when returning overdue books . . . but only during March and April." For such a rule to work, of course, data on people's hair colors would have to be in the system. When setting up a system, it is useful to think of all the library's special contingencies, and to make sure the data required to implement them are going to be in the database. Of course, any good system will allow manual overrides for such things as loan periods, loan limits, and fines.

ACQUISITIONS SYSTEMS

Of all the day-to-day processes in a library, acquisitions or buying materials is probably the most technically complicated to automate. Historically, it was the last of the major modules that vendors delivered. Serials management, looking after journal subscriptions and newspapers, is closely tied to acquisitions, and in Geac's case a serials subsystem was part of the acquisitions module.

Imagine that you are the librarian in charge of purchasing materials for a large university library. At the beginning of the fiscal year, your budget arrives and you allocate funds to support each of the teaching and research units in the university. This year, $50,000 has been allocated for the English and history departments.

First, your system will have to maintain two ledgers: funds committed and funds actually spent. To complicate matters, there are several layers of contacts involved in the book trade. There are the publishers, who maintain separate offices for book and journal production and sometimes more offices for different "imprints" or labels. Examples would include Taylor and Francis, Elsevier, Penguin Books, or any international publisher with offices in different countries and ranges of different types of publications. Such publishing houses maintain regional offices in the United States, Australia, India, and so forth. Journals issued under one office could be produced by another in Philadelphia, but books published by the same company and on the same topic might come from Britain or the Netherlands. Examples of different imprints would be Routledge, Viking, Penguin, Random House, and so forth.

Within the university, the book budgets for English and history are separate. In this case, you wish to order some books and journals that will help both departments. You split the cost between the two, and commit the funds to each budget. However, the British office wants to be paid in pounds sterling, and the American division in U.S. dollars. Your system must be capable of currency conversions and must have access to recent international exchange rates. When you commit the funds, the system calculates the result in the currency of your own country.

Then, an order is generated and transmitted to the vendor. Weeks later, a shipment of books arrives from the United Kingdom, but one you have requested is on back order. Meanwhile, the first journal issues are received. Soon, you receive an invoice, but it does not match the original order because not all of that order has been fulfilled. You update the committed funds ledger, and tell the system to issue checks accordingly.

When each issue of the journal arrives, its date of receipt is put into the system. The "cumulative holdings" for the issue are updated. Six months go by, and the fourth issue of the journal does not arrive. Your system knows the expected frequency of the journal's delivery, and after a few months, it can predict to within a few days the exact day of the month upon which to expect the magazine. It is well past due, so the system automatically issues a claims form for the publisher, asking for the missing issue.

Currency conversion, orders and invoices that never quite match exactly, multiple addresses for different divisions of the same publishing company, claims for missing issues, and even blacklists of unreliable vendors that purchasers should never use are all part of a truly clever acquisitions system. At the very least, it must have separate ledgers for committed and spent funds.

In this chapter, we have examined a small proportion of the technical aspects of ILS hardware and software functions from an operational perspective. That perspective would have been shared by a relatively small group of people: systems librarians, systems operators, and programming and support staff at the various vendors. The public, the library's users, remained the ultimate beneficiaries of library automation. That accords well with S. R. Ranganathan's law, "Save the time of the reader."

NOTES

1. Checkland, Peter. *Systems Thinking, Systems Practice*. Chichester, UK: Wiley, 1981. passim.

2. For illustrations, see "McBee Cards." http://valinor.ca/mcbee.html.

3. Breeding, Marshall. "History of Library Automation [Library Technology Guides]." Available at http://www.librarytechnology.org/automationhistory.pl. Accessed March 21, 2011.

4. National Computing Centre, Limited, J. D. Halliwell, and T. A. Edwards. *A Course in Standard Coral 66*. Manchester, UK: NCC Publications, 1977. See also: Inter-establishment Committee on Computer, Applications, and P. M. Woodward. *Official Definition of Coral 66*. London: HMSO, 1970.

5. For illustrations, see "Magnetic Core Memory." http://valinor.ca/core.html. Accessed November 5, 2010.

6. Berman, Robert. "Letter to W. Newman, York U. 4700 Keele." York University Libraries Fonds 066, York University Libraries. Departmental Records. 89-025. Series V: Circulation. Box 5: Geac (125) Plessey contract. At the time, B. H. Miller of York-Ryerson Computing Centre (YRCC) had written to Plessey, and Berman was replying.

7. The documents consulted are available in the university archives. York University Libraries Fonds 066, York University Libraries. Departmental Records. 89-025. Series V: Circulation. Box 5: Geac (125) Plessey contract. (126) Geac Monster Committee.

8. Berman, "Letter."

9. "A contract between Plessey Canada Limited, and York University Libraries." York University Libraries Fonds 066: York University Libraries. Departmental Records. 89-025. Series V: Circulation. (175).

10. Manson, Bill. Interviewed 2008.

11. Weicker, Reinhold P. and Siemens Corporate Research and Technology Inc. "Dhrystone: A Synthetic Systems Programming Benchmark." *Communications of the ACM* 27, no. 10 (October 1984): 1013–1030.

12. Vance, Ashlee. "China Wrests Supercomputer Title from U.S." New York Times, October 28, 2010. http://www.nytimes.com/2010/10/28/technology/28compute.html?_r=1&partner=rss&emc=rss.

13. U.S. Military Academy. "Proceedings of the 26th Military Librarians' Workshop held at the United States Military Academy, West Point, New York, 13–15 October 1982." In *Interservice Resource Management*. Ed. Charles A. Ralston: West Point, NY: U.S. Military Academy Library, 1984. p. 82.

14. Geac, *Policy Parameters for the Geac Library Information System*. Revised ed. Canada: Geac Canada, 1981.

15. McGee, Rob. *Request for Proposals for Integrated Library Systems*. Revised ed. [Richmond, VA]: RMG, 1992.

16. Monahan, Michael. Personal communication, 2008.

17. Examples include Schonbach, Avi. "Geac Computers." *Communications Standards Review* 13, no. 1 (1987). And Slonim, Jacob. *Building an Open System*. New York: Van Nostrand Reinhold, 1987.

18. Thomas, Keith. Interviewed December 2008.

19. Thomas, Keith. Interviewed December 2008.

20. Thomas, Keith. Interviewed December 2008.

21. Bagshaw, Don. Personal communication, 2009.

22. Monahan, Michael. Interviewed July 2008.

23. Monahan, Michael. Interviewed July 2008.

24. Monahan, Michael. Personal communication, 2008.

25. Monahan, Michael. Interviewed July 2008.

26. Sample MARC record from a training database, created using the Koha library system, 2008.

27. Furrie, Betty, Follett Software Company, Data Base Development Department; and Library of Congress, Network Development and MARC Standards Office. *Understanding MARC Bibliographic: Machine-Readable Cataloging*. 5th ed. Washington, DC: Cataloging Distribution Service, Library of Congress, in collaboration with The Follett Software Company, 1998.

28. American Library Association and Canadian Library Association. *Anglo-American Cataloguing Rules*. 2nd ed. Chicago; Ottawa: Authors, 1978.

29. Joint Steering Committee for Development of RDA Resource Description and Access. http://www.rda-jsc.org/rda.html.

30. "Overview." Joint Steering Committee for Development of RDA. http://www.rda-jsc.org/ Accessed April 6, 2011.

31. Guiles, Kay, cataloging policy specialist, Policy and Standards Division, Library of Congress. Personal communication, September 2010.

32. Lister, A. *Fundamentals of Operating Systems*. 3rd ed. London: Macmillan, 1975, 1984.

33. Himelfarb, Michael. "Exgeac Wiki" posting, January 2009.

34. Walton, Robert A. *Microcomputers: A Planning and Implementation Guide for Librarians and Information Professionals*. Phoenix, AZ: Oryx Press, 1983.

35. K.A. *Northwestern University Library File Description; File Name: Public Access Journal Records*. Chicago, IL: Northwestern University Library Systems Development, 1981. p. 1.

36. "LI700 Data Description." In *Notis-3 Application Programmer's Reference Manual*. Chicago, IL: Northwestern University Library Information Systems Development, 1982.

37. "LI700 Data Description." p. 3.

38. Harris, Marlene. Personal communication, 2009.

39. Bagshaw, Don. Personal communication, March 2009.

40. Bagshaw, Don. Personal communication, 2009.

41. Corbin, John Boyd. *Developing Computer-Based Library Systems*. Phoenix, AZ: Oryx Press, 1981. p. 2.

42. Corbin, John Boyd. *Managing the Library Automation Project*. Phoenix, AZ: Oryx Press, 1985.

43. Geac, *Policy Parameters*.

$$\underline{\quad 7 \quad}$$

Consolidation and Lasting Achievements

No automation decision looks brilliant ten years down the road.

—Bill Manson, librarian and former Dynix and Geac executive

The interaction among libraries and vendors has emerged in the narratives presented in this book, but it is also corroborated in the literature of the day. The process did not simply evolve without a great deal of reflection and scholarly appraisal.

THE BUSINESS OF LIBRARY AUTOMATION

Speaking in 1985, Jane Burke, then of NOTIS, had provided practical advice, not only for dealing with vendors in a contractual situation but also with other stakeholders such as city governments and with an eye toward the political realities of obtaining the requisite funding.[1] Over the years, consultants like Rob McGee, in addition to step-by-step advice for implementing automation projects, have also published works that take contractual obligations of libraries and vendors into account within the contexts of the broader computing environment and of political realities. The "locus classicus" is probably "Request for Proposals for Integrated Library Systems, which McGee's RMG Consultants Inc. published in 1982, revised a decade later, and continued to expand upon in related publications."[2]

While a great deal of creative collaboration was undoubtedly taking place, those involved in the sales process and those in executive positions were acutely aware of the business aspects of automation projects and of broader market conditions. In this chapter, salespeople, project managers, advanced development mangers, and other computer executives present their observations on the process of implementing ILS systems and on the era of consolidation of the 1990s. This era saw a shrinkage in the number of major vendors as new technologies were introduced; many corporate mergers took place, and the business model of ILS vendors was altered.

In 2008, Bill Manson was CEO of the Caledon Public Library in southern Ontario (which operated a Sirsi-Dynix Unicorn system) and vice president of a consortium of about 28 libraries, the Ontario Library Consortium; all were running off the same server. Manson had begun his career at the University of Calgary's library, half of whose building housed the university computer system, which used punched cards. Calgary had automation to produce multiple copies of catalogue cards and to type up on IBM paper-tape typewriters with 150 feet of paper tape feeding through the machines, which wound up on a spool mounted on the wall. He also remembers the initial Plessey Module 4 installation at the Calgary Public Library, where he was then employed, and the subsequent Geac installation. "They sold it to us without having any local staff in place, except the engineer, Brian Bowerman, who was working 20 hours a day. I think he was sleeping in the library."[3]

Manson reports that a few years later, the Module 4 was gone. Calgary had changed library directors with John Dutton taking over from Les Fowlie. Since the specifications for the Module 4 had not been fully explored, Manson suggests that Dutton felt the system would never be ready to go live. Calgary had decided to replace the system. When the Geac system was installed, a new computer room was in place with air conditioning and a raised floor, Halon gas fire extinguishers, and all of the requisites.

Before the 1978 Plessey installation, the library's in-house carpenter had designed, at the library's Memorial branch, an impressive wooden circulation desk that was designed to hold a copy of the library's card catalogue as well. In order to accommodate the Module 4's sleek, flush-mounted, circulation terminals, a rectangular hole had been cut in the desk. Manson remembers the carpenter's justifiable ire at seeing his invention defaced.

Calgary had brought two branches up on the Geac system; staff was linking book barcodes into the system. Every day at noon, the response time would decay because Manson decided to go to the computer room during his lunch break and play Adventure on the operator's console. It was slowing down the entire system. This demonstrates the challenge that computer resources posed: a relatively simple but transaction-intensive activity such as linking barcodes to books could be brought to a standstill by a text-based game running at a higher privilege level than the library system.

He credits librarian Margaret Beckman and Geac's head of sales, Robert Desmarais, with convincing Calgary to purchase the initial Geac system. Edmonton, its metropolitan rival further north within the province of Alberta, had recently purchased a system from CLSI.

Even without an online public access catalogue (OPAC), Calgary's system was transaction intensive for those days. Until the library upgraded to a Dual-8000, response time at the terminals remained unsatisfactory. "We could never operate for very long without encountering the [delay] message, 'No recognizable poll from host' at our circulation terminals," recalls Manson.

Manson recalls installing a series of successively larger machines: a Geac 6000, then an 8000, then a Dual-8000 system. Manson recalls problems getting the two systems to act in concert. Eventually, Calgary switched to a Geac 9000, giving Calgary one of the largest Geac Library Information System (GLIS) installations.

Manson left Calgary, going to work for Dynix. His territory included western Canada and any Geac site in Canada. Despite its shortcomings, "Geac was the Cadillac," Manson says. "It was the leading supplier of library systems. The academic panache of Geac was probably what carried it through."

Library systems are complicated and costly, and once installed, they are expected to run, with upgrades, for several years. Geac's Michael Monahan suggests, "Mass market solutions that run on PCs have to be designed for planned obsolescence . . . 18 months. That's not what ILS vendors do. [The sales cycle] is a marketing issue, and [so is] the scope of the problems they are trying to solve."[4]

Dynix decided to target Geac's customers who in the long sales cycle typical of libraries had reached the point of seeking upgrades to their existing ILS systems. "I was the designated poacher," Manson says. He remembers doing an impressive demonstration at a major public library that had been considering upgrading its Geac 9000 system. The computer Dynix bid was the Sequoia, and the Dynix sales team was able to demonstrate that all the features in their demonstration worked with real data at live library installations. At a demonstration at the Sequoia plant in Marlborough, Massachusetts, a Sequoia engineer demonstrated the fault tolerance of the system by pulling memory boards and disk drives from the system while it was running.[5] The pair of demonstrations became the model for subsequent Dynix bids.

Manson left Dynix for Geac shortly after Geac had purchased CLSI and, he was to be based in Newton, Massachusetts. He was put in charge of selling the LIBS Plus system, which was based on the older host-terminal architecture, even though client-server architecture was coming to the fore. The Plus system ran on Digital Equipment Corporation PDP mini-computers. Manson recalls, "The Geac and CLSI cultures never really meshed. They hired Charles Farley, who was iconically CLSI, as general manager of the libraries division."

However, though they had acquired CLSI's PLUS system in the takeover, Geac had another new library product and had been marketing it aggressively in the move to switch its customers from the now outdated GLIS system, which was based on the company's proprietary 8000 and 9000 hardware. The new product was called Advance. It had been modified from a system running at the University of Hawaii, and its original name had been "Aloha.

Bruce Park and David A. L. Smith had based the Advance system on PICK and UNIX. Like some of other programmer-executives mentioned in previous chapters, Park was given to flashes of inventiveness. Manson alludes to what he calls "cross-company" legends about Park's writing program code on cocktail napkins in hotels.

Dynix was apparently not terribly concerned that a system so like their own was being developed in Hawaii. "One of the corporate articles of faith around Provo, Utah is that Dynix allowed Park to obtain the University of Hawaii contract," Manson recalls.

It was the first for Advance, and it was a university system. Dynix had decided to concentrate upon the public library market. Some of the Dynix marketing people felt that the Hawaii contract would be too labor intensive for Park's start-up company. At that point, Dynix seemed poised to capture a large part of the market because it had a UNIX-based system and excellent hardware upon which to run it.

Though Geac had a version of UNIX running on its 9000, Manson recalls that the company had never attempted to sell it to sites. The technical means were there because a ZOPL-to-C cross-compiler had been written and a test version of the GLIS system had been ported to an Intel 300 computer, which ran IBM's Xenix variant of UNIX.[6] Though Manson was used to the PICK-based system that Dynix used, someone else was charged with selling Geac's Advance product. Geac had emerged from a period of interim receivership, having been rescued by Ben Webster's Helix Investments. Meanwhile, Ameritech had bought NOTIS. But, Manson says, the "Baby Bell" telecommunications company did not act definitively to develop or sell the NOTIS library system.

The real difference in many ways between Geac and Dynix was that people who had been involved from the beginning were librarians. Jim Wilson had been head of circulation at Brigham Young University, so he knew from the beginning what a system had to do to be a circulation system. The clash was between the user people and the programmer people; but there was no way in Dynix that there would be a group within Dynix shipping out white-papers. They were there to ship a product, and the product was going to be responsive to user tasks. Geac fell out of the market when it started to be obsessed with itself as an industry leader, rather than a market leader. Libraries have no money and high demand; it's a dumb business to be in. . . .

The only reason it makes any sense is if you are a dominant force, and that's one reason they had the shakedown. As long as there are five of you trying to eat each other's lunch, nobody is going to win. You will end up spending all your resources on development that will never pay off. That was one of the issues that was there with Marcel Bernard, who would ask, "How many more systems will you sell if you put this feature in?" and the answer could be, "none," or "we'll sell fewer if we don't put it in." There's no revenue there. "Revenue minus cost minus future investment equals profit." That would be up on the board at meetings.

A high level of dedication was common among employees of all of the system vendors. Manson remembers a company legend that one Dynix executive had been working out details of a sales contract while waiting in the hospital for the imminent birth of his wife's and his child. By the time Manson came on board, Geac was under the control of a new president, Stephen Sadler. Manson recalls being struck by some similarities with the Dynix environment in which he had been working. The office of one of Geac's senior managers was full of Japanese artifacts, he recalls. One of the hallmarks of Dynix culture was that at least two top Dynix executives had done their missions for the LDS Church, in Japan. "There were even inside jokes in Japanese in the Dynix software."

CHANGING BUSINESS MODELS

Why did some systems succeed during the 1990s, despite economic downturns and rapid technological changes? Bill Manson suggests,

Geac was both a hardware and software manufacturer, and when the money went out of the hardware business, that really changed the business model. UNIX became the be-all and end-all, and the computers became commodities. IBM and HP salespeople would ask me what they could do to help with a sale. I would say, "Just cash your commission check promptly; otherwise stay out of it." I don't want the hardware to become the issue in the sale. The hardware doesn't matter. Whereas, for Geac, the hardware was critical until they got to the Advance work, and to Vubis.[7]

He also said, "What CLSI was depending on for its cash flow was selling hardware, at outrageous prices. It went back to the days when CLSI had made modifications to the DEC equipment. No automation decision looks brilliant ten years down the road."

Writing in 1989, Michael Schuyler of the Kitsap Regional Library in Bremerton, Washington, had suggested that for Geac, the era drew to an end when the company's focus shifted from engineering to marketing. By contrast, Manson suggests that concentrating on dominating the industry, rather than particular market niches, led to Geac's loss of prominence in the library automation market, in which had hitherto been a formidable force. Overall, the company's annual revenues continued to spiral upwards, as did the value of its stocks.

Michael Monahan had started at Geac in 1976 and had been, in a very real sense, the founder of the group of programmers and librarians that would become its Library Systems Division (LSD), whose directorship was long led by Hans Kleinheinz. Following a period of interim receivership in 1987, Geac's president Bill Bearisto had demoted

Kleinheinz and made Monahan the de facto chief of LSD. By the Christmas party in 1987, because Geac hadn't been paying lease payments, cars were repossessed. "Every year, the company went through a hiring freeze, then record sales, but this was a wake-up call," Monahan says.[8]

There followed a dramatic rescue of the company by a group of Montreal venture capitalists, Helix Investments, led by Ben Webster, and a shakeup among senior Geac executives. In addition to Drury, the new executives would include Nick Haley, formerly of a successful company called Computer Associates, and new presidents like Stefan Bothe and Stephen Sadler. The company's new organizational structure was matched by a new marketing image, characterized by a change in the corporate logo. Henceforth, the wordmark "Geac" would be written in Pantone 288 blue ink, which was very close to IBM's Pantone 286 blue, instead of its traditional orange. The new letters were of solid Gothic type and angular, while the older ones had been rounded and orange, and at one time, set in an "outline" font with white inside. At this time, the company's library and banking divisions were still the major contributors to the company's sales and support income streams. Monahan suggests that historically, the library division had risen to prominence in part because of lack of pressure from senior management.

The division largely succeeded because it didn't get much attention. It had to generate its own money to keep it going, but it didn't have expensive people from the Harvard Business School running it. They weren't told to double their departments within a year. Some very good sales people didn't want to touch libraries because they couldn't figure out how to sell to them. The net result was that the division did not have the same pressures on it, but it became the largest division in the company. That was a shock to Geac's senior management.[9]

In a 1983 publication, Canadian Writer D. Thomas had described the computer companies that had settled in suburbs of cities like Ottawa and Toronto. Geac at various times occupied buildings on Markham's Dennison Street, John Street, Beaver Creek, Steelcase Road, Valleywood Drive, and Allstate Parkway. Thomas mentions the company only in the context of its banking and library operations.

The Toronto suburbs of Mississauga, Markham, and Don Mills are the preferred lairs of the multi-national computer companies, but they also shelter a number of smaller, Canadian-owned firms that have successfully laid claim to a share of the computer market. Geac Computers International supplies computer hardware and software for library and banking needs.[10]

This is the only mention of Markham or of Geac in Thomas's book. At the time, the computer spotlight in Canada focused on companies like Gandalf, makers of a world-renowned series of modems, and Dynalogic, which succeeded in getting mini-computers to read floppy disks and had paired up with the McBee company, whose punch cards had been used in accounting and in libraries for many years.[11] Nor were library systems much on the radar of Geac's senior management, who had, over the years, always had other "vertical markets" in mind as prospects for longer term growth. Monahan elaborates,

At the time Geac went into interim receivership the only business line that was making money was the Library Systems Division. What they didn't understand was that they had a business that had tremendous barriers of entry and that they were on the other side of the barriers. The library market isn't expanding; there won't be a 30–40% growth market. It doesn't expand when the economy is good, but it doesn't shrink either. It is stable, it is counter-cyclic, and it's got a very long sales cycle, but also, a very long retention cycle. You've gone through that. You've got products that are inside some of the biggest and best libraries in the world, and the truth is that of all the market niches that Geac was into, it was the only one that you could have walked into a client anywhere in the world and they might not have your system, but they would know about it. That wasn't the case in any other segment except perhaps credit unions.

The key to Geac's early success had been its focus on the customer's problems and their solutions. Arguably, this is the same service ethos that characterized the library environment. Monahan explains,

At beginning, although Geac was selling custom solutions, it became clear that with a small amount of hardware engineering, you could deliver a lot more by in some cases "tweaking" and in others interfacing hardware. In 1976, Geac was beginning to do hardware but out of the genesis of the HP 2100. In the beginning, Geac was what would be called a "custom enterprise solution" company. Gus German didn't talk bits and bytes. He asked, "What's your problem? He'd then say, "For this amount of money, we'll solve your problem." And if you didn't like it, you could have your money back. It wasn't the way most systems were sold then. Then, systems were thought of as hardware.

(One of the company's first projects requiring hardware had been a system for the Simcoe Board of Education.) According to Monahan, the process involved developing specifications to meet the customer's needs, then implementing them by producing software that matches the specifications. "If you start on the basis of 'It's got to solve your problem,' at some level, you forget about the specifications, but you become very very close to the client. You have to make sure they are happy with what is being delivered." From the perspective of the 2010s, German's philosophy seems remarkable prescient. Almost every company, across a wide variety of industries today, purports to sell "solutions."

German's philosophy pervaded the company. You needed to understand the customer's problem, then ensure you had an engineering solution for it. In Chapter 2, Unilinc's Rona Wade had expressed what many customers felt about the optimism of designers and the confidence that optimism inspired in customers. Wade recalled how Geac's Hans Kleinheinz had always seemed ready to promise "We can do that." Like Manson, who emphasized how Dynix had sought to demonstrate that its systems actually worked, Monahan stresses that engineering solutions or at least the knowledge of how to solve them were essential pre-sale ingredients. Before Kleinheinz had promised Wade that Geac could implement federated searches across individual and collective catalogues, Monahan and his programmers had examined the problem and figured out how it could potentially be addressed from a technical standpoint. "One of the good things about libraries is they always write everything down. If there was a 'we can do it now,' it always ended up on my desk. We wouldn't agree to do something if we didn't technically know how to do it."[12]

While several librarians have stressed the development of standards like MARC as the greatest achievements of late 20th-century library automation, Monahan offers a different perspective. This again emphasizes finding technical solutions that were, in some respects, ahead of the general computing industry. Asked what might have been the industry's greatest accomplishment, he says,

[For me, it was] the work done on user interfaces. OPAC. CLSI's came out in 1982. People at Guelph were checking the status of books and placing their own holds in the late 1970s. There weren't many industries where the customer could find out the status of something without asking the company. MARC records are a poor-man's HTML invented during the 1960s. Libraries were ahead of the curve in the 1980s, they are definitely behind the curve now. Amazon has the easiest search interface. They went from not having anything to having the benchmark.

PRODUCT MATURATION

Library customers wanted products that worked. Manson recalls visiting several customer sites shortly after Geac had bought CLSI and was selling its PLUS system. According to Manson, the system had hardware and software troubles. The portable data capture units would catch fire if you left them plugged in overnight. Manson went to a customer and tried to convince them that a new team was in place and all the problems would soon be solved. The customer directed Manson's gaze out the window, announcing that in the corn field he would find the grave of the last salesman who had tried that pitch.

The key, Manson decided, was to find some satisfied customers to interview. He dialed one that the Geac/CLSI staff had recommended, and was elated when the secretary said she would put him right through to the chief librarian, Dennis Day. Without any preliminaries, the CEO began, "He picks up the phone. I don't hear 'Hello.' I hear 'I will never do business with your company again.' " Manson adds, "This was the happy customer." Theoretically, taking over a company means acquiring its existing customer list and continuing to honor existing service contracts with those customers. This can be a significant source of revenue for the purchasing company. As well, satisfied customers will be more likely to "migrate" to software supplied by the new parent company.

I knew then, we've got a problem with our product, and we've got a problem with our customer communications. In buying CLSI, Geac had bought a customer list, but it was a list of people that were livid because the new product didn't perform. We'd come to the conclusion that those who were left as our customers had one of two problems—they were either broke or stupid.[13]

Today, the ILS has become, in his opinion, "commoditized": "A cup of Unicorn is the same as a cup of Innovative Interfaces," he says. "The open source solution provides some control over the development, but today, we are as close to a 'turnkey' environment as possible."

COMPETITION AMONG VENDORS

The systems we have been describing have all been designed for medium-sized up to the largest of libraries. Several choices existed for small to medium-sized libraries by this time. InMagic, dBASE, and general purpose database management systems (DBMS) were obvious choices. InMagic provided the more costly but more library-oriented solution. The disadvantage of dBASE was that it was really not designed for repeating fields like subject headings or multiple-authorship fields. InMagic was marketed to small libraries by distributors such as Phipps Associates in Canada; but none of these systems could handle the online transaction-processing demands of a large multiworkstation library. As well, PC-based systems had few ways of communicating with one another unless they were part of local area networks (LANs). In the Microsoft DOS world, those required special LAN software such as Novel Netware in order to work in concert with one another.

Follett Software, a spin-off from the book-publishing company; Athena; MOLLI; Winnebago; Mandarin; and an array of similar PC-based library automation packages were also on the market. MOLLI and Athena were eventually bought by Sagebrush, which was bought in turn by Follett along with Winnebago Spectrum. By the middle of the first decade of the new millennium, Destiny had become Follett's flagship product. One of the early smaller systems, Vancouver-based SydneyPLUS, is also still operative. From almost 100 smaller library systems launched during the 1990s, the market coalesced down to a handful of companies.

Of the larger systems that had begun in the mini-computer era, several continued to exist in the mature market of the 21st century. Similar corporate mergers and acquisitions narrowed this vertical market niche as well. In 2005, Sirsi bought both Dynix and Data Research Associates (DRA), while Endeavor, Innovative Interfaces Incorporated, and a very few of the pioneers continued as independent companies. Geac took over CLSI in 1993 and was itself bought by Golden Gate Capital in 2005. The going stock price for purchases of this nature was about $11 per share. This represents a drastic drop from the heyday, when Geac stocks soared at over $75 a share, but Geac had grown to a billion-dollar company.

HYTELNET, developed by Peter Scott, was an online directory of library OPACs that were available over the Net. Access to these catalogues was, at the outset, text only, and accomplished using the command line program Telnet. Remote users telnetted to the library's computer, where they were greeted with a login screen. Once logged in, users could see the library software's text-based interfaces. HYTELNET listed the computer vendors for each available catalogue because users needed to know the commands for each system in order to proceed. Today, with the adoption of the Z39.50 protocol, and with fairly standardized Web screens, it is no longer necessary to learn different sets of commands. Moreover, most library catalogues simply use Web browsers as their end-user screens, so beyond learning the different options available on various OPACs, most users would find the interfaces comfortable, or at least recognizable.

HYTELNET is still available over the Web, a snapshot of library automation, frozen in time on September 4, 1997.[14] The directory contains only those libraries that made their catalogues available through Telnet. The American Library Association's *Yearbook* series provides better overall totals for the numbers of library OPACs.[15] Nevertheless, a look at HYTELNET is illustrative. In the United States alone, there were 1,090 libraries whose catalogues were listed in the directory. In Australia, there were 51, in Canada 108, in New Zealand 9, and in the United Kingdom 128.

The world of library automation vendors was not always a "peaceable kingdom," despite the collaboration that characterized the marketplace. Michael Monahan recalls an unusual series of legal wrangling following Geac's successful bid for the Miami-Dade County library system. The losing bidder, CLSI, obtained an injunction against the contract. Geac eventually won, on the legal issue that one cannot litigate regarding contracts before they are signed, only after. In the event, the Florida judge ordered the bidding reopened, and Geac won again.

Miami had done what looked like the best evaluation any library had ever done. Four teams worked individually on the applications. Only at the end would anyone know what had won. Geac had won on all the eval areas, and all the teams agreed. Geac had had no contact with Miami and had not helped frame the RFP. The idea of being sued baffled Geac. After speaking to some people at CLSI, [I concluded that] they felt the process had been flawed because they expected to win. They were outraged. They felt something terrible had happened. Government purchasing is complex. It is not unusual that losing bidders might take action. It's not unusual that the guys doing the evaluations get it wrong.[16]

THE AGE FACTOR

Library automation has always been a niche market within computing and consists of smaller niche markets. School libraries and smaller, rural public libraries have different needs from larger public libraries, academic libraries, and special libraries. Regardless of type, local requirements may mean that particular libraries are more or less demanding in their requirements for system functions and features. A consortium serving all of these types of libraries needed software to handle the most demanding institution in the system. The microcomputer helped.

By the mid-1980s, the microcomputer was coming onto the market. By the time the vendors had perfected systems that ran on mini-computers, the death knell of the era had been sounded. The cost of computing hardware had dropped to the mere thousands of dollars, and the business models behind library automation vendors that had led the field during the past decades were no longer viable. Those that could adapt survived, and the systems they sold became more standardized in look and feel and greatly improved in capacity. The era of invention and of close collaboration among vendors and clients was drawing to a close. ILS automation had matured. Complacency over the fact that ILS worked so well may have signaled the top of the curve. If today, libraries are behind the curve, and the Googles and Amazon bookstores have captured the edge, it may be because, ironically, the problems the ILS were designed to address have been solved.

Reflecting upon his time at what had been CLSI's offices in Newton, Massachusetts, Bill Manson recalls, "By the time I got there, everyone had gone from being 20 years old to being 40 years old. That's a different culture. And they had faced possible bankruptcy three times."[17] Manson says the "wild and crazy" days of CLSI were over before the company's takeover by Geac.

We began this book with Arthur C. Clarke's and Alfred North Whitehead's comments about technology and magic; but there is another sort of magic at work in any fresh start-up enterprise. It has been described in a Geac tagline as "the power of working together," but ironically, almost by the very act of introspection that produces such maxims, the magical flame appears to be snuffed. Diane Koen, former Geac project manager, and former vice president of sales at Ovid, finds the phenomenon fascinating.

I'd like to understand the life cycles of these technology companies. What is, typically, the life of the growth phase, or the exciting phase, or the "we're all in it together" phase? How long does that last? Is it five years, is it seven years? During that magical period, everyone simply "gets it," but they can't tell you what "it" is.

Koen suggests, "You know that you're successful as an organization and as a team when the administration or management or owners of the company don't bring in people and consultants to ask you, 'What do you think you're doing? How do you see success? What is your culture?' " she muses. "There was never anything like that at Geac or at Ovid, when we were growing, and developing, and really connecting with the customers, because . . . we knew, or rather, we didn't know what we were doing, but it worked."

That period of initial enthusiasm and cohesiveness seems to peak when companies reach a new developmental phase.

It's interesting that when you get to mature companies, that are either growing really quickly, merging with others, bringing in other organizations, like buying CLIS or buying Advance. And then that people begin to question. "What are we doing? Why are we here?" And then, the "revolving door" of consultants start coming in. The really magical time of both companies that I worked for was when no one had to ask, "Why are we here?"

The minute that people begin to question their raison d'être, that magical period is gone. But the flip side of this is that, when things are working, people in the organization aren't even aware that there is such a question, Koen's suggestion works well within the theory of cybernetics, of communication and control, which posits that we learn primarily from negative feedback. Only when an organization no longer appears to be achieving its intended goals or when it strays from its course is corrective action necessary. Oddly, when a company is on course, it seems, nobody knows the destination. Be the waters rough or smooth, they just concentrate on the act of sailing, sailing for the pure joys of discovery and good seamanship.

Michel Vulpe offers a different perspective. He remembers well the uncharted turf upon which library and museum automators had to tread in the 1980s and 1990s. A long-term Geac employee, Vulpe was seconded to the Smithsonian Institution for several years, working with the likes of David Bearman, himself associated with the development of machine-readable cataloguing, especially the MARC record form for archival materials. Upon leaving Geac Computers, Vulpe and a few colleagues launched out on their own armed with a conviction that customer needs should drive software production and knowing that the things learned in automating the Smithsonian, the Vatican, and the banking sector could be generalized and offered as document management systems for all manner of industries and government settings. In May 2009, Vulpe's Infrastructures for Information Inc. (i4i) made the news when a Texas jury awarded it $200 million in compensation over its patent dispute with Microsoft Corp.[18]

Mr. Vulpe and Stephen Owens had formed i4i in 1993, and by 2009, it supported a numerically small but influential and significant client list, including the U.S. Food and Drug Administration. It operated from a loft-like office above Toronto's Spadina Avenue in an area filled with secondhand computer parts shops, bordering on Chinatown. With about 30 employees, i4i is reminiscent of the ILS vendors of the mini-computer era.

Perhaps, he suggests, the maturation cycle of a company has not so much to do with the age of the company but with the age of its employees.[19] He suggests that the venture capitalists and large corporations that began purchasing library automation companies represented a generation that did not understand the library marketplace or, in some cases, the computing industry. A generation later, however, this may no longer be the case. Even wizened executives today have had years of experience with computing. Nevertheless, the passion and drive that motivate people in their twenties and thirties to work long hours for the intellectual challenge more than the financial rewards may be the elusive quantity Koen wishes to "bottle."

ADVANCES IN COMPUTING AND INFORMATION SCIENCE

Linda Farmer is a Toronto-area library consultant who has worked for Infomart and the Financial Post as well as for Geac. Along with the other librarians we have encountered, she believes that the standards that were perfected during the late 20th century are of lasting value. However, she suggests, new computing techniques may make even those obsolete.

Librarians contributed controlled subject headings . . . but that was before the Internet. The concept in libraries is that we must find everything, and if we miss something it is the end of the world. Hyperlinks and ranking can solve these problems. There is a problem with languages, and that is why I was so involved with authority control. UTLAS was better at that than OCLC. [It was] the metadata concept although we didn't call it that. Standards for input. But now, librarians are on metadata schema committees. Full text, used well, is more effective than controlled vocabularies. However, certain metadata should still be linked to an authority source for controlled subject vocabulary. There is still a challenge there, but it is becoming less and less important.[20]

As her own authority, Farmer cites a work by the contemporary philosopher David Weinberger, author of a book called *Everything Is Miscellaneous*.[21] Farmer summarizes Weinberger's perspective, one that she has increasingly come to share. In the new digital environment, nothing is "grouped." You cannot foresee how people will use it. Taxonomies, hierarchies, and thesauri can all help with problems of context, but often the end users simply have no desire for accuracy.

Hiking bivouacking bushwalking . . . those are all equivalent terms. People get confused . . . if they put in hiking and get bivouacking. Librarians are good at explaining, but patrons don't want to know. However, Wikis do that. Both the precursor of and the successors to ILS are the document management systems, being used for pure digital collections. There are schemalogics and other systems with sophisticated full document management systems. With a good taxonomy, they take the digital content and do groupings. You can impose or create an hierarchical control to supplement full text. And there are "folksonomies" and "clouds" that allow users to tag items themselves. At first I thought, "this is a travesty." But [these new systems] keep track of how many times people assign words, clouds, with words highlighted, and they can tell if something is skewed. All these things I always thought were truisms or veritable truths bibliographically are just being shot down. Librarians do precoordinate indexing, but the creators of digital material typically do not. So now they are talking about programs to do metadata extraction. We are trying to suck from a fire hose of information. What's interesting is that [with] information with smaller and smaller units tied together to create digital objects, mixes and matches, you're going to need metadata to tie these things together and to create meaning; without that, they're like dreams![22]

InMagic, which began as a database more suited than most to library applications, embraced the "knowledge management" and "social-networking" movements of the late 1990s and early 21st century. In 2008, the company listed its services as including "information management, library and social knowledge network solutions." Capturing and preserving knowledge assets of companies, promoting corporate intelligence gathering, handling multiple formats, and building "enterprise management solutions" were now among its selling features, along with the traditional one of "managing large volumes of information and content."

Meanwhile, full-text retrieval, data visualization, streaming media, campus information repositories, Wikis, blogs, and virtual reality software like Second Life began changing user expectations of integrated knowledge management systems. The new era holds promise for libraries and archives to become publishers in their own right of digital collections in many media, with a true dialog between user and publisher becoming possible.

By the end of the mini-computer era, many vendors were switching to UNIX and Structured Query Language (SQL), a standardized operating system, and a standard family of "relational" database programs. Thus, both the software that ran the machine's basic functions, and the applications programs themselves, were becoming more similar to one another. The positive aspect of this is that systems are becoming technically similar, as are the capabilities or "functionality" that they offer.

At the beginning of the 21st century, a well-rounded systems administrator in any library needs to know about UNIX, some flavor of SQL, and Web servers such as Apache and Microsoft Internet Information Server (IIS). Additional knowledge of digital library, document management, Web design, and other applications software may also be required; but at bottom, most ILS on the market, whether proprietary to some vendor or "open source," are pretty much the same. The ILS marketplace has reached maturity even as it becomes eclipsed by a new range of Internet services.

During the 1980s, librarians were at the forefront of automated service development. Advances in computing, in communications, and in user expectations have altered the picture significantly. To paraphrase a prescient Australian systems librarian's 1992 prediction, the information world is increasingly looking like the Internet, "with a few odd library things hanging off it." And, as Barry also suggested, automated means of describing, retrieving, and distributing recorded information are rapidly being developed. Are the OPACs and ILS of the past decades totally obsolete in the new environment? Farmer thinks not. "The ILS is morphing," she says. "Libraries still need a local system, but the technology is 15 years out of date. With digital objects, the workflow has changed. To take licensed data, external data, and to integrate all this to a so-called OPAC—that's the future."[23]

END OF AN ERA

Almost as soon as the mini-computer era began, the seeds of the next revolution had been planted. Telecommunications developments culminating in global acceptance of the Internet protocols and the miniaturization of computers themselves were already underway. As early as 1978, Hiltz and Turoff had written a book called *The Network Nation: Human Communication via Computer.*[24] By 1983, there were many articles and a few monographs exploring the uses of microcomputers, today's desktop workstations, in library applications. As a result, many of the technical challenges that needed to be dealt with in the mini-computer heyday of the 1980s were bypassed by overall progress just as they reached their maturities. However, on the data-processing side, the 1980s have left a rich legacy, which is still being felt as the second decade of the 21st century begins.

As computing systems shrank in size and increased in capacity, mainframe computers, the mainstay of campus automation during the 1970s, increasingly gave way to mini-computers, making it possible for libraries to assume responsibility for their own data processing. Throughout the 1980s, mini-computers achieved prominence and developed in power. The super-mini-computers of the early 1990s were perhaps the final flowering of this technology, which still cost libraries hundreds of thousands, if not millions, of dollars to acquire and use.

Concurrently with microcomputer technology implementation, standards such as MARC, communications protocols like the Z 39 family, and the seven-layer ISO Open Systems Interconnection specifications continued to develop, laying the foundations for the Internet's ascendency during the early and mid-1990s. With the shift to microcomputers and end-user-oriented computing, database integrators like Thompson or Ovid continued to acquire and merge their offerings and to perfect their end-user interfaces.

Throughout this era, librarians contributed in significant ways. They were hired as analysts, instructors, customer service representatives, advanced development, marketing and bid-writing specialists, and sales personnel by major ILS and database vendors. Librarians and archivists contributed to standards committees, and the unique nature of library data—which required variable length records in distinctly searchable fields, multilingual character sets, and rapid transaction-processing speeds—pushed the development of products and standards in ways uncharacteristic of other industries, for example banking. Library systems user groups were instrumental in pushing the vendors into developing innovative solutions.

Mini-computers communicated with many more than a hundred users at a time, and did so without the benefit of the Internet. Unilinc, an Australian library consortium that used a Geac 9000, one of the largest and fastest mini-computers, could converse with over 512 terminals across an 800-mile radius, with end users typically noticing no more than two-second delays at the farthest reaches of the networks. Unilinc could also exchange data over wide-area networks, like the Internet, with other library computers around the globe. Such machines had to optimize disk storage, communications throughput, and rapid data processing along with managing user interfaces. In nontechnical terms, they had to talk to many people at once, do what they wanted, and tell them understandably and quickly when and how well the tasks had been completed. Today, specialized software and hardware, often not even in the same physical locations, combine to produce that result.

While the file servers of the early 21st century could still be classified as mini-computers based on their sizes, the era of widely distributed computing predicted by Sun Microsystems marketing people during the mid-1990s has largely been realized. During that period, Sun had adopted the tagline "The computer is the network."[25] Stand-alone all-purpose mini-computers are no longer much in the picture. Disk servers and communications servers located around the Internet have taken over the storage and end-user communications functions; and some early 21st-century laptop computers, which are more powerful than the mightiest of the mini-computers of the 1980s, do not even have internal disk drives (e.g., Apple's Macbook Air).

Another way of looking at the development of library automation would be to relate software and conceptual developments to the computing and communications hardware and methods available at given times. To do so would invite speculation about the role of technologies in scientific developments—which leads to two questions: "Does the availability of a technology lead to new ways of thinking about workplace automation problems?" And "Does the perception that there are problems to be solved, for which current technologies provide no answers, lead to new technical developments?"

The answer to both questions, the one about chronological periods and the one with the chicken-or-egg problem of technology and science, must be a noncommittal "sometimes." As was seen, particularly in the case of Geac Computers International, sometimes the problems of automating libraries and banking institutions led to the creation of new hardware. For the most part, developments in the broader field of computing and communications led to the application of new technologies to the problems of library automation. In both cases, creative thinking, much of it by librarians themselves, came into play. Inventing new ways to use technologies is no less "invention" than is the creation of the machinery itself.

As library automation moved from concept to reality and reached maturity, many of the pioneering companies and nonprofit institutions merged or simply ceased to exist. Why did some survive and others fail? In some instances, the solutions these companies and institutions provided were no longer required. Others failed due to management problems.

Some companies acquired others to augment the range of products they could offer. Other companies were sold because the principals wished to take their profits and retire or go on to other challenges. In some cases, similar products were acquired and supported through the remainders of their life cycles; and the existing customers of one system "migrated" to the product line the company wished to promote.

Some of the original library automation companies succeeded because they came to dominate market niches. Others sought to broaden their customer bases by addressing the needs of different niche markets. Innovative Interfaces Incorporated came to dominate the large university library, city library, and regional consortium niches. Follett Software, which initially sought to support school libraries, acquired the MOLLI, Athena, and Winnebago systems and by the early 2000s was seeking to migrate all those customers to its Destiny line of software. By early 2011, Follett was offering only its Destiny line of software.[26] MOLLI had been developed for hospital libraries, and Sagebrush had acquired both it and Athena, also designed for small-scale projects, before being acquired by Follett. Another of the "originals," Dynix, merged with a newer company, Sirsi, and still competes in the large- to medium-scale niche.

Meanwhile, some companies survived the Internet revolution by adopting UNIX or Windows as their operating systems, and by adopting client-server computing models. Surviving companies began relying upon database engines built around some variety of Structured Query Language (SQL) for their workhorse or "back-end" processing, and Web browsers for their user interfaces. These companies started developing "scalable" products that could be tailored to both small- and large-scale automation projects.

During the 1960s and 1970s, when much theoretical work and several practical projects were conceived, those fortunate few libraries that were automated usually relied upon campus or municipal mainframe computers for their data processing. The major reason for the growth spurt of the 1980s can probably be found in the availability of mini-computers, machines small and inexpensive enough to be installed by libraries themselves, or by groups of libraries forming a regional consortium. During this period, one key factor was that librarians themselves took charge of the development, implementation, and ongoing function of their systems. These librarians and programmers had to deal with many technical problems, as well as attendant workflow and societal issues. Most of the technical issues are no longer of concern, because of advances in computing in general. The social issues, such as patron privacy, job displacement among library staff, and customer satisfaction, will always be of interest, so long as people use technologies to attain their organizational ends.

The 1990s saw the democratization of computing. What was formerly an arcane science administered by lab-coated priests and riddled with esoteric jargon became a distributed global communications, entertainment, and learning environment. This shift was foreseen in the mid-1980s, when microcomputers began talking to one another over dial-up telephone lines, and bulletin boards, newsgroups, and mailing lists like L-Soft's popular Listserv™ became available outside the corporate offices and campus computing centers.

The development of library automation systems through mini-computers and the rise of commercially viable systems, "integrated" or "turnkey" systems, were the forerunners of what are today called "enterprise solutions." They automated all of the major daily processes and work flows involved in running libraries. Because libraries have needs that are similar to, but vastly more complicated than, those of other businesses, few people in the mainstream computing industry had sought to address those needs. It took librarians and academics, working with computer programmers, to specify and then deploy automation solutions for libraries. For the most part, the library automation features we take for granted today were developed during this period. The intricacies involved in providing ILS and database solutions that are taken for granted today— an insight into the social and business environments under which those activities flourished—and the personalities of individuals and their first-person narratives have been illuminated to some degree in the narratives of the present work.

The events of the era were enacted by a remarkable collection of passionate and highly creative people, who included a company vice president of advanced development who came to work barefoot and stood on his head when he wanted to solve particularly difficult technical challenges. It included field engineers who fixed computers using HO gauge model railroad components and Reynolds Wrap, operators at customer sites who invented simple improvements that surprised system designers, and programmers who suddenly found themselves managing whole deployments in far-off countries. Many of those people went on to illustrious careers, notably Sir Tim Berners-Lee, inventor of the World Wide Web, who had first worked as a programmer at Plessey.

The 1980s saw the rise of what would become today's "integrated" library systems. Then called "turnkey" systems, they gradually progressed from circulation systems, to full MARC cataloguing and acquisitions systems, to ones that incorporated almost every aspect of library operation. Library automation, which does not deals with information about the manufacture of some specific product or the delivery of some service, is different. The information it manipulated was itself the product.

CONCLUSIONS

In 2005, Golden Gate Capital, a California-based company, had purchased Geac and divided it up into smaller companies addressing different markets.[27] The old Geac LSD became part of a company named Infor, and it continued to market the company's Vubis ILS. In the autumn of 2008, Elizabeth Fenwick sat in her rural Ontario library's office, pondering over several competing bids for a new ILS. She and the CEOs of neighboring town libraries had been considering open source solutions like Koha or Evergreen as well as the offerings of the major ILS vendors. In the end, she found herself selecting the latest version of Vubis. It cost about a tenth of the price it might have fetched two decades earlier. It was supplied by Infor. In the end, as Rona Wade had done two decades earlier, Fenwick had selected a product that promised a better "integrated federated search" capability. That is, she wanted a system that could look at various databases and information sources, and display them to the user seamlessly.[28]

Beginning in the 1960s, mainframe computers, and the concurrent development of cataloguing standards like MARC, AACR2, and ISBD, had provided the conditions for the development of large "union" catalogues, like those offered by UTLAS, RLIN, WLN, and OCLC. The enormous cost of mainframe computers had forced libraries to band together into regional consortia, or to be dependent upon campus computing centers for their processing needs.

During the late 1970s, technical developments and organizational goals had combined to create the conditions for the ascendency of commercially feasible stand-alone integrated library systems. Just as social and technical factors had combined to create the conditions for the mini-computer era in library automation, several factors combined to bring the period to an end. The profit margins in computer hardware dropped drastically with the availability of more powerful and much less expensive microcomputers. The business plans of major vendors, especially of those who either built their own hardware like Geac or provided "turnkey" solutions by acting as "original equipment manufacturers" and building systems using other companies' hardware, had to change.

Graphical user interfaces and object-oriented programming, first pioneered within the UNIX world by Xerox and rapidly adopted by Apple and Microsoft, radically changed user expectations of human-computer interaction. The look and feel of windowed systems, with abundant color graphics, drop-down menus, pop-up windows, and a variety of typographical and design elements, made text-driven systems look antiquated. Within a generation, end users found the work flow cumbersome, even if the text-driven systems were more efficient than the windowed systems then on the market.

Along with these developments came productivity tools, then called "fourth-generation" development tools, which made programming itself more rapid and cost-effective. Relational databases like Oracle and SQL created new technical benchmarks against which customers evaluated vendors. The old "flat" file structures that underlay many integrated library systems were deemed archaic by the customer base, who now understood how a single relational database could eliminate the necessity for separate "modules" to handle acquisitions, circulation, cataloguing, and catalogue lookups. Perhaps most strikingly, the availability of reliable high-speed data communications networks and the ultimate dominance of the Transmission Control Protocol/Internet Protocol in the early to mid-1990s made truly distributed computing possible on a global scale, rendering the need for mainframes and super-minis obsolete for small to medium-sized computing applications.

As the first decades of the 21st century progress, a few large union catalogues like OCLC's continue to remain viable, and the regional consortium continues to fulfill some of its former roles. However, the contemporary consortium's value rests less upon its provision of shared cataloguing than upon its ability to act as a middle person in negotiating database contracts and as a provider of shared expertise, training, and cooperative services like virtual reference, interlending, and mutual support.

Moreover, the ILS, while still essential to the operation of contemporary libraries, has become merely one facet of the overall "enterprise-wide" computing environment of libraries. As more and more content switches from print to digital, circulation systems are becoming more like electronic commerce systems, associating transactions with charges to libraries and their clients. The online public access catalogue, now based on standard Web browsers, is becoming a "background" job, with "discovery layers" and "federated search" facilities coming between it and the user. With the increasing popularity of open source systems based on the LAMP model, Linux, Apache, MySQL, and scripting languages like Perl, Python, PHP, and Java, the vendors of integrated library systems are facing changes in their business models once more.

However, the technical and social challenges addressed and overcome during the mini-computer era still underlie library automation. That they were met so successfully makes it possible to overlook them. Truly advanced to the point of becoming commoditized, they are truly indistinguishable from magic. They were the inventions of the age of mini-computers, corresponding roughly with the 1980s, and a remarkable and sometimes interchangeable group of librarians and programmers were their parents.

Today, continued reduction in size of technology that can transmit information occurs almost daily. Handheld devices allow persons to send and receive e-mail, purchase and read books, and more that is yet to come. Our civilization is advancing even more rapidly with what Whitehead suggests are "operations we can do without thinking about them,"[29] consigning the mini-computer to yesterday's magic.

By the end of the mini-computer era, most of the basic challenges of ILS systems had been solved, albeit not universally. The hardware-based business models that had served companies like CLSI and Geac well were no longer operable due to drastic price reductions and concomitant increases in computing power. Computers and to some extent their software had become commodities. In efforts to switch to UNIX systems with Web browser user interfaces and Windows workstations, companies had rushed products to market; and those products had problems. The vendor consolidations of the 1990s had resulted in companies having multiple, formerly competing product lines to sell, and while that meant bigger customer lists, some of those customers were dissatisfied with their existing systems. The companies that throve during the period tended to be ones like Innovative Interfaces and Sirsi/Dynix, for whom libraries were the principal market.

Ironically, by perfecting the ILS to the point of appearing to be "magical" or commonplace, librarians may have lost their place at the cutting edge of development to online bookstores and Internet search companies. Google and Amazon are not successful because they allow librarians greater functionality, but because they do so for end users. With the advent of "smart" telephones, tablet computers, and Wifi, even desktop, laptop, and personal digital assistant computers appear to be becoming redundant for many users. The next phase of library automation may well involve the provision of research databases, archival materials, and bibliographic information, seamlessly and transparently, to the patron's fingertips via wireless telephones and tablet computers. The development of the ILS was a remarkable collaborative effort, in which designers and librarians as customers played often interchangeable roles. That process continues, but with new challenges and opportunities taking the fore. In our concluding chapter, librarian Louise O'Neil explains some of the ongoing innovation taking place in the field.

The industry's quest for high-speed, reliable, and relatively inexpensive transaction processing solutions and the demands of the library world for such capacities coincided with the era of mini-computers. While the special software needed to run libraries was being invented by vendors like CLSI, Geac, and their competitors, mini-computers were being perfected as well. However, within a few short years, the technological and communications restrictions of the 1970s and 1980s were no longer factors. Micro-computers were becoming commonplace, and the Internet was making it possible to distribute workloads among many small client machines, connected on demand to larger servers in geographically disparate locations. Did super-mini computers like the Geac 9000 exemplify a "sunset phenomenon"? Was it the epitome of its kind of machine, the mini-computer, just when microcomputers took over? "The sun is always brightest when it sets, because that's where it stops," Keith Thomas observes. "It couldn't possibly get any brighter."

NOTES

1. Burke, Jane. "Automation Planning and Implementation: Library and Vendor Responsibilities." In *Human Aspects of Library Automation: Helping Staff and Patrons Cope*. Clinic on Library Applications of Data Processing, April 14–16. Urbana-Champaign: University of Illinois at Urbana-Champaign, 1985. pp. 46–58.

2. McGee, Rob. *Performance of Turnkey Library Systems: A Contractual Approach*. Rev. ed. [Richmond, VA]: RMG, 1982. Revised 1992. And McGee, Rob. "Starting Over: Re-Inventing the Integrated Library System and the Library Automation Industry." Paper presented at "RMG's Nineteenth Annual Presidents' Seminar: The View from the Top," ALA Midwinter Conference, Denver, CO, January 23, 2009.

3. Manson, Bill. Interviewed October 2008.

4. Monahan, Michael. Interviewed July 2008.

5. Mark, Peter B. "The Sequoia Computer: A Fault-Tolerant Tightly-Coupled Multiprocessor Architecture." In *International Symposium on Computer Architecture*. Marlborough, MA: 1985.

6. Geac later, during a purge of excess equipment, sold a pair of Intel computers that had been used for this pilot project. They are currently in the author's personal possession.

7. Manson, Bill. Interviewed October 2008.

8. Monahan, Michael. Interviewed July 2008.

9. Monahan, Michael. Interviewed July 2008.

10. Thomas, D. *Knights of the New Technology: The Inside Story of Canada's Computer Elite*. Toronto: Key Porter Books, 1983. p. 823.

11. Thomas, D. *Knights*. passim.

12. Monahan, Michael. Interviewed July 2008.

13. Manson, Bill. Interviewed October 2008.

14. "Hytelnet: Archive of Telnet Sites." http://www.lights.ca/hytelnet.

15. American Library Association. *Yearbook of Library and Information Services*. p. v.

16. Monahan, Michael. Interviewed July 2008.

17. Manson, Bill. Interviewed July 2008.

18. Hartley, Mike. "The Man Who Took on Microsoft—and Won." *Globe and Mail*, May. 25, 2009. Court documents show that i4i claimed Microsoft infringed on its patent in a "willful and deliberate" manner when it created its Word 2003, Word 2007, .NET Framework, and Windows Vista software. In the autumn of 2010, the case was referred to the U.S. Supreme Court.

19. Vulpe, Michel. Interviewed January 2009.

20. Farmer, Linda. Interviewed February 2009.

21. Weinberger, David. *Everything Is Miscellaneous: The Power of the New Digital Disorder.* New York: Times Books, 2007.

22. Farmer, Linda. Interviewed February 2009.

23. Farmer, Linda. Interviewed February 2009.

24. Hiltz, Starr Roxanne, and Murray Turoff. *The Network Nation: Human Communication Via Computer.* Reading, MA: Addison-Wesley Pub. Co., 1978.

25. Sun's tagline is cited in several works, including Batty, Michael. "The Computable City." Paper presented at the Fourth International Conference on Computers in Urban Planning and Urban Management, Melbourne, Australia, July 11–14, 1995.

26. Follett Software Company. "Library Management." http://www.follettsoftware.com/pg57/library-management. Accessed March 20, 2011.

27. "Golden Gate Capital to Acquire Geac Computer Corporation for Approximately US$1.0 Billion, Cash Price of US$11.10 per Share." http://www.geac.com/object/pr_110705.html.

28. Fenwick, Elizabeth. Personal communication, 2009.

29. McGee, Rob. *Request for Proposals for Integrated Library Systems.* Richmond, Victoria: Chicago: Bethesda, MD, 1982, Revised 1992.

8

The Future of Library Technology

Louise O'Neill

In essence, libraries are about the interaction between people and information. They are not necessarily about technology, even in futuristic scenarios. In her broad review of fiction about the future of libraries, Katherine Pennavaria observes that most such works are really stories about current or anticipated changes in culture and society and the resulting changes in the roles of libraries and librarians—they are not really about libraries and librarians per se. Nevertheless, these same works often incorporate, almost coincidentally, descriptions of impressively prescient information-related computer technology (given the state of technology at the time), such as Vannevar Bush's Memex.[1]

With the growing and indisputable influence of computer technology on libraries, speculative fiction is largely replaced by predictions, well grounded in recent technical developments and an emerging view of the purpose of libraries and librarians with respect to technology. It is not surprising that much of the speculation about the future of library technology focuses on the potential inherent in the adoption of influential technologies such as Google, Wikipedia, and other Web 2.0 and Web 3.0 phenomena to further the aims of library service. There is no question that Internet-based social-networking and crowd-sourcing applications will have a growing impact on libraries and librarians, but their range of influence goes much farther. They are not strictly "library" technology.

This chapter is primarily about the future of library technology that has been developed specifically for library-related use. It is the kind of technology that has been covered in the preceding chapters, most notably integrated library automation systems (ILS). The impact of non-library-specific technology on libraries will also be considered briefly at the end.

INTEGRATED LIBRARY SYSTEMS

Emerging developments for ILS technology include the following:

- Open source software
- Increased focus on library users' experience of technology

- Description and discovery tools
- Nonlocal information resources and delivery
- Mobile and ubiquitous access

Open Source Software

Open source software is software for which the programming code is freely available on the Internet. The code can be added to, modified, and unreservedly shared among a community of programming users. Open-source ILS, such as Evergreen and Koha, share these characteristics.

In contrast, the ILS described in the preceding chapters began as locally developed applications that became commercialized and therefore proprietary. Vendors of proprietary applications do not normally reveal the software code that underlies their product. If customizations that require change to the underlying code are desired by libraries, then the vendor must do it, usually for a fee and not necessarily as quickly as the library might like. More recently, some vendors have made application programming interfaces (APIs) available. APIs reveal part of the code and allow for some customization to be made.

It would be easy to conclude that open source ILS are in fact a regressive trend, a full-circle return to the days when libraries wrote their own software programming from scratch to keep track of circulation and other processes, before commercial vendors became involved. However, there are three significant differences: (1) the code is not being written from scratch—the code is already available and is usually useful "out of the box," although it can be developed further if desired; (2) the code is not kept within one institution but is used and shared among multiple locations; and (3) library staff are not on their own in implementing and operating the system, but instead there is often enthusiastic external community support and in some cases third-party technical support companies who may even specialize in particular open source products.

Open source ILS are undoubtedly part of library technology in the future. The lines between proprietary products and open source products will continue to blur as vendors increasingly encourage customers to develop their systems via APIs. However, the lines will not converge unless vendors make all of their code freely available because they have found a business model that does not depend on keeping the source code secret.

Increased Focus on Library Users' Experience of Technology

The development of computer-supported library technologies clearly began as a means of automating library work processes, especially to support circulation of materials, acquisitions, and cataloguing—computers are particularly useful in supporting close adherence to bibliographic standards in an organized fashion. There was little thought for the impact of the technology on the library user. Even library patron accounts were mainly to do with keeping track of loans and fines, not with providing personal information to users about the status of their relationship to the library. Now, however, library technology is becoming increasingly client focused. This trend can only be expected to rise, at least partly in response to the increased competition from (and comparison with) more user-friendly technologies and the availability of library-like services, and also as a result of increasing awareness that products should be tailored to the users' perspective, not the librarian's.

Hence, many libraries now perform usability studies, hold focus groups, and actively solicit feedback in other ways to ensure that library websites and other computerized services support their users in easily achieving their objectives. To mitigate the labor-intensive aspects of these exercises, perhaps future library technology will automate both the collection of standard Web evaluation metrics (e.g., the number of clicks on a page); capture, report, and analyze other objective user data such as cursor movements; embed user feedback queries that may pop up when the user appears to be having difficulty (instead of making the user find and use a suggestion box); and perform text analysis of suggestions and produce a concise report. Personalization of Web pages could be used not just to allow the user to set his or her own preferences, but it could also enable analysis of trends and emerging conventions that could then be applied to the home page and other key pages, and correlate with usage patterns and use of information resources. This may in turn lead back to more customized suggestions for the user in addition to better overall design.

Description and Discovery Tools

Discovery tools (aka "front ends") are intuitive user interfaces that are layered over traditional online public access catalogues (OPACs) within ILS, which often are more reflective of cataloguers' practices. Discovery tools offer user-friendly and sometimes even user-contributed features and content, such as faceted searching, book cover graphics, tag clouds, personalization features, and user reviews and ratings. Content from electronic journals and other sources are seamlessly integrated into search results. Search results are often clustered and sometimes adapted to the Functional Requirements for Bibliographic Records application (i.e., they are "FRBR-ized").

While vendors have developed discovery tools primarily for their own proprietary ILS (such as Primo from Ex Libris, Encore, and Rooms from Sirsi-Dynix), most can be used with other IL. Some discovery tools have been developed by non-ILS vendors that are also ILS independent. These include Aquabrowser, Endeca, and WorldCat Local.

If discovery tools represent a significant advancement now, how could they evolve further in the future? Discovery tools only identify or deliver search results in the form of documents, not the information itself. A significant library technology–related shift will occur when library interface tools are largely capable of delivering information itself in response to a query, instead of or in addition to documents that contain the information. The significant shift is that it is information itself that becomes the focus of the discovery technology; the document that contains the information may simply become an aspect of the metadata that describes the information. The discovery tool will become a discovery and delivery tool, a "one-stop shopping" experience, and libraries will begin to move away from their orientation toward documents.

Descriptive cataloguing may undergo a similar paradigm shift. Local cataloguing of materials locally has given way to copy cataloguing and consortial sharing of records at many libraries, but each item must still be catalogued by someone, somewhere. Software such as METS ALTO can detect various metadata fields (e.g., author, title, and publisher) and could thus be used to populate fields in a bibliographic record. Computerized text analysis and artificial intelligence techniques could be used to extract subject headings according to a given thesaurus and taxonomy, with a resulting output into a useful format such as an automatically generated MARC record, complete with

Library of Congress (LC) call numbers and subject headings. Coupled with smarter search engines that integrate user-generated tags and folksonomies, the role of the cataloguer-librarian will change dramatically from describing and classifying the item to calibrating and "teaching" the software by correcting any errors it may have made in the generated subject headings.

Nonlocal Information Resources and Delivery

A catalogue is a list. Therefore, a library catalogue was originally a "list" of items held by a library. However, the library user's primary reason for consulting a library catalogue is not so much to see a partial list of what is owned by an individual library, but simply to find information or a particular item. If, once discovered, what is sought is made readily available, it is unlikely to matter to the user who owns it. "Clearly, the typical integrated library system (ILS) will no longer be the centerpiece of a library's online offerings. Rather, a centralized finding tool will be the focus."[2] This approach is currently exemplified by WorldCat Local, which almost seamlessly allows discoverability of resources within all its considerable holdings, and provides location information.

Mobile and Ubiquitous Access

Discoverability and deliverability of library resources via mobile devices, particularly handheld devices such as cell phones, represent the ultimate in convenience and service to library users at their place and time of need. What could be more of a time saver than displaying the call number of a book on one's cell phone when searching the shelves, instead of looking up titles in a catalogue and scribbling information on scraps of paper? What a welcome service to a researcher facing a deadline to be able to find and read a critical journal article on a cell phone!

Many ILS now feature a user interface for mobile devices, and the ability to download and read e-books on such devices is commonplace. In the future, as a matter of course libraries will optimize Web sites to work well in a mobile interface by repackaging the content to, for example, display critical pieces of information such as call numbers clearly, and integrate with online reference services so one can contact a librarian for assistance on the spot. A few libraries are using the vendor APIs to develop their own products, for example the District of Columbia Public Library's iPhone portal, available for free from the iPhone application store.

As electronic book readers such as Amazon Kindle and Sony Book Reader become more "book-like" in look and feel, the shift from printed paper to e-paper display will accelerate. The implications of this shift for the future of library service are tremendous but not imminent. Many libraries, particularly large research libraries, will not be able to give up shelves of printed books, journals, and so on anytime soon. But the need for shelving will undoubtedly dwindle, not to mention the need for circulation desks, loan policies, and fines (when the loan expires, the item is automatically "returned").

The growth of library service delivery via mobile devices is inevitable, but risky. The user's awareness of the library, or the fact that it is the library that is responsible for his or her access to resources, is significantly diminished. As a result, the financial, administrative, and political support required for most libraries' survival will falter. Future library technology may, however, address that dilemma by automatically ensuring that the user is aware that it is the library that is helpfully fulfilling his or her need. For example, a brief "Thank you for using ____ library" may appear at the bottom of the interface, or perhaps the user will receive a follow-up message listing the user's search strategy and results. Access to a librarian, or at least a friendly librarian avatar, should always be a click away. Automatically generated suggestions as to what else the user might be interested in (as is done on commercial Web sites) could also messaged or "remembered" by the system the next time the user logs in.

Ironically, cell phones with digital cameras may also be of use onsite in libraries because they can be used to read two-dimensional barcodes with no need for transponders or transceivers, possibly replacing radiofrequency identification (RFID) technology for self-service loans.[3]

OTHER LIBRARY TECHNOLOGY FUTURE DIRECTIONS

Institutional and Digital Repositories and Open Access

Institutional repositories (IRs) are electronic collections of theses, dissertations, journal articles, and other types associated with a particular institution, usually an academic or other research-oriented institution, which represent the intellectual output of that institution. Many IRs are created and hosted by libraries, and their contents are freely available via the Internet. A digital repository is broader in scope and may include digitized collections as well as links to electronic subscription services and other third-party products.

However, repositories are evolving rapidly from the inert storehouses implied by their name to highly interactive services buoyed by advances in computer technology, notably high-performance computing and the increasing ability to store and process massive amounts of data and large files. While data librarianship is nothing new, now librarians are becoming curators and providers of data sets as well as documents, prepublication and still in use by researchers. "Large collections of content, such as datasets, will dot the landscape. Virtualized storage technologies will be the norm. Cloud computing will be widely implemented for a range of applications. . . . In this environment, interoperation between repositories and service technologies will be a pressing priority. A range of strategies for ensuring that information is passed effectively between repositories and other campus systems will be in place. . . . As a result, library infrastructure will tend to blend with campus infrastructure as campus infrastructure becomes broadly distributed and less and less localized. . . . Controlling the technology environment within which library content and services are delivered will be an increasingly outmoded operating strategy."[4]

Technical interoperability between repositories is highly desirable in ensuring that the users find what they want easily, but that approach may also result in the disappearance of library-specific technology itself. This will be discussed further below.

Libraries as Publishers

Libraries have often published materials on a small, occasional scale: bibliographies, local histories, and books on special collections. Now open source publishing technology, notably Open Journal Systems (OJS) software, is enabling libraries to publish electronically on a much greater scale. Publications may include digital reproductions of rare books and e-journals produced by students and faculty who want a low-cost way to make their work available to all on the Internet. "Libraries are not replicating traditional publishing . . . they are frequently working with publishers and editors looking for the opportunity to translate their traditionally published titles to the emerging networked environment of information exchange."[5]

Academic libraries are leading the trend for library publishers, but there is the potential for the technology to be used by other types of libraries, especially if it grows in functionality. For example, public libraries may use it to support community publishing.[6]

ADOPTION AND CONVERGENCE OF LIBRARY AND NONLIBRARY TECHNOLOGIES

In a world of networks and web services, library technology must be compatible and interoperable with other technologies. While library technology was originally quite distinct when it was developed, today much of what ILS do are copied by other software products such as database applications, content and document management systems, workflow systems, and transaction systems. They do not detract from the value of an ILS that integrates all of these workflows and functionalities well, but there may also be advantages for an organization if a particular type of application can be used for multiple purposes, instead of integrating a whole separate application suite (i.e., an ILS) that duplicates a functionality that may already have been purchased, for example a transaction system that could handle circulation of materials.

Perhaps the most likely force for convergence of technologies is the development of the semantic Web and, for libraries, its use of the intelligent agent that "gathers information or performs some other service without the immediate presence of the user."[7] The intelligent agent can search for information on the Internet on behalf of the user, much as Web crawlers do now using keywords, but the intelligent agent will also gather information about the information (metadata!) incorporated via semantic Web technology such as Web ontology languages. Coupled with user information that it already possesses, the intelligent agent could offer very intelligent responses to a user's information needs.

Furthermore, the intelligent agents can improve their results over time by learning from human feedback (making use of artificial intelligence) and inferring similarities in relationships and meaning across Web ontology languages. For example, an intelligent agent could, over time, be expected to learn that the word " rich" in one ontology is often synonymous with "wealthy" in another.

Finding information effortlessly via semantic Web technologies is of obvious interest to library users, but it won't remain within libraries. If it works well, it is likely to become ubiquitous.

FUTURE LIBRARIANS AND TECHNOLOGY

What kind of librarian can work alongside an intelligent agent, tutoring it where necessary to find and package information tailored to the user's needs and preferences, perhaps without even being asked? What kind of librarian will be able to accept looking for information not just in one's local collection, not even in all library catalogues, but within the whole of the world's information resources? What kind of librarian will be able to work effectively in a library beyond walls—interconnected with and embedded into everything else, as ubiquitous as the technology that it uses?

Such librarians won't be driven by technology, contenting themselves with adopting the latest cool social-networking tool to library services in "me too" fashion. They know that if they do that, technology will marginalize or simply replace them. In the face of acceleration of computer-based capabilities, librarians' enduring and possibly even increasing relevance as a profession depends on their agility, not just in adaptation but also in foreseeing and influencing the potential uses of technology. Not only must librarians influence human software vendors and developers, but also they must now prepare themselves to shape and even lead the development of technology that replicates and automates librarians' expertise in bringing people and information together.

It is not just a matter of thinking outside the box; it is also necessary for librarians to be strongly aware of technology and to develop insight into its potential uses for library service. For example, any good reference librarian knows that articulating the true reference question is half the battle. Could librarians contribute to the creation of an expert tool based on a good reference interview, to help the user think out what he or she is really seeking? The information resources themselves are easily deliverable by technology, but this sort of library information service is not (yet). Gaming technology and the use of immersive, virtual environments provide a promising platform.[8]

This is not to say that future librarians must become more like computer technicians or programmers. Currently, many systems librarians are required to perform patently technical tasks that they are not educated to do, requiring more than a casual knowledge of UNIX, Oracle, or Perl. Is this a good use of a librarian's time? Wouldn't programmers, developers, and systems analysts do it all better? Future librarians will need to focus on the big picture—the what and why of technology—and supervise technical staff with the detailed technical knowledge to bring it about. Or, perhaps librarians will exert their influence to reward vendors who develop mature products with intuitive administrative interfaces that don't require technical training. The trend toward software as service (SAS) will assist this process.

If the role of future librarians in the face of future library technology seems ambiguous, it reflects the fact that technology itself is becoming ambiguous. Just as the phenomenon of cloud computing (making use of indeterminably located computed resources somewhere on the Web) grows, so librarians must practice cloud librarianship—where the touchpoint will not be an institution, a licensing agreement, a Web site, a software application, or any definitive markers at all. Cloud librarians will be comfortable with that ambiguity, and will know how to find and instantiate information from within the evanescent environment of the Internet, applying the same criteria as they always have to what they find: scope, content, authority, and timeliness. Cloud librarians will find, use, and influence ambient and increasingly ubiquitous technology in the same way. In doing so, they will make it library technology.

NOTES

1. Pennavaria, K. "Representation of Books and Libraries in Depictions of the Future." *Libraries and Culture* 37, no. 3 (2002): 238.

2. Tennant, Roy. "Demise of the Local Catalog." *Library Journal* (July 15, 2007): http://www.libraryjournal.com/article/CA6457238.html.

3. Story, Louise. "New Bar Codes Can Talk with Your Cellphone." *New York Times*, April 1, 2007, sec. Business, http://www.nytimes.com/2007/04/01/business/01code.html?ex=1333 080000&en=8bb1180541c7a895&ei=5088&partner=rssnyt&emc=rss.

4. Association of Research Libraries. "The Research Library's Role in Digital Repository Services: ARL Digital Repositories." http://www.arl.org/news/pr/repositories-3feb09.shtml. p. 32.

5. Hahn, Karla L. *Research Library Publishing Services: New Options for University Publishing*. Washington, DC: Association of Research Libraries, 2008. http://www.arl.org/bm~doc/research-library-publishing-services.pdf.

6. American Library Association. "ALA." http://www.ala.org/ala/mgrps/divs/pla/plapublications/platechnotes/institutional.cfm.

7. Dent, V. F. "Intelligent Agent Concepts in the Modern Library." *Library Hi Tech* 25, no. 1 (2007): 109.

8. Surprenant, T. T., and C. A. Perry. *The Academic Cybrarian in 2012: A Futuristic Essay.* 2003. http://alpha.fdu.edu/~marcum/supernant_perry.doc.

Index

About the Author

CHRISTOPHER BROWN-SYED is Editor of the journal *Library and Archival Security*. Dr. Brown-Syed is a former employee of the pioneering library systems vendors Plessey and Geac, who has taught in graduate schools of library and information studies in New York, Arizona, Michigan, California, and Illinois. He currently teaches at Seneca College in Toronto, Canada.